Frank S Russell

Russian Wars With Turkey

Frank S Russell

Russian Wars With Turkey

ISBN/EAN: 9783337299286

Printed in Europe, USA, Canada, Australia, Japan

Cover: Foto ©ninafisch / pixelio.de

More available books at **www.hansebooks.com**

RUSSIAN WARS WITH TURKEY

BY

MAJOR FRANK S. RUSSELL

14TH HUSSARS

FORMERLY OF BALLIOL COLLEGE, OXFORD, AND OF THE STAFF COLLEGE

WITH TWO MAPS

CEDANT ARMA TOGÆ

HENRY S. KING & CO., LONDON
1877

(The rights of translation and of reproduction are reserved)

PREFACE.

THE following pages lay no claim to originality, in them will be found no new theories of history—no startling discovery in the science of either war or politics. They are simply intended to lay before the public some passages in the history of the past, and from them, if possible, to give a glimpse of the future.

The wars of 1828 and 1829 are given in detail; the account of them is derived from the works of Count Moltke, Colonel Chesney, Fonton, Valentine, Allison, and others. These campaigns, which hitherto have been but little noticed or read, would be most interesting, if only as an abstract study of the art of war. They have, however, another claim to attention—sooner or later, if not in the days of the present, as is most probable, certainly in those of the next generation, there will be other battles under other leaders, but fought over the same battle-grounds and between the same nations.

Monarchs, generals, armies change, but rivers, mountains, and the principles of strategy remain the same.

Until the day comes—and may it be far distant—when the word England is but the geographical expression for a foggy 'little island set in stormy seas,' Englishmen have reason to look with anxiety to the East—they have interests to guard, possessions to defend; hence the history of the past seems to be well worth their study. There are some now amongst us—the Cleons of our time—who would recommend a policy which savours of the selfishness of China coupled with the isolation of Japan, who would endeavour to separate political from strategic considerations. These men may be honest and sincere, they may be politicians, but certainly they are not statesmen.

While the following pages are being sent to the printer for the last time, the news has arrived that the representatives of the Great Powers have finally presented their reduced and now irreducible demands to the Porte. If these conditions are rejected, war appears imminent—if accepted, as they afford no certain guarantee whatever for the better government of the Christian subjects of the Turk, war can only be postponed.

Paris: January 18th, 1877.

CONTENTS.

PAGE

INTRODUCTION 1

CHAPTER I.

THE EARLY WARS UP TO 1828.

Treaty of Carlowitz in 1699—War of 1709—Treaty of Pruth—Peace of Passarowitch—War of 1735—Siege of Azoph—Details of war—Continuance of war in 1738 and 1739—Defeat of Count Wallis at Belgrade—Success of armies of Czarina—Thirty years' peace—War of 1769—Successor of Romanzoff—Continuation of war—Treaty of Kuchuk Kainardghi—War of 1787—Siege of Ismail—Continuation of war—Peace of Jassy—War of 1806—Exploit of Admiral Duckworth—Peace of Tilsit—War of 1810-11—Siege of Rustchuk—Defeat of Turks—Conclusion of peace between Alexander I. and the Porte—Events from Peace of 1815 to 1828 14

CHAPTER II.

THE POSITION AND RESOURCES OF THE TWO COMBATANTS AT THE OPENING OF THE WAR IN 1828.

Position of Russia in Europe in 1828—Position of Turkey—Condition of her army and her fleet—Convention of Akkerman—Forces available to be brought into the field by Turkey—Forces available for invasion by Russia—Disposition of forces at opening of campaign—Lines of defence possessed by Turkey—The Pruth—The Danube—The Balkans—Büjuk Chekmedgé . . 55

CHAPTER III.

THE CAMPAIGN IN EUROPE IN 1828.

Reasons why operations were delayed—Method of Russian advance —Passage of Danube— Siege of Brailow— Peculiarities of Turkish defence of fortresses—Advance of Russians towards Varna—Strategy of Turks—Schumla—Siege of Varna—Attempts at relief—Fall of Varna—Contests before Schumla— Retreat of Russians to the Danube—Operations of 6th Corps in Wallachia—Siege of Silistria 71

CHAPTER IV.

REMARKS ON CAMPAIGN OF 1828 IN EUROPE.

Campaign commenced too late—Russian force too weak—Army should have marched on Varna—Diversion to Schumla a mistake—Strategy of the Turks—Tardiness of Grand Vizier— Results of Campaign in Bulgaria—General Geismar and his operations 97

CHAPTER V.

THE CAMPAIGN OF 1829 IN EUROPE.

Situation at commencement of year—Resources of Russians— Diebitsch—Resources of Turks—Commencement of hostilities Capture of Sizeboli—Naval exploit of Turks—Siege of Silistria —Diebitsch's march on Schumla and subsequent operations— Battle of Kulewtscha—March across the Balkans—Capture of Adrianople—Position of Russian army at Peace of Adrianople —Signature of Peace 108

CHAPTER VI.

REMARKS ON THE CAMPAIGN IN EUROPE OF 1829.

PAGE

The character of the Russian operations—Remarks thereon—Extracts from Appendix to Count Moltke's book on sickness in the Russian army—Field-marshal Diebitsch 138

CHAPTER VII.

THE CAMPAIGN IN ASIA IN 1828.

State of affairs in Asia in winter of 1827-28—Attitude of Persia—Russian preparations for invasion of Asia Minor—Resources at her disposal—Alternative methods of attack—Preparations of Turks—Commencement of campaign—Fall of Kars—Outbreak of the plague—Capture of Akhaltsikh—Defeat of the Seraskier—Capture of other fortresses—Conclusion of campaign—Remarks 156

CHAPTER VIII.

ASIATIC CAMPAIGN OF 1829.

Preparations of Turks for campaign—Threatening attitude of Persia—Consequent precautions of Paskewitch—Turkish attempt on Akhaltsikh—Successful defence and results—Letter of Paskewitch—Defeat of Hadgi Pacha—Defeat of the Seraskier near Kainly—Retreat of Hadgi Pacha—Fall of Erzeroum—Check of the Russians at Khart—Final defeat of the Seraskier—Retreat of Russians—Conclusion of war—Remarks on campaign—Conditions of peace 164

CHAPTER IX.

WAR ON THE DANUBE OF 1853 AND 1854 AND PREVIOUS EVENTS FROM PEACE OF ADRIANOPLE.

Relations that existed between Russia and Turkey after 1829—Revolt of Mehemet Ali—Victories of Ibrahim Pacha in Syria—Assistance given to Turkey by Russia in 1833—Russian forces quit Constantinople—Second revolt of Mehemet Ali in 1839—Intervention of Allies—Danger of an European war—Strategical position of Jaffa and Acre—Bombardment of Beyrout and Acre—Convention of 1840—Occupation of Principalities by Russia in 1849—Events that occasioned Crimean War—Assurances of Nicholas—War on the Danube in 1853; success of Omar Pacha—Siege of Silistria—Retreat of Russian Army—Landing in the Crimea—War in Asia and fall of Kars—Peace signed—The Treaty of Paris 179

CHAPTER X.

THE RESOURCES AND ARMED STRENGTH OF RUSSIA AND TURKEY AT THE PRESENT TIME.

Events connected with Eastern Question from Treaty of Paris up to present time—The Russian army—Russian railroads—Roumania, Servia, Montenegro, and Greece — Resources of Turkey—Turkish Army 204

CHAPTER XI.

THE CHANCES OF SUCCESS POSSESSED BY EACH COMBATANT IN THE EVENT OF WAR.

Divergence of views on the subject—To ensure success a large force required by Russia—Probable Russian system of invasion—Time required by the various Corps to reach the Danube and

Schumla—Lines of defence to be occupied by the Turks—Line of the Danube—Schumla—The Balkans—Selimno Pass—Flanking column by Servia—Time required to reach Adrianople—Probable date when Constantinople would be threatened—Reasons why Schumla cannot be disregarded—Alternative plans of operation—Difficulties of railway transport—Importance of Schumla—Description of the position of the Chekmedgès—of that of the Dardanelles—of the position in Asia Minor—Opportunity lost by Russia in 1876—Concluding remarks . 254

CHAPTER XII.

THE POLITICAL ASPECT OF THE EASTERN QUESTION.

Importance of Austria in a Russo-Turkish war—The Slaves—Policy of Austria—How the action of Austria might be neutralised, externally and internally—Slavonic question—Danger to Austria—Limits of Bulgaria—Interests of England—Traditional policy of Russia—Essentially aggressive in its character—Various lines of policy open to England—Which it is her interest to adopt—Unfortunate natural antagonism between Russia and England—Advantages of the policy suggested . 288

APPENDIX 309

RUSSIAN WARS WITH TURKEY.

INTRODUCTION.

It is a common saying that history repeats itself; perhaps it might be said with greater truth that, as in the common occurrences of life, so also in history, similar causes produce similar results. It now seems as if there is to be another of the many successive conflicts that have taken place between Russia and Turkey within the last hundred years. The same causes are at work, the same symptoms are visible. On the one side the misgovernment and tyranny of the oppressor, coupled with lamentation and cries for aid on the part of the oppressed: on the other side sympathy for suffering brethren of the same race and religion, and indignation against their taskmasters. On the one hand a rapidly decaying and bankrupt power, existing, as it were, on the sufferance of its neighbours, but possessed of, perhaps, the most fertile and highly favoured territories of the earth, whose fertility they turn to no account, and whose advantages they neglect; and these highly favoured lands inhabited by people antagonistic in religion, in habits, in feelings, the dominant race far inferior in numbers, receding in civilisation, intolerant, unyielding; the subject race rapidly increasing in numbers, advancing in prosperity, and daily more and more ambitious for the sovereign power, for which they are still unfitted. On the other hand a gigantic and powerful empire, with great resources still undeveloped, with territories whose sterility is their bane, and whose vast extent is their weakness, peopled by races but half civilised and more than half fanatic—races obedient to the dictates of a single man, but with prejudices so strong and feelings so deep, that this man, great as is his power, sacred as is his person, if he values his life cannot afford to disregard them. And as it were within the grasp of this mighty nation, there is a land flowing with milk and honey, which would supply all that in their own land is wanting, whose conquest would alike coincide with the tenets of their religion, with the dictates of their feelings, and with the consideration of their material advantage.

In truth, one may say, however sincere be expressions of peace-loving rulers, however earnest the endeavours of highly skilled diplomatists, it may be possible to postpone but it is wholly impossible to prevent these wars between Russia and Turkey, that are as natural in their origin as they are historic in their recurrence. Whether the year 1877 will or will not see another campaign on the banks of the Danube, and on the slopes of the Balkans, we may rest assured that so long as the crescent flies on the dome of St. Sophia, so long as the Muscovite empire remains united, there must be sooner or later a contest for very existence between the 'Colossus of the North and the Sick Man of the South.' The Eastern question will still be unanswered, and there will still be a dormant volcano which one day will convulse Europe.

Ever since the year 1453, when the Turks conquered Constantinople, it may be said that they have been in almost a chronic state of dissension or war with their Christian neighbours. Up to 1683, when Mahomet the Fourth besieged Vienna, the tide of their conquest was advancing; since then it has been slowly but certainly receding. On three successive occasions their naval power has been destroyed by the combined fleets of other nations, and twice has England participated in this destruction. In 1571, at Lepanto, the fleets of Spain, Genoa, Malta, Venice, and Pius V., combined to destroy their navy; again in 1770 they were defeated by the fleet of Russia aided by Englishmen, in the passage of Scio; once more, fifty-seven years later, in 1827, at Navarino the Turkish navy was annihilated by the united fleets of England, Russia, and France. The Turks have not unfrequently been called 'our ancient allies;' it will be found on referring to history that they might with greater truth be called 'our ancient enemies,' as up to 1840 we were nearly always allied against them.

England has always had a considerable interest in Eastern affairs, both on account of her commerce and for her vast possessions in the East; but that interest has increased within the last fifty years, in a degree scarcely realised at the present time. As our Indian empire has been added to, as it has become yearly more and more bound up with the associations, the feelings, and the fortunes of Englishmen, so have our interests in the East become magnified, and our solicitude as to how they may be best protected has become hourly more and more intense.

It is remarkable to note the comparative indifference with which our fathers, grandfathers, and great-grandfathers heard of a war between the Russians and the Turks, and the complacency with which they witnessed the near approach of Russian armies to Constantinople. It will be asked, why is there not this indifference now? Why are we more anxious, more solicitous, more nervous than those who have gone before us? The answer is plain. In those days neither the overland route to India nor the Suez Canal had been established; our communication to India was round the Cape, and hence the conversion of the Black Sea into a Russian lake, and the preponderance of Russian power and influence in the Mediterranean were important only so far as they affected our commerce, and indirectly prejudiced our position and general prestige. It is needless to remark that the case is very different now to what it was in 1791, or even in 1829, and those who attempt to argue that because our ancestors were indifferent, we should be so likewise, start from false premisses, which must lead to mistaken conclusions.

While, however, the position of England has materially altered within the last fifty years, it cannot be said that the positions of either Russia or Turkey have changed within the last hundred and fifty. The former State is, undoubtedly, more powerful for attack, the latter is weaker for defence, but as regards interest and causes for disagreement they are precisely the same as they have been for the last two centuries. Russia is still somewhat cut off and isolated by the very existence and geographical position of the Ottoman empire, and would derive enormous benefit from an extension of her southern territory. Turkey still hideously misgoverns her subjects and ill-treats her Christian population, though from all accounts not so much as in former days, not more than Russia herself ill-treats some of the inhabitants of her subject and recently subdued provinces. Turkey still occupies the position described as follows, by Sultan Mahmoud: 'The Franks envy us our possessions in Europe, and must sooner or later drive us into Asia. This would have been done twenty years before I mounted the throne had it been possible to divide Constantinople between them; but like a beautiful female captive, she has remained inviolate in the bosom of banditti. They cannot yet agree whose prize she is to be.'

But while the positions of Russia and Turkey have remained almost unchanged, the position of Austria, as will be shown in a future chapter, has altered in a degree, if possible, more striking than that of England. The events of 1866 and 1870 have bequeathed a legacy of danger to the Court of Vienna such as she cannot ignore or disregard.

As before remarked, until there is a complete and radical change in the entire state of affairs in the East, wars between Russia and Turkey are inevitable and must recur as often, if not indeed oftener, than they have done in the last hundred years. It is therefore especially desirable that we should thoroughly realise the character of these contests—that we should study alike their political and their strategic aspect, and should be fully prepared for any eventuality which the course of events may bring about.

When we look back we find that since the year 1709 Russia has made war against Turkey no less than eight times, namely:

> From 1709–1711.—Single-handed.
> „ 1735–1739.—In alliance with Austria.
> „ 1768–1774.—Single-handed.
> „ 1787–1791.—In alliance with Austria.
> „ 1806–1807.—A short time in alliance with England.
> „ 1810–1812.—Single-handed.
> „ 1828–1829.—Single-handed.
> „ 1853–1855.—Crimean War.

In these eight contests Russia has invariably been the aggressor, and nearly always has added to her territory. In fact, to quote the words of a distinguished writer on Eastern affairs in the year 1854: 'A reference to the map will show that Russia has advanced her frontier in every direction; and even the Caspian Sea, which appeared to present an impediment to her progress, she has turned to advantage by appropriating it to herself. It will be seen that the plains of Tartary have excited her cupidity, while the civilised States of Europe and Asia have been dismembered to augment her dominions. It will be seen that the acquisitions she has made from Sweden are greater than what remains of that ancient kingdom; that her acquisitions from Poland are as large as the whole Austrian empire; that the territory she has wrested from Turkey in Europe is equal to the dominions of Prussia, exclusive of her Rhenish provinces; and that her acquisitions from Turkey in Asia are equal in extent to all the smaller states of Germany, the Rhenish provinces of Prussia, Belgium, and Holland taken together; that the country she has conquered from Persia is about the size of England; that her acquisitions in Tartary have an area equal to Turkey in Europe, Greece, Italy, and Spain; and that the territory she has acquired within the last sixty-four years (since 1772) is greater in extent and importance than the whole empire she had in Europe before that time. . . . .'

'The power and resources of Russia lie in the countries to the west of the Volga, not in the wilds of Siberia; and her empire in Europe has been nearly doubled in little more than half a century. In sixty-four years she has advanced her frontier eight hundred and fifty miles towards

Vienna, Berlin, Dresden, Munich, and Paris; she has approached four hundred and fifty miles nearer to Constantinople; she has possessed herself of the capital of Poland, and has advanced to within a few miles of the capital of Sweden, from which, when Peter the First mounted the throne, her frontier was distant three hundred miles. Since that time she has stretched herself forward about one thousand miles towards India, and the same distance towards the capital of Persia. The regiment that is now stationed at her furthest frontier post on the western shore of the Caspian has as great a distance to march back to Moscow as onward to Attock on the Indus, and is actually further from St. Petersburg than from Lahore, the capital of the Punjab. The battalions of the Russian Imperial Guard that invaded Persia found, at the termination of the war, that they were as near to Herat as to the banks of the Don; that they had already accomplished half the distance from their capital to Delhi; and that therefore, from their camp in Persia, they had as great a distance to march back to St. Petersburg as onward to the capital of Hindostan.'

Whatever opinion we may entertain of the intentions, the wishes, and the character of the present ruler of the Muscovite empire and of his government, no one, we may add, who has watched their career can have other than a high one; no one can question their sincerity: nevertheless facts and history remain, and the traditional policy of a mighty empire, which possesses patriotic and faithful children, cannot change in a day or suddenly become unaggressive and peaceful after having been for centuries the reverse.

Alison has remarked that 'such are the natural strength and incomparable local advantages of Constantinople, that it has, both in ancient and modern times, enabled the empire of which it formed the head to survive the usual causes of decay, which after the lapse of a few generations generally prostrate the most powerful Asiatic monarchies.' No one who studies the history of the last century can fail to be struck by the truth of this reflection,—it is impossible to avoid feeling the greatest astonishment that the Turkish empire has so often and miraculously survived the destruction which on so many occasions has apparently impended over her. Eight times she has been in danger from Russia: twice, in 1711 and 1739, she has saved herself by force of her own arms; twice, in 1774 and 1829, has she been saved by the plague; once, in 1807, has she been saved by accidental circumstances; and three times, in 1791, 1812, and 1853, has she been saved by the intervention of other powers. In truth a succession of marvellous escapes—fortunate perhaps for her, but most unfortunate for other nations, since indirectly, from her gross misgovernment, from her apparent helplessness, and the temptation she affords for attack, Turkey is the chronic and inveterate disturber of peace in Europe. She and her antagonist Russia were the only disturbers of the great fifty years' peace; again they brought that peace to a close, falsifying the fond dreams of Utopian believers in the efficacy of international exhibitions as harbingers of a terrestrial Millennium. Now, again, are they threatening to inflict on Europe, for the third time within fifty years, the horrors of an Eastern war.

The 'Eastern Question' has been defined 'as the question whether Russia will have Constantinople or whether she will not.' This is a concise, and not altogether an inappropriate definition, but it is not sufficiently complete or exhaustive; to it also might be added how the Turks can be made to govern properly, or, if that is an impossibility, how they may be satisfactorily replaced. Until these questions are solved, and indeed for some time after their solution, should that time ever arrive, all history bearing on the East must be replete with interest and instruction. From the earlier conflicts, which are summarised in the following pages, but little can be learnt from a military point of view. In those days the science of war had made but little progress in Europe, and the East was even then far behind the West in enlightenment. As remarked by Frederick the Great, the Russians and Turks, when fighting, resembled 'a number of one-eyed men thrashing a number of blind ones.' Still physical characteristics remain the same, the sea still retains its position, and obstacles, which did not prove insurmountable formerly, most certainly would not be insurmountable now, as some believers in the Turks and in their powers of defence would imagine. When we come to the campaigns of only fifty years ago—those fought in 1828 and 1829—within the memory of some living men, we find in every way much that can with advantage be studied; likewise at the commencement of the Crimean War there were many remarkable events of both a political and a strategic significance. Thus in looking back and pondering over what has gone before, we must not fail to remember that the past is little else than a reflection of the future, while history is the mirror in which this reflection may be seen.

Since the above pages were written, affairs in the East have taken an unexpected turn, illustrating more than ever the truth of the saying that 'history repeats itself.' The reader can judge for himself as to the aptness of the parallel between the situation now and what it was fifty years ago.

In 1827 the misgovernment and barbarities of the Turks had utterly disgusted Europe, had converted their allies into enemies, and had deprived them of either material or moral support. Then it was also a case of oppressed nationalities, the Greeks being the sufferers instead of the Slaves. Russia, as now, came forward as the philanthropic and disinterested champion of the sufferers from misrule, and was aided by England and the great Powers in her charitable efforts. A conference was assembled at London, and the delegates of the Powers there represented, ignoring the fact that 'there were

Turks in Turkey,' arranged the affairs of the Ottoman Empire to their own satisfaction, but without consulting the Ottomans. They suddenly found that they had reckoned without their host—to their advice, to their suggestions, remonstrances, menaces, and armed demonstrations, the Divan showed itself equally indifferent. There followed Navarino—that 'untoward event' as it was termed in the Speech from the Throne of the following year; even this somewhat energetic demonstration failed to induce the Turk to swallow the wholesome dose which his kind physicians had prepared for him. The converse of the *Malade imaginaire*, although fearfully sick, he refused to acknowledge his sickness. The French and English ambassadors left Constantinople and retired to Corfu, while Russia was left mistress of the situation. This situation was, however, by no means an enviable one —even in those days the Russian army was not, as a whole, the same as the splendid guards that kept watch over the Emperor's palace at St. Petersburg—even in those days there existed defaulting contractors—corrupt officials—gunpowder that would not ignite— guns that would not go off, and stores that existed only in the bills which the Government had paid for them. Austria became alarmed and began to intrigue; England, though loyal and true as ever, was by no means eager to convert Constantinople into a Russian stronghold; France was not a whit more anxious to encompass the same end. In fact, the Emperor Nicholas found that, though moral support was apparently freely accorded him, as regards material assistance he must rely on his own resources. Nevertheless, his word was pledged, his prestige, and perhaps his life, were at stake, and hence there followed the war of 1828. Time alone can show how far the parallel will hold good to the end.

CHAPTER I.

THE EARLIER WARS UP TO 1828.

Treaty of Carlowitz in 1699—War of 1709—Treaty of Pruth—Peace of Passarowitch—War of 1735—Siege of Azoph—Details of war—Continuance of war in 1738 and 1739—Defeat of Count Wallis at Belgrade—Success of armies of Czarina—Thirty years' peace—War of 1769—Successor of Romanzoff—Continuation of war—Treaty of Kuchuk Kainardgi—War of 1787—Siege of Ismail—Continuation of war—Peace of Jassy—War of 1806—Exploit of Admiral Duckworth—Peace of Tilsit—War of 1810-11—Siege of Rustchuk—Defeat of Turks—Conclusion of peace between Alexander I. and the Porte—Events from peace of 1815 to 1828.

It would be difficult to trace out separately, or even to summarise, all the various wars in which from time to time the Turks have been engaged since they entered Europe. In point of fact they were for centuries more or less at war, which was carried on vigorously or not according to the means they happened to have for waging it. Their neighbours were their enemies, and all Christendom combined against them as against a common foe. Russia did not appear as their separate and definite antagonist until the commencement of the eighteenth century, but since then the contest between these two nations has been continually renewed at short intervals.

About the year 1694 there occurred the last great united alliance against Turkey, in which all the Eastern Powers of Christendom joined; the war lasted more or less for about five years, and was at last brought to a close by a treaty of peace, which was concluded between the Sultan and the Czar, then Peter the Great, in 1699, at Carlowitz; at that time, through the intervention of England, an armistice for thirty years was agreed on between the belligerents, and Turkey, having had the worst of the conflict, ceded Transylvania and Hungary to Austria, and portions of what is now the south of Russia, including Azoph, to Peter the Great.

This may be termed the first serious commencement of the decay and fall of the Turkish empire, as it will be chronicled in the pages of some future Gibbon. Notwithstanding this formal treaty and solemn armistice, we find a few years later, in 1709, another war breaking out between Russia and Turkey. This time the armies of the Czar were defeated, and in the hour of his need Prussia and his other allies deserted him; he had thus to accept the best terms he could get, and to renounce all the advantages he had gained in 1699. In 1711 the treaty of Pruth was signed and matters remained *in statu quo* until 1720, when we find the Muscovite and Ottoman empires, strange to say, allied together against Persia. In the meantime it may be remarked that the Turks had been engaged in a desperate conflict with the Venetians and Austrians, and had been signally defeated.

In 1711 they besieged Corfu, but were repulsed with loss; in the same year they lost Belgrade, which was then termed the key of the Turkish Empire on the western frontier. Prince Eugene, in command of a large force of Austrians, besieged the fortress and defeated an army of 180,000 men which hastened to its relief. The result was the peace of Passarowitz between the German Empire and the Porte, signed in the following year.

As before stated, in 1720 Russia and Turkey were allied together against Persia; this alliance, however, was not of long duration. Turkey became alarmed by the progress of Russian arms, and was with difficulty restrained by Austria and France from declaring war. In 1722 peace was proclaimed between Russia, Turkey, and Persia, and a convention signed, in which many advantages were conceded to the Czar. This peace likewise did not last long, for in 1735 the Empress Anne, seeing, as she thought, a favourable opportunity for recovering some of the advantages given up by the treaty of Pruth, discovered a pretext for declaring war with the Porte, and induced Austria to join her in hopes of a share in the spoil. This war was of such great duration and of so serious a character that it merits more than a passing notice. The actual and formal rupture between the Porte and Russia did not take place till the spring of 1736, although in the previous year every preparation had been made for war. At first the Emperor of Austria attempted mediation between the Czarina and the Sultan; but finding his efforts vain he preferred to join the Russians and to aid in the dismemberment of his Mussulman neighbour.

The campaign commenced with the siege of Azoph, some details of which are narrated as follows by Sir Edward Cust in his 'Annals of the Wars': 'Marshal Münnich, who had been appointed to the command of the Russian army, commenced operations in the month of March, having assembled six regiments of infantry, and three of cavalry, together with 3,000 Cossacks of the Don, at St. Anne, about eighty leagues from Azoph. On the 27th Münnich passed the Don and began his march with so much precaution and silence that he arrived near Azoph without having been perceived by the enemy; and he immediately attacked and carried by storm two castles on the river-side without the loss of a single man. On April 3rd, the Russians carried the fort of Lutick with little loss. He now gave over to Count Lacy the care of blockading and taking the town, and left the camp for the grand army that was formed on the Dnieper, where he arrived on the 18th, and found himself at the head of from 50,000 to 54,000 men.

'On May 19th, Münnich sent off five detachments, each composed of 400 dragoons and 150 Cossacks; and as the steppe-land was one vast unbroken plain, they had orders to march within sight of each other, so as to unite whenever the force of the opposing army should make it necessary. They had marched only about two leagues when they came up with a body of Nogay Tartars, whom they attacked and routed. They had gone about two leagues farther when General Spiegel, who commanded, was obliged to unite his detachments as quickly as he could, since he suddenly found himself in presence of about 20,000 men advancing upon him. Spiegel had just time to form square, ordering the front rank to dismount, when these attacked him with most horrid yells, and poured forth a flight of arrows. Münnich, apprised of the danger in which Spiegel was, put himself at the head of 3,000 dragoons and 2,000 Cossacks, and marched rapidly to his relief. As soon as the enemy perceived his approach, they retired with great precipitation, leaving 200 dead on the field. It was ascertained from the prisoners taken that the Khan, with an army of 100,000 men, was encamped at twenty leagues from the spot, and that the body that had retreated was under the command of the Kalga Sultan, or generalissimo of the Tartars of the Crimea. On the 26th the Russians were encamped on the side of the river Kalantshi, when on a sudden they were attacked and surrounded by these troops, but at the first shot fired from some field-pieces the latter all fled with precipitation to the lines of Perekop.

'The Marshal determined to force these famous lines, and, marching all night, came upon them suddenly at break of day, to the astonishment of the Tartars, who had known nothing of his movements, and were astounded when they saw the Russian force formed up in six columns for the attack. These lines were extraordinary works, nearly two French leagues in extent from the Sea of Azoph to the Black Sea. There was but one entrance, and six towers of stone, mounted with cannon, flanked the approach. The ditch was twelve toises broad and seven deep, the height of the parapet seventy feet, and its thickness in proportion. The troops advanced boldly to the ditch, under the command of Manstein, but on arriving there found it more deep and broad than they could have expected: nevertheless, they threw themselves into it and assisted one another to climb the parapet under an exceedingly brisk fire of the enemy. The Tartars, now finding the affair serious, did not wait for the Russians to reach the top, but betook themselves to flight, leaving no impediments to the free passage of the lines.

'On June 5th the Marshal advanced into the Crimea. The Tartars harassed them incessantly in the march, but scampered away immediately they were attacked. As they advanced they soon found water to fail. The natives, who fled from the villages, burned all the forage and spoiled the water of the wells. The absence of all water (for rain water is the only resource of this country and very scarce) caused the troops to suffer a good deal, and much disease ensued in consequence. On the 26th Münnich advanced upon Baktchi-Serai, and on the 27th they repulsed the enemy and entered the town. He had intended to proceed to Caffa, but his army was so reduced that he resolved to return to Perekop, where he destroyed the lines, and on August 28th returned to the Ukraine.

'Count, now Marshal, Lacy commenced the siege of Azoph on May 15th. On the 19th Admiral Bredal, who had come down the Don with fifteen galleys and a great number of other vessels, arrived off Azoph. The Turkish fleet, under the Capudan Pacha, Dgiannon Conja, entered the Sea of Azoph to succour the place, but the mouth of the Don is so barred with sands and shoals that neither fleet could get near each other. The works against the place continued by sap till June 13th. During this time the besieged made continual sallies, which were repulsed. The Marshal himself, in one of them, was nearly taken prisoner, and received a gun-shot wound in the thigh. On the 18th the usual accompaniment of a Turkish siege took place. One of the largest powder magazines exploded, by which more than 100 houses were thrown down, and 300 men lost their lives. At midnight, on the 28th, the assault was given, and although two mines were sprung the besiegers effected a lodgment, so that on June 29th the Pacha governor requested a capitulation, and Lacy, after leaving a garrison in the town, marched away to rejoin Münnich in the Ukraine. It was at this siege that the effects of the discipline which Münnich had established in the Russian armies were made curiously apparent. Sickness prevailed in the camp to a great extent, occasioned by intemperance and a general disgust for the service.

'To remedy this evil the Marshal issued an order forbidding anyone to be sick, on pain of being buried alive!'

In addition to the operations related above, the Empress Anne had directed an army against the Turkish territories of the Kuban. In this campaign she was also successful, and before the close of 1836 the entire district had submitted to her.

In the year 1737 the war was continued with unabated vigour. Sir Edward Cust gives the following account of the operations of the Russians:—'Marshal Münnich took the field towards the end of April, and found his army to consist of 63 battalions and 145 squadrons, which might be reckoned at 60,000 or 70,000 men. There were in the artillery-train 62 guns of siege and 11 mortars, besides 165 field-pieces and 16 howitzers. On July 10th they were within three leagues of Ochzakow, where they came to blows with some Turks of the garrison, who had sallied out to the number of 15,000 men. On the 11th he began the siege between the river Dnieper and the Black Sea, and had the governor known what he was about at this time, and made a sally, he could have foiled the Russians, and forced them to retire; but a powder magazine blew up, which buried 6,000 men in the ruins, and threw the whole garrison into consternation. Münnich chose this moment for an assault, and finding his troops unwilling to face the flames, he opened a battery upon his own soldiers; so that the place was at length carried by men who feared the enemy less than their own terrible general. It surrendered at discretion on July 13th.

'In the meantime Marshal Lacy advanced again into

the Crimea with about 40,000 men. On June 28th, supported by a fleet in the Sea of Azoph, he crossed an arm of the sea by a bridge, and marched along the narrow strip of land that stretches as far as Arabat. The Khan, who never imagined the Russians would enter the country on that side, had posted himself with all his troops behind the lines of Perekop, which he had taken care to have repaired, and trusted to be enabled to dispute more successfully than had been done the year before. He now found them of no use, for Lacy was in full march for Arabat, without the loss of a single man. The Khan thought to rectify his mistake by posting himself with all diligence across the narrow spit of land formed by the Sea of Azoph on one side, and the Putrid Sea on the other. As soon, however, as Lacy heard that the Khan had arrived at Arabat, he caused the Putrid Sea to be sounded, and found a means of crossing through it, to the astonishment of the Khan, who forthwith retreated to the mountains. It was not the Khan alone who judged of this enterprise in marching along the spit of Arabat as a rash one. All the generals except Spiegel represented to Lacy that he ran the risk of seeing his whole army perish. The Marshal answered that there was danger in all military enterprises, but that he did not see more in this than in others. However, he begged their opinion as to what they thought best to be done. They unanimously replied, " To return with all possible speed." Upon which Lacy rejoined, that since the generals had a mind to return, he would have their passports made out accordingly; and called for his secretary to deliver them without delay. He even commanded a party of 200 dragoons to be their escort to the Ukraine, there to wait his return. It was three whole days before the generals could prevail on the Marshal to relent, and forgive them their presumption in proposing a retreat to him. On July 25th Lacy was within a few miles of Kara-su Bazar, which was immediately abandoned.'

After the operations as above related were brought to a successful issue, there was an attempt on the part of the Turks to retake Ochzakow, which failed, and also a naval action in the Sea of Azoph of an indecisive character. While, however, the Russians were thus engaged on their southern frontier, and had achieved considerable success, their allies the Austrians had not been so fortunate. With that timid and undecided policy, which seems to be inseparable from the traditions of the Viennese Court, the Emperor at first did not throw himself into the contest with vigour or determination, and when his troops actually were engaged, by his interference with his generals, he caused their defeat. Marshal Seckendorff had been placed in chief command of the Imperialist troops, and he framed a plan of operations which was to commence with the capture of Widdin, and to be seconded by an advance of the Russians towards the Pruth. Neither of these operations were carried out, and at the close of the year 1737 the Ottoman forces remained master of the situation, while Seckendorff was disgraced.

During the years of 1738 and 1739 this war still continued. It will afford some idea of the strength and resources of the Turkish empire in those days, as compared with her present condition, if we consider that for nearly four years she was opposed single-handed to the combined forces of Russia and Austria, and although she suffered many reverses, still in the end she maintained her position, and certainly the integrity of her empire, against them both. The year 1738 was marked by a Russian invasion of the Crimea under Marshal Lacy, who crossed the Sea of Azoph in July, almost dry-shod, with an army of 35,000 men. The Khan of the Crimea assembled an army of 40,000 men to resist the invasion, and being assisted by a storm in the Black Sea, which dispersed the fleet intended to supply the Russian army, he succeeded in repelling the invaders, who were forced to retire without any practical result beyond the destruction of the lines of Perekop. At the same time Marshal Münnich, with about 50,000 men, was engaged in operations on the banks of the Dniester, but eventually was forced to retire. The Austrians were not more successful on the borders of Transylvania. Here the Turks had taken the offensive early in the year, and soon captured Orsova. The campaign closed with the retreat of the Imperialists and by the disgrace of Konigsegg, the general who had replaced Seckendorff as generalissimo.

In 1739 the war was again renewed, and again proved unfavourable to the fortunes of the Emperor of Austria.

Count Wallis, who had been placed in chief command of his army, assembled an army of about 56,000 men, besides cavalry and artillery, near Belgrade, and in June encountered the Turkish army at the battle of Crotska, which is thus described by Sir Edward Cust:—

'The Grand Vizier with his whole force had taken post on two hills between the defile and the village of Crotska. The Prince of Hildburghausen formed the first battalion that cleared the defile into square, whilst the left wing passed along a narrow path, and extended itself on the heights overlooking the Danube. In this position the Imperialists withstood repeated attacks from the Turks, who assailed them, with far superior numbers, from five in the morning till sunset, when Wallis ordered a retreat under cover of the approaching darkness. The Imperialists were hampered by the defile in which the Grand Vizier had caught them. On their side four generals were killed and five wounded; and 7,000 men, with 400 officers, were left dead on the field of battle. In this desperate conflict both parties sustained considerable loss, but the Turks displayed new skill in the art of war. Instead of tumultuous and unconnected attacks, they fought in the greatest order and in regular bodies; and when broken they rallied with speed and activity. This was due in a great measure to the admirable discipline they had received from Count Bonneval, a French military adventurer, who, after having served in the navy and army of France with distinction, took afterwards an Austrian commission, and subsequently became a Mussulman under the appellation of Achmet Pacha. He was meditating a return to Christendom when he was surprised by death, eight years later than the present events. His memoirs are amusing and curious, as showing the rewards attendant upon those who adopt service among Orientals.

'The Imperial flotilla under Admiral Pallavicini fell down the Danube to co-operate with the army, so that when Wallis retreated the admiral found himself exposed to severe handling from the Turkish batteries, and only regained Belgrade on the 24th in a most dilapidated condition. The Imperialists took up so strong a position at Kinza, and placed their artillery with so much skill, that on the following day he repulsed a considerable body of troops headed by the Grand Vizier. Wallis, however, seized with despondency again, retreated during the night, and occupied the lines of Belgrade; when, being still alarmed at the appearance of some Turkish irregulars, and deeming himself unequal to the defence of this strong position, he recrossed the Danube the following night. The Turks now instantly advanced against Belgrade, and the Grand Vizier, investing the place on the side of Servia, commenced the siege in form. He summoned the garrison to surrender on July 29. The Earl of Crawford, who served as a volunteer in the Imperial army, signalised his courage in an extraordinary manner on the occasion, and was dangerously wounded.'

After the defeat of the Imperial army at Crotska, the Turks invested Belgrade and prepared to push their successes to the utmost. No opportunity, however, was afforded them for any further triumphs over the Austrians; the Emperor and his advisers, appalled by such a series of disasters, were only too glad to conclude a separate peace, by which Belgrade, Servia, and other portions of territory were handed over to the Porte, which now was left to engage Russia by itself.

While their allies had suffered such defeat and humiliation, the armies of the Czarina had been far more fortunate. Count Münnich, with about 60,000 men, invaded Turkey from the side of Poland, and after a series of operations succeeded in utterly routing the main Ottoman army at the battle of Cho-czim on August 28th, 1739. Peace soon followed, and the Sultan, notwithstanding his recent defeat, succeeded in making almost as advantageous terms with Russia as with Austria; the former relinquished Belgrade, the latter Azoph, while it was arranged that Muscovite vessels of war should not appear in the Black Sea, and that commerce should be carried on by Ottoman vessels. This treaty, by some called the convention of Belgrade, by others that of Nissa, was signed in 1739, and remained in force for thirty years, until 1769, when the partition of Poland took place.

As this was a violation of existing engagements, and was calculated to alarm the Divan for the integrity of its own territories, the reigning Sultan determined to take the initiative, and having been promised assistance by France—an assistance, it may be remarked, never really accorded him—he declared war. The conflict which resulted was most disastrous to Turkey. The Crimea was invaded, Romanzoff's armies were most successful on the Pruth, Ismail and Bender were captured, and in 1770 the Turkish fleet was destroyed in the Bay of Tchesme, by Elphinstone, an Englishman in the Russian service.

The details of this war, disastrous in its results, and nearly productive of the destruction of the Ottoman empire, are of so complicated a character that it seems unnecessary to do more than indicate shortly their general bearing. Little was done in the first year of the conflict, 1768, beyond preparations and concentration of troops. Early, however, in 1769, two Russian armies under Prince Gallitzin and General Romanzoff respectively commenced operations on the north-west and northern frontier of Turkey. At first Gallitzin was defeated, but by the middle of September the Russians had obtained so great a success at Cho-czim, on the Dniester, that by the end of the year they had subjugated all the open country north-west of the Danube. It may be remarked that this great Russian victory was principally caused by the extraordinary rashness of the Turks, who crossed the Dniester to attack their enemies without having secured their communications in rear, or made corresponding attacks on the enemy's flank, and who, when on a sudden flood of the stream and the consequent destruction of their temporary bridges, were 'left in the air' and utterly routed.

After their successes of the 1769 campaign the Russian army under the supreme command of Romanzoff retreated behind the Dniester, while the Turks on their part concentrated behind the Danube. Early in 1770 both combatants crossed the rivers before them and advanced to attack. Romanzoff first encountered an Ottoman army under the Khan of the Crimea between the Pruth and the Larga. The Turks here occupied an intrenched camp, and could not be attacked; but fortunately they were induced by repeated challenges to descend into the plains, and there were utterly routed. Romanzoff next met the main Turkish army of a nominal strength of 150,000; this force he also defeated on the banks of the Pruth at Kagul on August 2nd, and ultimately drove it across the Danube. This great victory was soon followed by the fall of Bender, on the Dniester, the great Turkish fortress of the north, and with this capture the campaign of 1770 ended. Romanzoff established his headquarters at Jassy, and remained master of Moldavia and Wallachia.

During the three following years this apparently endless war was continued; in 1771 the Russians invaded the Crimea and conquered the entire peninsula, while the unfortunate Khan escaped to Constantinople, and it is stated died of grief. The Turks also made a counter attack on the Danube and captured Giurgevo, but were defeated in the Dobrudscha; on the whole, this year ended without any very decisive results to either party in the Danubian provinces, though it may be said that on the whole the Russians had the advantage.

In 1772 the war languished in the early part of the year, and in the autumn an armistice was concluded, but neither party being agreed as to the terms of peace, in 1773 the contest was renewed with all vigour.

The operations of this and the following campaign are somewhat interesting, as the Russians started from much the same base as they would now occupy in a Turkish war. They had possession of the entire territory north of the Danube, and their operations very much resembled those which afterwards took place in 1828 and 1829, both as regards preliminaries and results.

On June 18th and 19th, 1773, Romanzoff crossed the Danube near Brailow, defeated a Turkish army, which he encountered ten days later near Silistria, and then at once proceeded to besiege that fortress. On the approach, however, of a large Turkish army the siege was raised, and the Russians recrossed the Danube between July 2nd and July 5th. There they remained until October, when they again recrossed the river in two divisions; one of these recommenced the siege of Silistria, while the other moved on Varna and attacked it. They were repulsed from both these places, and by December had to retrace their steps into winter quarters in Wallachia without having achieved any decisive results. It is stated that at this time, as also in other wars, the superiority of the Turkish over the Russian cavalry was most remarkable, and contributed more than anything else to cause the retreat of the invading army.

In 1774 the Russians were more fortunate than in the previous year, and all but succeeded in actually reaching Constantinople. This time the Russians again crossed the Danube in several columns, the principal passage being effected at Turtakai, which had been captured by Suwarrow in the previous year. The Turks, as on several other occasions, did not attempt to defend the line of the Danube, but concentrated their forces in Bulgaria, while the garrisons of Rustchuk and the other fortified towns threatened the Muscovite communications. The disorganisation, however, of the Turkish army rendered any military plans, however well devised, entirely futile. The Grand Vizier was shamefully defeated on June 20th by Kaminski and Suwarrow, and was deserted by almost all his army. He shut himself up in Schumla, and his government sued for peace. Now, as fifty-nine years later pestilence came to the aid of the Turks, this was fortunate, since, in addition to external dangers, some of her principal possessions, Egypt, Tripoli, Greece, and Syria, revolted from her; it may truly be said that the Ottoman Power was never in greater straits than now, and that the Russians had never a better chance of reaching the Bosphorus. In fact, nothing retained the Turk in Europe but the appearance of the plague, which broke out with unexampled malignity, spread from the Neva to the Euphrates, and entirely paralysed both the combatants.

At last, in 1774, the treaty of Kuckuk Kainardghi was signed between Catherine II. and Abdul Hamid; by this Russia obtained free navigation of the Black Sea with the passage of the Dardanelles, provided only one ship of war was kept in the seas of Constantinople. She acquired Azoph, Taganrog, Kertch, and the Kinburn, her frontier was advanced to the Bogue, she obtained the sovereignty of the two Kabardas, and the Crimea was made independent, with a view to its future annexation. This treaty was even more important in its consequence than its conditions at first seemed to indicate, since by it alone Russia obtained that ascendancy in the Caucasus, and in Georgia, which led to their subsequent conquest and to the conversion of the Caspian into a Russian lake.

The peace proclaimed in 1774 only lasted about twelve years, as the Empress Catherine placed a large army under Potemkin on the line of the Caucasus, while Suwarrow threatened the line of the Danube; she then concluded an alliance with Austria for the partition of Turkey, and in the meantime seized the Crimea. The Sultan, in presence of the great danger that was threatening him, acknowledged the sovereignty of Russia in the Crimea, but thereby wholly failed to avert the storm; at last, seeing that it was inevitable, he took the initiative, and declared war in 1787. The coalition against the Porte was at this time almost as formidable as it had been fifty years before. The Emperor Joseph of Austria looked forward to a large extension of territory on his eastern frontiers, while the Empress Catherine was to have Byzantium as the seat of the empire of the East, Egypt being offered to France as the price of her connivance.

The Austrians were first in the field, and also, as events turned out, were first out of it. Four Imperial armies assembled in the spring of 1788 for the invasion of Turkey, one at Cronstadt in Croatia under General de Vigne; a second at Peterwardin in Hungary under General Langlois; a third under General Febris on the borders of Lithuania; and a fourth in the Bukowine under the orders of the Prince of Coburg. The Russians, on the other hand, had concentrated a force of 150,000 men by June 18 on the river Bug, and prepared in the first instance for the siege of Ochzakow, to be followed afterwards by an invasion of Turkish territory.

The Austrian army commenced operations soon after February 10th, 1788, when war was declared; they were opposed by the Grand Vizier, who at the head of about 200,000 men had taken up a commanding position, first near Silistria and afterwards at Belgrade, which latter fortress the Emperor was peculiarly desirous of capturing.

Operations of no very great importance were carried on until August; on the 7th and 8th, however, of that month, the Ottomans boldly assumed the offensive, and after a sanguinary battle at a place called Temeswar, near old Orsova, defeated the Austrians with great loss. The success, however, was not followed up with the ability which caused it to be achieved, and by the end of October the Vizier had to conduct an unfortunate retreat from the position he had previously gained, and in November an armistice was concluded for an indefinite period.

While these events had been taking place on the borders of Transylvania, the Russians, who likewise had a Swedish war on their hands, had also been engaged with the Turks, and had achieved considerable successes. The Ottomans had been defeated in an attempt to retake Kinburn, both Cho-czim and Ochzakow had fallen after desperate sieges, and in some slight naval engagements in the Black Sea victory had equally remained with the Muscovites. At this time a Scotchman, Admiral Greig, was in chief command of the Russian fleet in the Euxine, and it is related that nearly all their principal naval officers were British subjects. So high an opinion did the Empress Catherine entertain for British seamanship that she named the notorious Paul Jones to the chief command of her fleet in the Baltic, an appointment which caused sixty British officers in her service to resign their commissions.

The year 1789 did not dawn hopefully for the prospects of the Turks; as usual their unsuccessful generals were first made the victims of popular discontent at national disasters. Jussuf Pacha, the Grand Vizier, was seized at the head of his army, carried to Constantinople, disgraced and subsequently murdered. These vigorous measures, however, in no way brought victory to the Crescent. The Turks were defeated in every quarter both by the Austrians and the Russians. Marshal Loudon, in command of the former, captured Gradisca in Croatia and subsequently reduced Belgrade; while Potemkin, the Muscovite general, made himself master of Bender, having previously defeated an Ottoman army in the open field. In fact, so great were the misfortunes of the Porte in the year that, if there had not been an insurrection in the Netherlands which partially paralysed the Austrian empire, it is more than probable that Constantinople would have actually fallen before the armies of the allies.

Early in 1790, on February 20th, the Emperor Joseph expired, and with him all energy on the part of Austria in prosecuting the Turkish war. The contest, it is true, was renewed in the spring, and an action favourable to the Ottomans took place at Giurgevo; but on July 27th the Court of Vienna made a separate peace at Reichenbach, the conditions being the renunciation of the Muscovite alliance, and the *status quo*. Thus the Russians were once more deserted, and left to continue the contest single-handed.

Up till quite late in the autumn of 1790 the armies of the Empress Catherine continued inactive; this was owing, it is stated, partly to the state of the health of their mistress, who was as determined as ever on the conquest of Constantinople, but was unable to spare sufficient energy for the direction of affairs. In October the operations commenced, and consisted mainly of two operations. In the first place there was a struggle between the Black Sea and the Caucasus. Butah Pacha had advanced with 50,000 men from Anapa to invade the Muscovite territory; he was met by General Herman near the river Kuban on October 10th and utterly routed. The other operation took place on the Danube, and was the celebrated siege and surrender of Ismail by Suwarrow. The following graphic account of the capture of this fortress is taken from Sir Edward Cust's 'Annals of the Wars:'—

'It was late in October when Suwarrow received reinforcements and supplies, with this brief and peremptory letter from Potemkin: "You will take Ismail, cost what it may." This strong fortress was the key of the Lower Danube, and, on account of its importance, a garrison of 13,000 men, the flower of the Turkish troops, was posted there to defend it. The works had lately been much improved and strengthened in a most masterly manner, under the able direction of a Spanish engineer officer. It was the only fortress of any value that remained to the Turks in those parts, and there was nothing between it and Constantinople but the intrenched camp at Schumla, and the difficult passes of the Balkan mountains. A fleet of galleys under Admiral Ribas invested Ismail by water, and Suwarrow completely surrounded the fortress by land, after which he summoned the Turkish governor, who returned a haughty defiance.

'It was already the month of December, not the time for making a regular siege, during the fogs and rigour of that most inclement region; but it was not suited to the genius of this rudest and roughest soldier of fortune to undertake any slow and regular process of military science. He therefore surrounded the place with batteries constructed on every spot of ground which could answer his purpose, and armed them with the heaviest battering cannon and mortars, as well as with every kind of machine that could carry any form of hostile projectile, while forges for heating balls were constructed everywhere, to pour destruction into the devoted place. The dreadful roar of a most stupendous bombardment awoke the garrison at five o'clock in the morning of December 25th. At seven such showers of red-hot shot, bombs, and carcasses had been already thrown that, thinking the enemy to be cowed, the Russian commander determined to try the effect of an assault by brute force. Twenty-three thousand men, divided into eight columns, one of which was led by Suwarrow in person, and each column appropriated to its particular point of attack, advanced against the fortress, while the Russian galleys, mounting 567 guns, played upon it from the river. A most desperate conflict ensued for three hours. Ismail looked like a volcano in action; it was a most dreadful battle.

'At length the assailants were repulsed; the galleys rowed away with a terrible loss in men and officers; the Turks sallied out upon the retiring columns to swell the bloody rout with the sword and ataghan. Suwarrow was seen exhibiting the most extraordinary valour in his own person, to reanimate his troops and recall them to the fight. To allow his men time to recover their spirits, or perhaps to bring up fresh troops, he determined to distract the attention of the Mussulmans by a fresh bombardment from all the batteries on land and from the galleys by water. The assault was then renewed, but the Russians were again and again driven back.

'At last one earth-battery was carried, Suwarrow being the first to apply the scaling-ladder, and, with a standard in his hand, he mounted, and planted it on the work. It is reported of him that, when he was leading or driving his people to the assault, he cried out, " Brothers, no quarter to-day, for our bread is scarce." The first line of works was at length carried, but the contest was still dreadful, for the Turks strained every nerve to recover what they had lost, and totally dismissed from their minds the preservation of life. Fresh reinforcements had arrived to the Russians, whilst the Ottomans were wearied and worn down by this long and continual conflict, and these were now at last beaten back to the defence of the second parapet; this they defended as desperately as they had done the first, and they then showed as bold a front behind the third parapet as they had done at the first and second.

'At length, an hour after sunset, the third line was carried, and a torrent of savage and irritated Muscovites led on by Suwarrow, as at the first, burst into the very heart of the city, and began a carnage that lasted through the night, accompanied by horrors of which humanity could scarcely endure the recital. Many Turks, incapable of witnessing them, and to shorten their own misery, rushed desperately upon the bayonets of their enemies. The rising sun in Ismail exhibited such a scene as had never before shocked the eyes of the beholders. About 30,816 Turks of all ages are said to have perished in the storm and subsequent massacre. The gallant old Seraskier Pacha who had held the chief command was found pierced with sixteen bayonet-thrusts. Six or seven Tartar princes of the ancient family of Gheraí also perished.

'The Russians are believed to have lost 13,000 men in the assault, including an amazing number of officers, some of them of the highest rank. The Prince de Ligne was wounded, and the Duke de Richelieu had a narrow escape—both of these had been volunteers. Suwarrow's despatch on this occasion was in his usual laconic style, and addressed to the Empress: "Mother, Ismail is at your feet." The bloody trophies taken at Ismail were displayed in an ostentatious and grand triumph at St. Petersburg, and the Czarina said sarcastically to Sir Charles Whitworth, the British Ambassador, on the occasion, "Since the King, your master, is determined to drive me out of St. Petersburg, I hope he will permit me to retire to Constantinople." Nothing now appeared to be in the way of that long-coveted object. The Grand Vizier with his dispirited army retired into the defiles of the Balkan, and Russian detachments under Prince

Galitzin, Prince Repnin, and other generals, crossed the Danube, and drove every Turk that dared to show himself out of Bulgaria.'

In 1791 the war was renewed between the Russians and Turks, and again the latter suffered great disasters. On April 6th the Ottoman army was signally routed by Prince Galitzin, afterwards it was again defeated near Matchin on July 9th; similarly, in the province of Kuban, the Muscovites achieved a great but most sanguinary victory on July 3rd.

These were the last actions of this war, which, it is stated, for carnage and cruelty exceeded any other that had been recorded in history. The Turkish army was practically disbanded, and the road to Constantinople lay open, hence no course was open to the Sultan but to sue for peace and to accept such conditions as the Empress Catherine might choose to dictate. It was indeed fortunate for Turkey at this juncture that the defection of Austria, the exhaustion of the Russian exchequer, and the action of England prevented the Czarina from carrying out her avowed intentions of conquering Constantinople, certainly there was nothing whatever to prevent her legions from marching straight to the Bosphorus —and probably nothing but the certainty that such a step would involve a European war, for which she was ill prepared, prevented her raising the Russian standard on the dome of St. Sophia. On August 4th the preliminaries of peace were signed, and on January 9th the following year the peace of Jassy was concluded. By this treaty Russia advanced her territory in Europe to the Dniester, and acquired important rights and concessions in Asia.

Between 1792 and 1806 the ever-recurring contests between Russia and Turkey were suspended—the wars of the French Revolution and the rise of Napoleon allowed the Eastern question for a time to lie dormant. National antagonism, however, of so violent a nature as that existing between the Muscovite and the Turk must soon find a vent in action, and Napoleon was not slow in turning their antagonism to account. Through French intrigues, a difference was easily excited between the cabinets of Constantinople and St. Petersburg, and, although the former yielded on all the points of difference, the Emperor Alexander, now absolutely without the shadow of an excuse, caused an army of 80,000 men under General Michelson to invade the Danubian provinces. At first brilliant success attended his arms, and the Turks were driven across the Danube. The victories, however, of Napoleon in the West rendered a further advance impossible, since every available man was required elsewhere. In this juncture England came to the aid of Russia and helped her both by land and sea. An expedition was sent to Egypt, and Admiral Duckworth made the celebrated passage of the Dardanelles with the fleet. Neither of these ventures were fortunate in their results, the expedition to Egypt ended disastrously, and Admiral Duckworth, having had Constantinople for more than a week at his mercy, was so long beguiled by the promises of the Divan, that finally he had to execute a somewhat ignominious retreat.

This incident in our naval history seems to deserve more than a passing notice, especially as it illustrates what has frequently been said of the foreign policy of England, that she loses by diplomacy what she has gained by the sword. Napoleon, seeing the importance of an alliance with Turkey and thereby of neutralising a large portion of the Russian army, had sent one of his most skilled diplomatists, General Sebastiani, to Constantinople with orders to get up a war by all the means in his power. Bonaparte's choice was a happy one, and his instructions were carried out with equal ability and success.

It is unnecessary to recount the various stages of the negotiations which ultimately brought matters to such a crisis, suffice to say the aid of England was so urgently required by Russia that Sir John Duckworth, then cruising off Ferrol, with four ships of the line, was ordered to unite with a squadron of three line of battle ships and four frigates, lying in Besika Bay, and to force the Divan by threats of an immediate bombardment of Constantinople to accept the Russo-English and renounce the French alliance. Favoured by a fair wind the gallant admiral sailed through the Dardanelles, notwithstanding the cannonade which the formidable batteries on its shore directed on him; with but trifling loss he reached the sea of Marmora and delivered an imperative ultimatum to the panic-stricken government of the Sultan. Words can scarcely describe the terror and amazement of Constantinople; the capital was utterly defenceless; the sea batteries were unarmed; and the population rose in insurrection, loudly demanding the heads of Reis Effendi and of the French Ambassador, whom they considered the causes of their misfortunes. Sebastiani was, however, equal to the occasion; disregarding alike his own personal danger and the threats of the English admiral, he counselled temporising and delay; a few days were all that was required to arm the batteries and to render the capital safe. The brave but unwary English sailor fell into the snare; day after day was passed in the exchange of diplomatic notes and negotiations; meanwhile the Turks were making Constantinople safe and were cutting off the retreat of their enemies; at last after the lapse of four days the British admiral perceived his danger, and to save his fleet had to retire. The passage of the Dardanelles was again forced, this time also successfully, but with considerable loss, and, except for the impression it made on Europe, this gallant expedition was as to results entirely fruitless.

This war, on the whole disastrous to Turkey, was concluded by the peace of Tilsit, then, thanks to the intervention of Napoleon, she escaped the loss of Moldavia and Wallachia, which were occupied by Russia temporarily, as it was termed, but which otherwise would have been ceded to her. It may be remarked, however, that secret clauses were added to the treaty signed at Tilsit, and that by these the partition of the Turkish empire was arranged between

Alexander and Napoleon. Previous to the invasion of Russia by the Grand Army in 1812, as will be seen hereafter, the Czar deemed it politic to reveal these secret clauses to the Divan to ensure their neutrality in the approaching contest. In this he was perfectly successful, and subsequently for many years to come the influence of England replaced that of France in the council-chambers of Constantinople.

The peace arranged at Tilsit did not last long, any more than those which had preceded it. As before remarked, ever since 1807 the Russian troops had remained in occupation of the principalities, but, in the beginning of the year 1810 the Czar, now being relieved from his Swedish war, deemed it an opportune time formally to annex these provinces, and he at once commenced preparations still further to increase his dominions. The army of the Danube was increased to 100,000 men, 30,000 of whom were cavalry, a young and active general Kamenskoi was placed in command of it, and was directed to cross Bulgaria and the Dobrudscha early in the year before the unhealthy season had commenced or the Turks had time to collect their forces for a serious resistance.

So early as March 14th the Russians attempted to cross the Danube opposite Ostrova, but were foiled in their attempt, and did not finally effect the passage till May. The 3rd of June found them at Bazardjik, where they defeated a small force opposed to them, the Turks, according to their custom both in previous and in subsequent wars, having abandoned the line of the Danube and concentrated on Schumla. The Muscovite general, after this first success, divided his army into two columns; with one he made an attempt on Varna, the other he despatched under Langeron to occupy Bulgaria north of the Balkans, and to reduce the inland fortresses. The attack on Varna failed, whereupon the Russian army concentrated and moved on Schumla; here they were also unsuccessful, and after a blockade of three weeks had to retire to Rustchuk, which had previously been besieged by a detached corps. The siege of this fortress, and of its *tête de pont*, Giurgevo, together with the efforts made by the Ottomans to relieve it, occupied until September 26th, when finally the place surrendered, the Pacha in chief command being permitted to retain his 'horse-tail,' and to march out with other honours.

The incidents of this siege, as is the case with the defence of nearly all similar fortresses occupied by Turks, were most curious and striking. So early as August 3rd the Russians attempted to execute an assault, but were repulsed with enormous loss; there were the usual cruelties on both sides, including decapitation of prisoners, and the application of the knout. Had the Grand Vizier been false to his national characteristics, and shown any real energy after the departure of the Muscovite army from Schumla, the latter would probably have been forced to recross the Danube; as it was, he deputed to his second in command, Muktar Pacha, the task of relieving Rustchuk. The relieving army encountered a force of Muscovites sent to meet them at Battin on August 7th, and were defeated with a loss of 6,000 prisoners, 178 flags, and 14 guns. The loss of standards on both sides, but more especially on that of the Turks, is a noteworthy feature in these wars —apparently a great number must have been carried by armies in the field. From all accounts, Russian armies have now gone to the other extreme, since in the Crimean war their regiments, it is said, brought no colours into action. Some minor subsequent operations on the Upper Danube brought the war of this year in Europe to a conclusion, and by October 23rd the head-quarters of the Russian army were established in winter quarters at Bucharest. In Asia the forces of the Czar were far more decisively successful than in Europe; although both the Persians and the Asiatic allies and subjects of the Sultan opposed them, a large portion of the shores of the Caspian as far as Lankaran were subdued and added to the empire of Russia.

The year 1811 was marked by an unwonted amount of energy on the part of the Ottoman Government, as from the events occurring in other parts of Europe there was every prospect of Russia being much embarrassed in her war with the Porte. The Turkish fleet, having been refitted, threatened a landing in the Crimea, and three distinct corps were despatched to encounter the Muscovites on the Danube. One advanced on the right to Turtukai, another on the left towards Widdin, while Achmet Pacha, the commander-in-chief, with the third, moved on Rustchuk and there entrenched himself. The Russian commander-in-chief, General Kutusov, had been obliged to assume a defensive attitude, five corps of his army having been despatched to the frontiers of Poland in view of disagreements with France. Their great weakness as regards numbers caused the Muscovites to be defeated, and on July 5th Rustchuk was abandoned, while the entire army recrossed the Danube, and entrenched themselves on the left bank. They were followed by the Turks, who also entrenched themselves, and thus the rival armies remained confronting each other until October 10th. Each made various sorties at different times, but neither achieved any important advantage. At last General Kutusov, having collected every available man, which raised his army to a strength of 35,000, took the offensive. His operations are related as follows by Sir Edward Cust:—

'General Kutusov now resolved, as the season was advancing, to carry into effect his long-matured offensive operations. He learned from the country people that the Turkish camp, on the right bank, was very bare of troops, and that even the fortress of Rustchuk was not properly garrisoned or defended. He therefore ordered General Markov to pass with 14 battalions, 2 companies of artillery, and a body of cavalry, from his camp at Slobodsca to the right bank, to endeavour to surprise the camp and the fortress. Leaving their tents all standing to deceive the enemy, this division marched away in the night of the 10–11th, but the flotilla did not come up as ordered, and accordingly only as many men were crossed as the pontoons could pass, while the Cossacks swam the stream on their horses. In consequence of these delays, it was the morning of the 15th before General Markov could report the passage of his entire force. Kutusov, displeased at this delay, ordered General Sabanajev to go and supersede Markov; but, before he could do so, the general was in full march, and as, happily for him, the Turks had not penetrated the intention of his movements, he reached their camp without being noticed, and threw it into complete disorder. They had not dreamed of being assailed on their own side of the river, and general consternation seized the Grand Vizier, and all his high functionaries, as well as the merchants and traders, who, as is usual in Eastern armies, thronged the encampment with the requisite supplies for the army. The rich tents and campaign furniture of the Grand Vizier, together with hosts of camels and numerous carriages, were all deserted, and their owners and keepers fled for their lives through the fortress of Rustchuk, and many of them never stopped till they reached Rasgrad and even Schumla. General Markov, like a true soldier, without giving a thought to the booty, seized the batteries, and turned the guns against the enemy's camp on the other side of the Danube; while Kutusov, seeing from the height of Slobodsca the whole course of events on the opposite shore, immediately ordered an advance of his entire army upon the entrenched camp before him.

'The result of this combined movement was a furious attack from the two sides of the river at once. The rush of the Muscovites to battle, as they dashed into the fight with loud cries, and amid the roar of eighty pieces of artillery, did not long leave the victory doubtful. The Grand Vizier, who had hastily got into a boat, and sought only his personal safety, sent a messenger to Kutusov to propose an armistice, which might be followed by a treaty of peace, but, not receiving a favourable answer, he escaped to Rustchuk, and thence to Constantinople. He might, perhaps, have been taken prisoner, but Kutusov, who was a great politician, as well as an artful strategist, and had been Russian ambassador to the Porte, is supposed to have known his man, and to have been convinced that he would prove useful at the Divan in accomplishing those further objects which the general knew were now aimed at by his sovereign. Tchappan-Oglou Pacha, a man of great bravery and considerable firmness of character and military ability, succeeded to the command of the army after the departure of the Grand Vizier.

'The position in which he was placed demanded the exercise of all his best qualities, and he now by his wisdom extorted the admiration of all. The Russians brought up every day a fresh supply of artillery, until 200 pieces played upon the Turkish camp. Nevertheless, the "son of the shepherd" resisted every offer of capitulation, and silently resolved to cut his way out of the dilemma by his own prowess. Provisions now began to fail in the Turkish camp; of forage there was none, and the horses were numerous; they were therefore sacrificed to the necessities of the army, and being so placed as to be exposed to the ceaseless tempest of shot, they were rendered available for the food of the soldiers. Their tents and useless arms in like manner served for fuel, but the Pacha still held firm.

'At length an armistice was negotiated; but it was not until December 4th that Tchappan-Oglou and his army finally quitted their camp in virtue of a convention, by which they were to evacuate it without their arms or cannon, and be quartered in the village about Bucharest until peace was concluded: 5,000 men with fifty-one guns surrendered, but some 120,000 had already perished by disease or by the cannonade, and a large number of the gun-carriages were burned and the guns thrown into the Danube. On the 14th Kutusov established his head-quarters at Bucharest, where the negotiations were concluded, and the Russian general-in-chief invited Prince Tchappan-Oglou to join him there, and treated him with great distinction. Such a result to the Russian arms on the Danube was most fortunate for the Czar at this critical period. Great Britain lent all her influence to induce the Porte to agree to terms, and successfully resisted all the endeavours of the French ambassador, Latour-Maubourg, to counteract this issue. The astonished Turk had now revealed to him the secret articles of the Peace of Tilsit, by which Napoleon had agreed to the destruction and partition of the Turkish empire, and to the further stipulations made at Erfurth with the same object; and the Divan, in view of this flagitious policy, now abandoned themselves unreservedly to Great Britain, whose ambassador regained all his former credit with the Porte.'

In concluding a summary of the wars of the first period and before dealing with those of a later date, and of a different character as regards their military peculiarities, a few words on the methods of warfare then practised by the Turks and their opponents may not be out of place.

The first thing that strikes one in reading the history of these wars is that the Ottomans, whenever they met the Russians in the open field, were invariably defeated. Their operations were as dilatory and tardy in their commencement as they were slow in execution. Their superior officers were by no means able and apparently were far too luxurious in their habits to be good soldiers. The next point is the extraordinary manner in which both sides alike made use of entrenchments; the Turks more especially appeared to regard the spade as their most valuable weapon, and, in place of rapid manœuvring and skilful combination, they had no thought of doing anything but moving slowly to a position, there fortifying themselves and making subsequent sorties. In former days, as in all their recent wars, Ottomans, whether regular troops, irregulars, or untrained inhabitants, have always fought brilliantly behind entrenchments; in fact they seemed especially to rely on this quality as their strong point and safeguard. The wars not unfrequently were little else than a succession of sieges, in which the Russians often had the worst of it. The Turks had little or no military science, and knew nothing of engineering, hence their attack on fortresses was by no means so brilliant as their defence. The arm in which they more especially excelled was their cavalry, and in this they were undoubtedly far superior to their opponents, the Russians, and continued to be so until quite recently. As regards discipline and *morale* but little can be said for the troops of the Sultan. The Janissaries, of whom the main portion of the Ottoman armies were composed, were alike turbulent in peace and unsteady in war. No Turkish army has ever yet fought a losing battle, and after a disaster the largest force generally melts away like snow. If we refer to any of the successful contests that the Russians have fought, we find that subsequently during the same campaign they had but little trouble, and that there was scarcely ever a drawn battle, as is often the case between European armies.

When we turn to the Russians and their combats with the Turks, but little is to be said; the Muscovite armies in those days were so well known throughout Europe that the characteristics of their soldiers were also thoroughly appreciated. The same stolid determination, the same cool courage and obedience, were exhibited on the Danube, in the steppes of Bessarabia, and on the slopes of the Balkans, as was shown at Zorndorff, at Eylau, and at Borodino; there was the self-same courage as that which finally repelled Napoleon, in 1812, and rendered battles in which Russian armies engaged the most sanguinary of the century.

The treaty of Bucharest finally brought this war to a conclusion; by this convention the Russian frontier was advanced to the Pruth, the navigation of the Danube was secured, and all the Turkish fortresses in Servia were demolished. Had it not been for the great and pressing danger which then menaced the Muscovite empire, there can be little doubt that terms far more severe, and territory far more extended, would have been exacted from the Porte.

After the fall of Napoleon, the weariness of wars and the desire for peace which possessed Western Europe seem also to have extended to Russia, since, up to the year 1828, we find her at peace with Turkey, although the pretexts for getting up a quarrel during that period were perhaps more numerous and certainly were more justifiable than frequently has been the case, either in former or in later years. In fact, Turkish misgovernment and cruelty seem about this time to have reached a pitch unequalled before or since. Insurrections and subsequent massacres appear to have been of no unfrequent occurrence; the struggle for Greek independence, which may be said to have lasted more or less from 1822 till 1830, was little more than a perpetual succession of atrocities perpetrated almost equally by both sides. Of these outrages the massacre of Scio by the Turks was the most celebrated and the most revolting. The slaughter lasted for ten days, and it is said that 40,000 persons of both sexes were put to the sword.

In July 1827 the treaty of London was signed by Russia, Great Britain and France, on behalf of Greece, and in October of the same year there was the destruction of the Ottoman navy by the combined fleets of these powers at the battle of Navarino. There then followed the campaign of 1828 and 1829, the only contest, by which the great European peace of fifty years was broken; strange to say, it was destined that these very same powers should again be the first to interrupt that peace, and the wars that have followed may be traced to that fatal interruption.

CHAPTER II.

THE POSITION AND RESOURCES OF THE TWO COMBATANTS AT THE OPENING OF THE WAR IN 1828.

Position of Russia in Europe in 1828—Position of Turkey—Condition of her army and her fleet—Convention of Akkerman—Forces available to be brought into the field by Turkey—Forces available for invasion by Russia—Disposition of forces at opening of campaign —Lines of defence possessed by Turkey—The Pruth—The Danube —The Balkans—Kuchuk Chekmedgè.

APPARENTLY the Emperor Nicholas had everything in his favour when he embarked in the war with Turkey in the spring of 1828. His prestige in Europe was at its zenith, his credit was excellent, his people were devoted, and his army was supposed to be highly trained and thoroughly efficient. He had no avowed enemies, but many faithful and devoted allies. Russia had temporarily outlived the suspicion and mistrust with which the constant aggressions of successive rulers had in former years caused it to be regarded throughout Europe. Prussia, then a second-rate power, was benevolently neutral, Austria not actually hostile, France was complacent and indifferent. England, led away by sympathy for the Greeks, and by a righteous indignation against Turkish barbarities, had become oblivious of the interests of her Eastern empire, and would have acquiesced in the transfer of the Muscovite capital from St. Petersburg to Constantinople almost without a murmur. Last, but not least, the Turkish fleet had been annihilated at Navarino, and Russia, mistress of the Black Sea, had the inestimable advantage of being able to feed and supply her armies by water transport. Nevertheless, if we look at the other side of the picture, the prospect was by no means so encouraging. Russia had not yet recovered the exhaustion caused by the wars of Napoleon, while her army had lost the efficiency which stood it in such good stead at Borodino and Leipsic. She had been engaged in a series of successful but most trying wars with Persia. Her military system had only just been reorganised ; Poland was still a thorn in her side, and Austria, although professedly neutral, maintained an attitude of hostile expectancy and thereby detained on the Transylvanian frontier a body of troops that would have sufficed to place the Russian standard on the dome of St. Sophia.

If, however, the condition of Russia in '28 was in some respects unsatisfactory, that of Turkey was infinitely worse. The war of Greek independence had been going on for six years, and had seemingly strained the resources of the Porte to the utmost, while it had estranged all the allies that, under other circumstances, might have afforded it assistance. The Ottoman navy, as before stated, had been destroyed on October 20th, 1827, by the combined navies of Russia, England, and France, and as regards the army, it was practically non-existent as a body, while what remained of it, by spreading disaffection, was a source of weakness rather than of strength. In order to explain how this was brought about, it is necessary to revert to the history of the Janissaries, and to the manner in which they were destroyed.

When the Turks first entered Europe, and their exploits carried terror into the courts of every Christian king, their battles were won, not by those who were born followers of Islam, but principally by compulsory renegades, the children of Christian parents, torn from their homes when young, and afterwards converted into staunch followers of the Prophet. These mercenary soldiers, Janissaries as they were called, soon discovered their power, and, like the standing armies of other countries in those days, not unfrequently ruled the sovereign whom they nominally served. But as their turbulence increased, their military valour diminished; discipline, the first necessity in an army that hopes for success, deserted them, and the only command they obeyed with readiness was the order to retreat. For three centuries they had been the support of the Ottoman empire, now they became its bane. Sultan after Sultan had attempted to cajole them, to conciliate them, to subdue them; but Sultan after Sultan failed; some lost their lives, others their thrones, others succumbed, but the power of the Janissaries and of their society remained supreme. At last there came a leader of the faithful, who combined boldness with prudence, cunning with moral courage. He formed a standing army on the European model, conciliated the Aga of the Janissaries, Hussein Pacha, and gave him command of it. This general renounced all allegiance to his class, and devoted himself to the service of his master. When the Janissaries after several mutinies broke out into open insurrection on June 14th, 1826, he aided the Sultan to rout and disperse them. Mercy was a quality but little strained in Turkey at that time, and certainly none was shown to the mutineers: their power was thoroughly broken, their chiefs were hung or exiled, and as a body they were no longer formidable, but nevertheless their disaffection was widely spread, their influence was still formidable, and as their members were scattered throughout the empire, they did much to weaken the power of the Government and to increase the danger then threatening the Ottoman state.

In point of fact in the year 1827, when the differences with Russia began to culminate, there was no Turkish army worthy of the name in existence; hence everything was to gain time in order to create one, and the Russian ultimatum of eighty-two articles, termed the convention of Akkerman, was signed on September 25th, 1827, although, as openly avowed afterwards, there was never for a moment any intention to hold to its conditions. In the meantime, every effort was made to raise an army, recruits were seized in all parts of the country, carried in chains to Constantinople, and there converted into a curious and hybrid force, which is described as follows in the Introduction to Count von Moltke's book, 'The Russians in Bulgaria and Roumelia'—' The army therefore was composed of men disciplined after the European fashion, wearing Russian jackets and Turkish trousers, with Tartar saddles, French stirrups, and English sabres; it consisted of Timariots, or troops giving feudal service—of troops of the line, whose service was for life, and of militia, who served only a term of years, of whom the leaders were recruits, and the recruits mere children. The system of organisation was French, and the instructors were men from all parts of Europe. The splendid appearance, the beautiful arms, the reckless bravery of the Moslem horde, had disappeared; but yet this new army had one quality which placed it above the numerous host which in former times the Porte could summon to the field—it obeyed.'

The same author thus sums up the condition of affairs at this period:—

'The Turkish empire, just before the outbreak of the Russian war, stood on the brink of perdition. The Turkish army had been destroyed by the Sultan at Constantinople, the Turkish navy by the Franks at Navarino. The Russians were waiting on the frontiers both of Europe and Asia, ready to advance. The French held the Morea, and Ibrahim Pacha was reduced to great straits. The Greek flag was free, and the Mediterranean was closed by all the maritime powers. In addition to this, the finances were much embarrassed, the population partly in open revolt, and all discontented. Well might the Sultan exclaim to his vizier, " Keep your wits together, for Allah knows the danger is great ! " '

It cannot be said that this picture is overdrawn ; but there was vitality still remaining in the system, and the certain symptoms of internal decay had not made themselves visible. Europe had not yet awoke to the inherent and hopeless viciousness of the Turkish rule, the subject races were still cowed and ignorant of their powers, and this—this and the plague—saved the Turkish empire.

It is not necessary to consider the actual available force which each of the two combatants could bring into the field. As is usual historians differ as to numbers, and in those days there were no official accounts of campaigns by which the statements or theories of individuals could be corrected. Moltke puts down the entire Turkish army at 180,000 men, under the following headings:—

Paid Infantry, including 6,000 Guards or Bostangis	60,000
Spahis (Cavalry)	10,000
Regular Cavalry	2,600
Artillery, &c., about	3,000
Irregulars, chiefly Asiatic horsemen	97,000

In all about 180,000, of whom at least one-third were cavalry. Chesney estimates the available Turkish force at considerably less, whereas Alison puts it at a somewhat higher figure. All, however, are agreed that the regular troops did not exceed 60,000, and that the great strength of the army lay in irregular cavalry, in which arm alone they were superior to their antagonists. The artillery was on the whole fair, being well served, but infamously appointed, the field guns were mostly drawn by bullocks, and as regards numbers were far inferior to those of the Russians, nevertheless the gunners fought with such bravery that the results were most satisfactory.

When we turn to the Russians we find a formidable and compact army assembled for the invasion of Turkey; but still a force far inferior to what could now be collected in a fortnight by means of railroads, and even in those days by no means proportionate to the resources and magnitude of the Muscovite empire. As the events proved, it was insufficient for the task before it; but still so superior to anything by which it was met, that, had it been properly led, a great and signal success must inevitably have crowned its efforts. With respect to the actual numbers, accounts, as usual, differ. Moltke says there were nominally 120,000, but only 100,000 effectives, and on the commencement of the campaign only 65,000. Imanitschew puts the number at 130,000; Witzleben at 95,000; and Alison at 158,800, including the Imperial Guard of about 20,000, and the 2nd Corps of about 31,000, neither of which arrived until the end of August. Chesney says there were 120,000 at the opening of the war. On the whole, therefore, it may be concluded that considerably under 100,000 effective men, and something over 300 guns were under the orders of Count Wittgenstein, when he invaded Turkey in May 1828.

On the sea the Russians were infinitely superior to their antagonists, they had in the Euxine alone sixteen line-of-battle ships, six frigates, and seven corvettes. The Turks had a few vessels remaining after the battle of Navarino, but these, with the exception of one solitary excursion, never ventured to show themselves outside the Bosphorus.

The only arm in which the Turks were greatly superior was their cavalry, and in this they certainly excelled. Their irregular horsemen were numerous and daring, they hung round the flanks and rear of the enemy's army, and invariably had the best of any encounter with their rivals. The Emperor Nicholas had practically ruined the Russian cavalry, which is now only beginning to recover from the effects of his endeavours to assimilate it to the cuirassiers of Kellerman, that saved the fortunes of France, at Marengo and Austerlitz. In place of bringing into Turkey Cossacks, whose hardy ponies could live on grass and endure all hardships, the Russian army was encumbered with heavy ponderous men on heavy ponderous horses, magnificent but useless, unable to live on the bad food, and soon broken down by the hardships of the bivouack and the march; in point of fact this cavalry before long ceased to exist, later in the campaign its place was supplied by Cossacks. The Turkish cavalry, although but poorly drilled and unable to manœuvre, were admirably suited for the requirements of a long campaign. Their horses were small and well broken, principally stallions of the Arabian breed; they could endure heat and cold, were accustomed to be picqueted out, and were only fed and watered once a day, a great matter when marches were long and forage scarce.

Having discussed the numbers and quality of the opposing armies we now have to consider the manner in which they were disposed. According to Moltke the Turkish army was divided as follows at the opening of the campaign :—

30,000 at Constantinople to keep order.
7,000 at the Dardanelles.
25,000 in various forts.
10,000 in Thessaly to check the Greeks. .
30,000 in Asia Minor.
26,000 in the fortresses of the Danube and Dobrudscha.
30,000 in reserve at Adrianople.
25,000 at Schumla.

In all probability the above estimate of numbers is very much exaggerated, and not a half of this force was in position when the Russians crossed the Pruth; the Asiatic troops more especially were late in coming up, and no fewer than 12,000 cavalry did not reach Constantinople until after the fall of Varna. According to Chesney, even so late as June 2nd there were only 13,000 cavalry and 19,800 infantry to cover the fortresses of the Danube, and to defend Roumelia from invasion. Before describing the Russian plans of operation, it is necessary to say a few words regarding the theatre of war.

In the year 1828—and the same may be said now—there are four distinct natural lines on which an invasion of Turkey by Russia might be resisted. The first is the line of the Pruth, the second the line of the Danube, the third the line of the Balkans, and, lastly, the positions which are termed those of Kuchuk Chekmedgè and Büjuk Chekmedgè, about twenty miles to the north of the Bosphorus, supposed by some to have been the place where Attila was checked in his march eastwards, and where the Huns were defeated by Belisarius. The first line—that of the Pruth—is practically untenable, and is never defended. It has the great disadvantage of being at right angles to the other bases of operations, and an army defending it is liable to have its flank turned, and its communications cut by any hostile force that succeeds in crossing the Lower Danube by Tulcha. In 1828 the line of the Pruth was not defended, nor yet in 1853; in fact, hitherto the Turks have limited their resistance in an invasion to the line of the Danube and the Balkans, or rather the entrenched camps in front of the latter, Schumla and Varna, the positions of Kuchuk Chekmedgè and Büjuk Chekmedgè have in latter years never yet been reached by an invader.

The Danube is a most serious obstacle to an invading army, since not only is the river a deep and rapid stream with steep banks on the Bulgarian side, but its course is studded with strongholds more or less formidable. The following were possessed by the Turks at the opening of the campaign:—Widdin, Nikopolis, Rustchuk, Giurgevo,

Turtukai, Silistria, Hirsova, Matchin, Brailow, Isakchi, and Tulcha. Of these Widdin, Rustchuk, Silistria, and Brailow were the strongest, largest, and most formidable; none were well armed, or well fortified, but the gallantry of the garrisons covered many deficiencies. There is no doubt whatever that in the face of a fairly large army well led a passage of the Danube from Wallachia must be a perilous operation, as was proved by Omar Pacha in 1853. In the campaign, however, of which we are now speaking, the Turks were too weak to attempt any of the counter strokes which alone can render the defence of a river successful.

The following detailed description extracted from Count Moltke's work, before referred to, will give a good idea of the peculiarities of this river, both in a physical and military point of view :—' Between Golubracz and Gladova, a distance of about forty miles, the Danube breaks through the limestone rock which runs from north to south between the Carpathians and the Balkans. At the former point, where there is an old Servian castle, the stream, which is not less than 2,000 paces wide, is suddenly narrowed to a width of only a few hundred paces, and pursues a very winding course between high and in many places precipitous walls of rock with a very rapid fall. At several points, especially Bilnitz and the Iron Gate (Demir Capu), its bed is crossed by reefs of rock which, when the water is low, rise above the surface of the river, and when it is high create prodigious whirlpools, always

F

rendering the navigation of the river difficult, and at those points impassable. On this point of the river's course are the Turkish fortresses of New Orsova (Ada-Kalessi, the Island Fort) and Gladova (Feti-Islam, the Triumph of the Faith). The width of the stream throughout this tract is on an average 600 to 900 paces, and on both sides lies an almost uncultivated, thickly wooded, and very inaccessible hilly country. Very little below the Iron Gate, however, the character of the stream changes altogether. On the Servian side, it is true, wooded heights still stretch along the right bank of the river as far as the boundary stream of Timock, but below that the mountains recede far away on either side, and the river flows on through a plain above a hundred miles in breadth down to its mouth. Lesser Wallachia, as far as the Aluta, and the north of Bulgaria are indeed traversed by a few chains of hills branching off from the high mountains, and are altogether less flat and low than the vast plains of Greater Wallachia, nevertheless they are on the whole level countries. There is, however, a very marked difference between the opposite banks of the river. On the Bulgarian side (all the way below Widdin) they rise steep and high immediately overhanging the stream, while on the Wallachian they are flat and muddy, with extensive meadows intersected by branches of the Danube, and overflowed whenever the water rises. As the river flows on, these low banks become wider and wider, and more and more marshy, and the islands larger and more numerous. Below Rustchuk there is only a single spot, at the mouth of the Dembowicsa opposite Turtukai, where the shore is firm and dry though flat, down to the edge of the river, which at that point is not impeded by any islands. Opposite to Silistria, too, a road passable at all seasons leads from Kallarasch to the Danube. In the Dobrudscha, too, the right bank is considerably the highest; the opposite low Wallachian shore is for the most part firm and dry down to the edge of the river as far as the Bortisa branch of the Danube, but the islands form a marsh covered with trees and rushes many miles in breadth, which is always flooded when the river is high. Hirsova is the first point at which the valley becomes narrower, and a passage across the river is practicable. At Brailow the left side of the valley of the Danube first begins to rise from the river in perpendicular terraces of clay of about eighty or a hundred feet high.

'From Brailow and Galatz there are roads across the wide marshes, practicable in the fine season, to Matchin, which place commands their débouches, and beyond which the fine picturesque tops of the Matchin and Betschepe mountains rise to a height of above 1,000 feet. Below Isakchi the Danube flows through its delta in three branches, of which only one, the Sulina, is navigable, and this is not above 200 paces wide at its mouth. The whole space, thirty miles in width, between the northern and the southern branches (the Kedrilleh and the Kilibogas) is covered by an unbroken waving sea of rushes ten feet high, above which only the rigging of the ships is visible.

The Danube below the Iron Gates, except where it is divided by islands into several arms, is nowhere under 900 paces in breadth and in many places it is more than double that width. In places it is as much as seventy or eighty feet deep, but at many points it is far shallower. Below Pesth, where a suspension bridge has been constructed, the mighty river is only crossed by one single bridge of boats, that at Peterwardein. Of the massive bridge built by Trajan at Gladova nothing now remains but the piers and a sort of tower on the Wallachian shore. At Tultscha the river is diagonally crossed by a sandbank which leaves a navigable channel only fourteen or fifteen feet deep. At this point a bridge on piles might be thrown across the main channel if the approach on the left bank were not rendered impossible by extensive marshes and islands overgrown with reeds. Everywhere else the passage of the river could only be effected by means of boats or pontoons. Although the fall of the Danube is not nearly so great below the Iron Gates, the current on an average does not even then run less than two and a-half miles an hour.

We next come to the line of the Balkans; these mountains are of no very great height, varying from 500 to 3,000 feet; they run east and west, parallel to the Danube, and have hitherto been considered formidable as obstacles, more from the few and bad roads that traverse them than from any difficulties which they themselves present. The passes are clearly marked on the map, and are now much about the same as they were in 1828, only considerably better and more practicable for artillery. From the fact that the Russians commanded the sea, the western passes were not taken into account in this campaign, although probably in the next war they will be turned to account. Moltke names the following roads as being alone practicable for troops at the time of which he writes:—

1. From Tirnova to Kasanlik—an easy pass which might be forced without much difficulty.

2. From Tirnova by Demirkapu to Slivno.

3. From Tirnova to Osman-Basari, thence by Kasan to Selmeid—and to Karnabat.

4. From Schumla by Tshalikarak and Dobroli to Karnabat.

5. From Kosludja to Pravadi or Jenikoi to Aidos.

6. From Varna along the coast by Burghas and Missivri.

For an army pivoting on the sea, as the Russians in 1828 and 1829, routes 4, 5, and 6 are the most important, and these might be easily barred by an army at Aidos, who could engage each column singly as it issued from the passes. In addition to these recognised and known roads there are also a number of paths or sheep-walks by which infantry can be easily conducted across the mountains It cannot therefore be said that the Balkans, if undefended, would offer a serious obstacle to an invading army, any more than the mountains of Bohemia in 1866, or the

Vosges in 1870 hindered the advance of the Prussians. In fact the real strength of the Balkans lies in the position of the entrenched camps of Varna and Schumla in front of them. As remarked by Moltke, so long as both or even one of these strongholds can be retained ' passing the Balkans will always be a hazardous undertaking.'

We come lastly to the positions of Kuchuk Chekmedgè and Büjuk Chekmedgè before spoken of. As these lines were neither attacked nor defended in 1828 and 1829, it is scarcely necessary here to allude to them, but as they will inevitably exercise a great influence in any future war where Constantinople is in danger, in another chapter they will be described in detail.

CHAPTER III.

THE CAMPAIGN IN EUROPE OF 1828.

Reasons why operations were delayed—Method of Russian advance—Passage of Danube—Siege of Brailow—Peculiarities of Turkish defence of fortresses—Advance of Russians towards Varna—Strategy of Turks—Schumla—Siege of Varna—Attempts at relief—Fall of Varna—Contests before Schumla—Retreat of Russians to the Danube—Operations of 6th Corps in Wallachia—Siege of Silistria.

THE Turkish Government had issued its Hatti-sheriff, amounting practically to a declaration of war, on December 18th, 1827; but no reply was made by the Czar until April of the following year, and neither the Pruth nor the Danube were crossed until May 7th and June 8th respectively. It is somewhat difficult to account for this delay in commencing the campaign. Moltke speaks of it 'as a great sacrifice made to political at the expense of military expediency.' It seems, however, that political causes scarcely afford a sufficient explanation. It was all important to the Russians to hasten the commencement of hostilities, not only because every day of respite granted to the Turks enabled them to reorganise their army, to strengthen their fortresses, and to mature their various preparations for defence, but there was another important reason for having a winter's campaign. During the month of January the Danube might be crossed on the ice without difficulty, and the country roads, which in rainy weather soon become impassable for heavy traffic and artillery, would, in a frozen condition, be admirable lines of communication. It cannot, moreover, be said that Europe was more hostilely inclined in December than in May; Austria was, if anything, more inclined to oppose a Russian invasion of Turkey in the latter than in the former month, and in both the remainder of Europe was equally passive and indifferent. We must therefore look to other than political causes for an explanation of the time of year when the campaign commenced in 1828. In all probability the great distances which have to be traversed by Russian troops in order to effect a concentration on the southern frontier, and the consequent time always required to carry out a mobilisation of their army, may be regarded as the first cause of the delay; and the second will probably be found in the stormy character of the Black Sea during the winter months. As Wittgenstein's army was almost entirely dependent for its supplies on water transport, it was far more important that the sea should be calm and the winds favourable than that the Danube should be frozen and the country roads hard.

The Russian army when it commenced operations was divided into three corps, to which the following duties were assigned:—The 3rd Corps, under General Rudjewitsch, about 38,000 strong, was to cross the Lower Danube, march through the Dobrudscha into Bulgaria, and thence direct on Varna. The 7th Corps, under the Grand Duke Michael, about 24,000 strong, with the siege train was to besiege Brailow and to cover the flank of the 3rd; while the 6th Corps, about 22,000, under Rothof, was to occupy Moldavia and Wallachia, take Silistria if possible, and generally protect the communications and flank of the remainder of the army.

On May 7th and 8th the 6th and 7th Corps crossed the Pruth with flags flying and bands playing; the common soldiery had all the enthusiasm of the Crusaders, and considered that they were about to engage in a sacred and religious war; the officers had all the confidence in themselves and the contempt for their enemies which are stated to have been the peculiar characteristics of the early followers of the first Napoleon. No difficulty whatever was encountered in crossing the Pruth, bridges were made at Falschi and Woduly-Isakchi, where bridges were established and permanently maintained. The 6th Corps occupied the principalities without hindrance. Bucharest was occupied by Cossacks on May 12th; and Crajova, the capital of Lesser Wallachia, on the 21st. On June 2nd a sortie from Widdin by a force composed, it is stated, of 4,000 infantry, 5,000 cavalry, and 10 guns, was repulsed by General Geismar at Kalafat, but beyond this and the occupation of a position at Turtukai, which prevented the passage of the Danube at Oltenitza, as had been intended, no attempt at resistance was made by the Ottoman troops north of the Danube. Exception not unfrequently has been taken to the policy of Wittgenstein in thus occupying Moldavia and Wallachia; it has been said that he thereby scattered his force, already too weak, that he wasted valuable time, and unnecessarily excited the jealousy of Europe. When, however, we learn that the Russian Staff compelled the inhabitants of these provinces to furnish 250,000 measures of grain, 40,000 loads of hay, 50,000 kilderkins of brandy, and 23,000 oxen for the use of the troops; also that 16,000 peasants were sent to make hay on the Danube, and that an enormous number of waggons and horses were put into requisition—we can scarcely question the wisdom of the measure, more especially if we consider that an army which did not command the left bank of the Danube above Brailow would be liable at any moment to have its communications and rear threatened by a hostile field force operating in Wallachia or issuing from Brailow itself, from Rassowa or from Silistria. Undoubtedly these fortresses might have been masked or reduced, and the command of the sea rendered the Russian army comparatively independent of other supplies; so on the whole the policy or impolicy of the course actually adopted must always remain an open question.

While the 6th Corps effected the occupation of the principalities, the 7th Corps commenced the siege of Brailow, and the 3rd prepared to cross the Lower Danube at Satunovo, nearly opposite Isakchi. The passage of this river was effected on June 9, but the success of the operation was owing more to bravery and good fortune than to skill and wisely devised combinations. The Danube at this point is only about 900 paces in width, and seeing that preparations had been made for a crossing here, the Turks had taken means to oppose it. A battery of about fifteen guns had been placed on the opposite bank, and about 10,000 men had assembled to support and aid the battery. In all probability the crossing would have been successfully opposed, had not some Zaporogua Cossacks been persuaded by the governor of Ismail to join the invaders; these new allies ferried about 1,500 light troops across the Danube unperceived by the Turks; the latter were taken in flank and disgracefully routed, leaving the passage of the river free. Not only was a brilliant success thereby achieved and an entrance into the Dobrudscha secured, but this feat of arms was followed by the immediate surrender of the fortress Isakchi, only 4,000 yards from where the river was crossed. From the insufficient defences of this town, and the absence of outworks, it is probable that no very protracted or formidable resistance could in any case have been offered by it. Still its immediate surrender was as disgraceful to the Turks as its possession was important to the Russians. The fortress contained large stores and eighty-five guns of heavy calibre.

This passage of the Danube by the 3rd Corps is interesting for many reasons. It shows the difficulties which attend the passage of that river, as well as the manner in which they may be surmounted. Count Moltke remarks that in the whole course of the Lower Danube, Satunovo was the only place where the Russians could cross; that as the left bank could only be reached by means of a dyke, which it took weeks to build, their intentions must become known to their enemies, who had ample time to frustrate them, more especially as the point selected was immediately opposite a fortress. Hence he deduces the conclusion that it would have been wiser to dispense with a bridge in the first instance, and only to collect materials for its construction, while the actual crossing was effected in boats at Reni or some place where no preparations had been made to oppose it.

We saw that the 7th Corps after crossing the Pruth on the 7th and 8th of May had marched to Brailow. The siege of this fortress is so remarkable an incident in the history of the war that it deserves special notice, all the more as it exemplifies the warlike peculiarities of the Turks, and the desperate manner in which they often conduct the defence of a place, when troops of another nation would only think of capitulating. It seems unnecessary to give a detailed description of the fortress or of the manner in which the engineers on both sides conducted the attack and defence. The introduction of rifled firearms has so entirely altered all the conditions of warfare as regards fortresses, that little can be learnt from what occurred at Brailow previous to the actual assault.

Suffice to say that Brailow at the time in question was a town of about 24,000 inhabitants, of whom about 7,000 or 8,000 were capable of bearing arms. It stood on the edge of the Danube, was not commanded on any side, and was surrounded by fortifications consisting of eight bastioned fronts with revetted scarps and counterscarps. According to Colonel Chesney, the height, or relief as it is termed, of these fortifications was greater than in any other Turkish fortress, and there was a castellated citadel flanked by eight round towers, defending the western front of the town. Although there were no outworks and no casemated protection for the garrison, this fortress was the strongest place on the Danube, it was also well provisioned, was armed with 278 guns besides mortars, and, all told, had a garrison of about 8,000 men—in short it was a hard nut to crack.

On May 11th the investment was commenced, and by May 25th the first parallel of the attack was completed; also five batteries had been erected by the Archduke Michael on the north-eastern side of the town. The Russians used every diligence in pushing on their works, and by June 6th their third parallel was finished at a distance of about 130 yards from the counterscarp. Up to this time the defence had been merely passive, being confined to a few insignificant sorties and desultory firing; now it may be said that the resistance of the Turks really commenced. In order to make up for the want of ricochet and proper breaching-batteries, the Russians had to employ mines, and by June 15th five were ready for explosion. During these operations, of which Count Moltke gives a detailed account, including a sketch, the works of the besiegers were much hindered by repeated sallies made with great determination and bravery. On the morning in question these mines were charged, and two columns of troops prepared to storm the place as soon as a signal was given by three rockets for the firing of the mines. Unfortunately a mistake occurred, and out of five mines only three exploded. Hence the column on the left had no breach before it. As from the smoke and confusion, the officers were unable to see the ramparts or their condition, all advanced boldly to attack, and searched in vain for a breach in the escarp. It is needless to say that they were utterly routed, in fact it is stated that only one man was left alive, he a sergeant, who was pushed into the Danube and saved himself by swimming. The right column, notwithstanding that they had a breach to storm, were not much more successful. The Turks fought with a vigour and determination perfectly unequalled, so much so that although the attack only commenced at nine o'clock, by half-past eleven the Russians were repulsed with a loss of about 2,000 killed and wounded.

It is probable that the defence of Brailow would have been even still more protracted had it not been for two circumstances—the defeat of the Turkish flotilla on the Danube and the surrender of the fortress of Matchin. On June 8th a Russian squadron of eighteen vessels, under

Vice Admiral Zaradowsky, attacked and defeated, with a loss of thirteen of their number, an Ottoman flotilla of thirty-two gun-boats, which retired from before Brailow up the Danube to Silistria, thus giving the Russians the command of the river. The surrender of Matchin was alike unexpected and inexcusable—it was a strong fortress and had only been subject to a slight bombardment; nevertheless, it capitulated almost at once. Count Moltke says that 'the badness of the defence was not to be attributed to military or local causes, but entirely to personal considerations!' In fact, there is little doubt that in this case, as in that of many other Turkish fortresses, the commandants had belonged to the Janissaries and were disaffected, also that they frequently preferred the Russian gold, to be acquired by a speedy surrender, to the Turkish bowstring, which was the almost inevitable consequence, whether the defence had been gallant or the reverse. Suliman Pacha, the Governor of Brailow, notwithstanding his gallant defence at the commencement and his reply to the first summons of surrender—'When the rampart is destroyed we shall form a living one of our bodies,' is not free from the suspicion of corruption. Colonel Chesney states, on apparently good authority—that of the Russian commander in Wallachia—'that the gates of Brailow had been opened by a golden key.' In any case the fortress capitulated long before it need have done so; the two unexploded mines were successfully fired on June 16th, and two days afterwards the surrender was finally arranged. The garrison were permitted to march out with 'bag and baggage,' and were allowed ten days to evacuate the place—a not unimportant condition, since thereby the 7th Corps was delayed for that time in its southward march when its support was much needed by the 3rd Corps. It is stated that there were provisions for several months' defence captured in the place, besides quantities of ammunition and nearly 300 guns, also that the siege cost the Russians, in round numbers, about 4,000 men, according to some authors 5,000.

The fall of Brailow was immediately followed by that of all the fortresses in the Dobrudscha, namely, Isakchi, Hirsova, Tultscha, and Kostendji. The capture of the latter place was peculiarly timely, as thereby the Russians got possession of a safe and fortified seaport, where their supplies could be landed, and where their fleet could rest in security. Of this advantage they were not slow in availing themselves, since almost immediately after its capture, on July 5th, a transport fleet of twenty-six sail from Odessa entered the harbour.

As remarked by Count Moltke, the defence of Turkish fortresses has hitherto presented two striking peculiarities as contrasted with the system of resistance carried out by other nations. In the first place, whereas the efforts made to check the approaches of the besiegers are most unscientific and feeble, the defence of the breach is most desperate, in fact the defence commences where with other armies it ends. Secondly, as a rule, in other countries forts held only by regular garrisons make a good defence, while inhabited towns usually capitulate as soon as they are subject to bombardment. This was specially noteworthy in the late war of 1870, for whereas Bitsch held out until the last, Soissons, Thionville, Strasburg, and other towns surrendered almost as soon as a few shells had burst in their streets. The converse of this has hitherto been the case in Turkey, and 'peaceful inhabitants' have made a far better defence than professional soldiers. Time alone can show whether modern arms have altered this peculiarity; possibly they have, and long-ranged weapons may have caused as great a revolution in the Turkish as in other methods of fighting.

We left the 3rd Corps having just crossed the Danube at Satunovo; by June 11th the whole of the force had passed over and was on its march southwards. Its progress, however, was necessarily slow, since it did not reach Karasu, near Trajan's wall, only 75 miles' distance, till June 25th; there it remained for eight days, awaiting the fall of Brailow, and then marched on leisurely towards Bazardjik. Here occurred the first fight of the war in the open field; it was a cavalry affair, and in this the Turkish horsemen showed that they were nearly as formidable as in the days when the Russian infantry were obliged to carry *chevaux-de-frise* in light carts for their protection. Hussein Pacha had sent on about 8,000 men, chiefly cavalry, to occupy Bazardjik; on the approach of the advance-guard of the Muscovite army the Turks evacuated the town and took up a position behind some hills in front of it, thereby forming what may be termed an ambush on the flank of the Russians. The latter fell into the trap and were driven back with a loss of nearly 12,000 men. Eventually, when the artillery of the invaders appeared, the Ottomans had to retreat; but this skirmish was by no means unimportant in its results, not only from the moral effect it produced, but likewise from the fact that the Emperor's army was thereby detained for nearly a week at Bazardjik, it not being deemed prudent to advance until reinforcements arrived from the 7th Corps, now set free by the fall of Brailow. A portion of this Corps joined the main army on July 11th, the remainder of which had been detached to watch Silistria on the 21st. Their places had been taken in front of that fortress by 10,000 men of the 6th Corps, who, after having vainly endeavoured to effect a passage of the Danube near Rustchuk, had been obliged to march round by Hirsova to get into their required position.

We therefore find, in the middle of July, that the Russian army was thus distributed:—

The 3rd and 7th Corps on the march through the Dobrudscha, advancing on Varna.

The 6th Corps partly (10,000 men) in front of Silistria, the remainder occupying Wallachia.

The Guards and 2nd Corps on the march southwards through Russia—these did not arrive until the end of August.

As regards numbers, Von Moltke gives the following estimate:—

At Bazardjik	24,000
In Wallachia and about	11,750
Before Silistria	10,750
Escorting troops on the flotilla and at halting-places in the rear	5,500
Before Varna	5,100
The Advance-guard at Kosludja	6,000
Before Anapa	2,000
Total	65,100

There is, however, great reason to suppose that these numbers are considerably under-stated; Imanitschew gives the numbers at 85,000, which, probably, is an exaggeration. And where now were the Turks? The question is by no means easily answered, as the official reports issued by the Ottoman Government are at all times few and far between, while they are even less to be depended on than those issued by the Russians.

From the commencement of the campaign the Turkish commander-in-chief had apparently made up his mind to adopt a Fabian system of defence—no attempt whatever was made to defend the line of the Danube and the first serious opposition afforded to the Russian advance took place before Schumla. There were, however, various skirmishes, in which the Turks were on the whole successful. First there was the affair near Bazardjik, previously mentioned, there was another cavalry encounter on July 12th near Kosludja, in which General Rudiger's force was severely handled, and lastly there were two rather serious skirmishes on the 14th and 15th before Varna, resulting in the repulse of the Russians. With respect to these contests, Count Moltke makes the following observations: 'The Turks in these skirmishes had hitherto acted with equal prudence and determination, and according to their own views they had everywhere beaten the Russians. They certainly expected that their adversaries would have brought larger masses of men into the field, and were astonished to find that with the enormous means at Russia's disposal only a few squadrons of horse and a handful of infantry were brought against them. Unimportant as was the result of these skirmishes, their moral effect was favourable to the Turks, and the confidence of the Russian cavalry diminished with the strength of their heavy parade horses.'

As before mentioned, it is wholly impossible to form even an approximate idea of the number and position of the entire Turkish army at this time; it is, however, tolerably certain that immediately in front of the Emperor Nicholas there were—

> In Schumla about 40,000,
> In Varna about 7,000.

In rear of these on the other side of the Balkans there were reserves variously estimated at from 25,000 men upwards, and there were of course large bodies of Ottoman troops in course of organisation, in addition to the garrisons of the fortresses of Silistria, Rustchuk, Widdin, Pravadi, &c.

THE POSITION OF SCHUMLA.

Up to July 16th the march of the Russian columns had been directed on Varna as the objective; on this day, however, their plans were changed, they joined the advanced guard under General Rudiger at Kosludja and marched on Schumla, weak divisions under General Suchtelen and Benkendorff being detached to watch Varna and Pravadi. The wisdom of this change in direction will be discussed hereafter; we will now confine ourselves to a narration of events as they occurred, a few words first are necessary to describe Schumla, inasmuch as this fortress occupies much the same position as regards Constantinople that Metz did as regards Paris before the late war.

The town of Schumla lies at the foot of a group of hills to the north of the Balkan range and separated from it by the valleys of the Kamtchik. In the year of which we write, it contained about 40,000 inhabitants, was unfortified, but had a line of outworks round it on a range of heights at a distance of about 1,500 paces from the town. When the Russians first appeared before it there were no detached forts; two, however, were subsequently erected during the siege. The position formed an entrenched camp of great natural strength, capable of containing from 30,000 to 40,000 men, and from its strategic situation of great importance, since, although it does not actually command any of the Balkan passes, a force issuing from it could act on the flank and rear of an army moving southwards. As the Russians had not a sufficient force to mask it and march on, as the Germans masked Metz in 1870, they were obliged to halt and commence a regular siege or rather investment, since the strength of the garrison and the well-known gallantry of the Turks behind entrenchments made an assault out of the question.

It seems unnecessary to enter into the details of this siege, or of the various affairs in the open which took place during its course. On July 20th a small Turkish force occupying the heights between Kisjila and Boulanlik behind the Pravadi river was attacked by the main Russian army, and was driven into Schumla. Before and after the investment of the fortress was completed, the Turks made many sorties, all of which were carried out with great gallantry, and with tolerable success, but without producing any very decisive result on the fortunes of either force. At last on August 3rd it became evident to the Emperor Nicholas, who had recently joined the army, that, if he wished to bring the campaign to a conclusion, he must direct his attention elsewhere. Accordingly he proceeded to Varna, taking with him reinforcements and twelve guns, and leaving Marshal Wittgenstein with the main army to continue the blockade and siege of Schumla, where for a time we also will leave him, and turn to the operations before Varna.

Varna is a seaport town at the mouth of the Devno; in 1828 it contained about 25,000 inhabitants, and for those days was strongly fortified. From its geographical position it was of peculiar strategic importance; not only did it afford an excellent base where supplies might be landed, but it also commanded the principal and shortest line from the Russian frontier to Constantinople. Count Moltke remarks that the whole force of an invading army ought to be directed against Varna, and that when Wittgenstein changed the direction of his march to Schumla he committed a fatal error, which was the ' turning point in the campaign of the year 1828.' As before mentioned, General Suchtelen had been detached to watch Varna with a weak division on July 14th, he remained in observation until August 3rd, having in the meantime had various skirmishes with the garrison, who under Capudan Pacha made frequent sorties. Towards the end of the month the Russian fleet anchored in Varna bay, bringing some detachments from Anapa, where a descent had been made, and about August 6th the siege was regularly commenced.

Notwithstanding the presence of the Emperor Nicholas himself, notwithstanding the arrival of the siege train from Brailow, and the co-operation of the fleet, it may be said that two months elapsed without the Russians being really nearer the capture of the place than they were when they first appeared before it. The Turks had succeeded in reinforcing the garrison, and had carried out an active defence with extraordinary bravery, and a very considerable amount of skill. There had been various encounters, almost amounting to battles, during the course of the investment, and not only did the besieged execute a succession of sorties and attacks on the Russian works with great determination, but a relieving army under Omar Vrione having been collected at Adrianople, advanced to raise the siege. After several sanguinary battles, in which both combatants exhibited great bravery, the superior quality of the Muscovite troops in the open field proved decisive, the attempt to raise the siege failed, and Omar Vrione was obliged to content himself with a position in observation outside. Had the quality of the Turkish troops been somewhat better, there can be little doubt that the battle of Kurt-Tepe, or Kurtesse as some call it, which was fought on September 30th, would have been a most disastrous defeat to the Russians. As it was, Prince Eugene, who then commanded them, had to retire on the night of the battle, and was only saved from the consequences of defeat by the enemy refusing to face him on the following day. Moltke remarks 'that although the attack failed, the moral effect which the courage of the Russian troops produced upon the Turks did much towards bringing the campaign to a successful issue.'

To return, however, to the siege of Varna. By October 9th the position of the Russian army became most precarious; winter was rapidly approaching, Schumla was unsubdued and could not even be invested, the Turks were daily increasing in numbers and confidence; unless Varna could be captured all was lost, nothing remained but a disastrous defeat in an enemy's country before a relentless enemy. What was to be done? Force of arms would certainly never cause the fall of Varna in time to save the Russian army; other means must be tried, and tried they were with admirable results—that never-failing instrument the *golden key* was again applied to the gates of this fortress, and it opened them with its accustomed success. The second in command, Jussuf Pacha, on this occasion was the traitor; the commandant, Capudan Pacha, refused to capitulate, and shut himself up in the citadel; however the result was the same, Varna surrendered unconditionally after a siege of eighty-nine days in all, twenty-seven of which were after a practicable breach had been effected. Whereas Jussuf Pacha was conducted away as prisoner of war, and afterwards received an ample grant of land in the Crimea from the Emperor Nicholas, Capudan Pacha was permitted to march out and join Omar Vrione on the Kamtchik, who on hearing of the fall of the fortress retired to Aidos unmolested.

We left Marshal Wittgenstein before Schumla on August 3rd, endeavouring to maintain an investment of the stronghold with forces scarcely sufficient for that purpose. Up to August 26th but little was done on either side beyond a few skirmishes, attacks on redoubts, and counter-attacks. Gradually, however, the Seraskier, who here was in chief command of the Ottoman troops, began to understand the danger of his enemies. And on the night of August 26th, although, as remarked by Count Moltke, a night assault is a phenomenon in Turkish military history, such was carried out on the Muscovite redoubts, and at the same time a very formidable onslaught was made on the main Russian position in hopes of breaking through it.

Thanks to the information given by a Bulgarian spy this attack failed, but it had the effect of causing the Russians to draw in their forces and to abandon the investment. This enabled the garrison to obtain supplies and to detach 14,000 men to join the Grand Vizier, who at last was advancing from Adrianople to attempt the relief of Varna.

On September 9th the Turks again attacked the Russian redoubts and once more were repulsed in consequence of previous information of their attack having been given by spies. Finally the Russians under Wittgenstein were compelled to remain entirely on the defensive, and they retained this attitude during the latter portion of September until the fall of Varna. During this period their sufferings were fearful; it is stated by Count Moltke that their cavalry, now reduced to about 3,000 men, lost on an average from 100 to 150 horses daily, and soon became almost dismounted—hence the foraging parties could no longer be protected from the Turkish cavalry who made repeated attacks on convoys. The infantry, encamped in an open plain, with the thermometer at 125° in the daytime, had to live on biscuit and bad beef, had no water for washing, with very little to drink, and suffered enormously, more especially when the cavalry were unable to perform the outpost duty. In fact the position of the Russian army was in the highest degree critical and even dangerous when Varna surrendered, and had it not been for the extraordinary supineness and incompetency of the Turkish generals, even that event would not have saved them.

Almost as soon as the Turkish prisoners had been safely cleared out of the town of Varna, the Emperor set sail for Odessa, and Wittgenstein commenced his retreat northwards. Both experienced many dangers: the Emperor was nearly blown into the Bosphorus. It is related that when the captain of the vessel proposed to run the ship ashore as the only hope of safety, Nicholas replied that he preferred death to falling into the hands of the Sultan; the wind then changed and the Emperor was saved both from death and captivity. Marshal Wittgenstein commenced his retreat on October 15th; so well had his movements been concealed that for a few days he was unmolested; then the Turkish cavalry proved as formidable as the Cossacks to Napoleon's grand army in the retreat from Moscow. The roads through Bulgaria, bad at any time, had become almost impassable, and by the time his wearied troops reached the Danube they had lost half their baggage and nearly a third of their number.

Before concluding the history of the twenty-eighth campaign it is necessary to say a few words regarding the operations of the Russian 6th Corps, which had been left partly in Wallachia and partly opposite Silistria, when the remainder of the army marched southwards. Silistria has on several occasions proved a serious obstacle to Russian armies, and in 1828 it was successful in resisting their attacks. At that time it contained about 24,000 inhabitants, but was scarcely better fortified than it had been when it endured the siege of Kaminski in 1770. The defences were principally earthworks, and were devoid of outworks or any of the more elaborate protection generally used in modern fortresses. Count Moltke remarks the 'position of the town is equally important in a strategical point of view, and unfavourable for the purposes of fortification,' and that the only means of converting it into a good fortress would be to erect strong outworks on certain heights which command the town and to erect a *tête-du-pont* on the left bank of the Danube.

The Russian army under General Roth arrived before Silistria on July 21st. At first the besiegers were not more numerous than the besieged, and therefore had to take up a defensive position. For seven weeks the two rival forces remained opposite to each other making mutual sorties and mutually engaged in entrenching their respective positions. At last, on September 15th, some reinforcements arrived for the besiegers in the shape of the 2nd Corps-d'armée, and thus enabled them to commence active operations; it was not, however, until nearly the end of October, when the Russian army was raised to 30,000 men by the arrival of parts of the 6th and 3rd Corps from Schumla, that the fortress could be invested. Then, however, the season was already too far advanced to prosecute the siege, and it was finally raised on November 10th.

On the other side of Wallachia the Russian army under

General Geismar, numbering about 10,000 men, had been compelled to remain on the defensive, and in fact had experienced some difficulty in retaining its position. The Pachas of Widdin and Rustchuk, the latter afterwards well known as Kuchuk Hamed, were men of considerable energy and daring. The former succeeded in collecting about 10,000 men, and the latter 8,000, and with these they commenced a series of desultory attacks on the Russians by means of the *têtes-de-pont* Kalafat and Giurgevo opposite Widdin and Rustchuk respectively. At first Kuchuk Hamed was the most active and made two rather formidable sorties on June 2nd and July 3rd from Giurgevo. These, however, were repulsed without much trouble and for a short time General Geismar was unmolested. Receiving information, however, from Greek spies that the Pacha of Widdin was meditating a raid, he moved up to Golenz near Kalafat, so as to watch and check the enemy's movements. From this point he was forced to retreat to the entrenched camp of Tchovoza behind the Schyll half way to Crajova on August 18th, having been attacked by superior numbers.

The Turks then overran Lesser Wallachia, carried off great stores of provisions that had been prepared for the Russian army, and did much mischief. After this they returned to Widdin, but made another sortie on August 27th, which forced General Geismar to retreat to Crajova, while the country was again ravaged. Nothing further occurred until September 24th, when the Seraskier of

Widdin, with a force of about 26,000 men and thirty guns, issued from Kalafat, marched round the right flank of the Russian force which was entrenched as before at Tchovoza, and threatened their communications.

The danger was imminent. General Geismar had only about 5,000 men on the spot, while his adversaries had, according to some authors, nearly five times that number, irregulars though they were; his own communications were in the greatest danger, and those of the main army were seriously threatened; the only hope of safety lay in a vigorous offensive, and this he adopted. In place of marching direct at the Ottoman army, who, according to their custom, had entrenched themselves, he marched on their communications with Widdin; the result was a serious cavalry encounter on September 27th, which concluded in a manner by no means decisively favourable to the Russians: both armies retained their positions at nightfall and prepared for the final and decisive struggle on the following day. For this struggle, however, General Geismar with the enormous odds against him could not afford to wait, he was indeed in a critical position, retreat was impossible, and a battle on equal terms was almost synonymous with defeat. Nothing remained but a night attack, and this he executed with the most perfect success. Orientals are notoriously careless in their outpost duty at night, the Turks have ever been negligent even beyond other Orientals; trusting to this the Muscovite commander caused his artillery to redouble its fire just before sunset as if to cover his retreat. He then waited till the enemy had had sufficient time to settle down to repose, and, dividing his force into eight columns, advanced to attack their camp. The attacking columns first came on the camp of the irregular cavalry, who without a single vedette fell an easy prey to the surprise—the vizier fled on a mule, his lieutenant on foot. The Turkish infantry, however, having had some notice of their danger, showed more steadiness, and for some time the fortunes of the day, or rather of the night, hung in the balance. At last the village caught fire and the rout of the Ottomans was complete; it was a 'sauve-qui-peut,' nothing was saved. At two o'clock in the morning General Geismar was master of the smoking ruins of Bojeles-chti, which was the name of the village, and of the trophies it contained. Among the latter were arms for 10,000 men, twenty-four standards, 424 waggons, and last, but not least, a letter from the Sultan giving orders for the complete destruction of General Geismar's corps.

After this signal defeat the Turks gave no more trouble in Wallachia—their demoralisation was complete, so much so that on October 25th, without being attacked, they evacuated the important *tête-de-pont* of Kalafat, which was immediately occupied by the Russians and fortified towards Widdin. During the winter the *tête-de-pont* of Nicopolis was also taken. Both of these were important captures for the operations of the ensuing campaign. During the winter there were a few minor operations on the Danube, but these belong to the war of the following year.

After the siege of Silistria had been raised, and Wittgenstein had retreated from before Schumla, it may be said that the campaign of 1828 was ended; both combatants returned to their winter quarters to reorganise their shattered armies. The Russians were disposed as follows:—

General Roth at Varna with the principal part of the 6th and 7th Corps; also occupying Pravadi, &c.

The Guard Corps in Bessarabia.

The 2nd and 3rd Corps in Moldavia and Wallachia.

It is stated that of more than 100,000 Muscovites that crossed the Pruth barely 60,000 were alive at the end of October. In truth, the losses of the campaign were great and the results were small.

CHAPTER IV.

REMARKS ON CAMPAIGN OF 1828 IN EUROPE.

Campaign commenced too late—Russian force too weak—Army should have marched on Varna—Diversion to Schumla a mistake—Strategy of the Turks—Tardiness of Grand Vizier—Results of campaign in Bulgaria—General Geismar and his operations.

In reviewing the events of the 1828 campaign in Europe we have the great advantage of possessing the criticisms of Count von Moltke, written at a time when his opinions were probably just as valuable as at present, but from the fact that the writer was comparatively unknown, were but little read or noticed. Count Moltke, at that time a captain, was attached to the head-quarters of the Russian army, and served with it through the campaign. Hence his remarks are deserving of special attention, not only from the subsequent reputation acquired by their author, but because he had special opportunities of personally seeing and judging of the operations which he thus criticises. Other authors have also added their observations, and, although but few have written much on these wars, and still fewer have attempted to draw practical deductions from them, nevertheless, if only as a statement of the other side of the question, their views are in many instances worthy of observation, all the more as Count Moltke, impartial as he undoubtedly is in a remarkable degree, from the circumstance that he served with the Emperor Nicholas's army, necessarily regarded events peculiarly from a Russian point of view.

The first point to be remarked as to the manner in which the campaign was conducted is the great mistake that was made in beginning it too late. As the Danube was not crossed till June 8th, and as the distance from the Lower Danube to Constantinople is at least 480 miles, it was quite impossible for an army to reach Constantinople until the middle of October, even supposing it marched with extraordinary diligence and encountered few or no obstacles on the road; when we consider that there were fortresses to be subdued and Turkish armies to be conquered, it may confidently be asserted that before the war was commenced its fate as regards a complete success was sealed. There is no distinct information as to why this fatal delay was incurred. Count Moltke attributes it to political causes, but does not state their nature.

The next point on which especial stress may be laid is the fact that the Russian army was far too weak for the task imposed on it; and this mistake Count Moltke considers to have had far more to do with the failure of the campaign than the delay. He says: 'If the Russian Government was guided by the recollection of the days when Münnich, Romanzoff, and Suwarrow with 17,000 Russians beat

160,000 Mussulmans, it should also be borne in mind that in the campaign of 1828–9 the Russians had not to fight the Turks in the endless steppes of Bessarabia, Moldavia, and Wallachia, but in the forests of the Balkan. On the former European tactics may have great advantage over undisciplined hordes, but in the forests of the Balkan the Turkish Spahi, with his long rifle, mounted on his quick horse, and supported by swarms of skirmishers on foot, is by no means a despicable foe. Moreover, experience of all former wars should have taught the Russians to expect an obstinate resistance from the Moslem behind stone walls.' He adds in another place : ' The campaigns of 1809–11 had shown that an army of 70,000 men in Bulgaria was so fully occupied by the lines of the Danube that it had no strength left to cross the Balkans ; nevertheless in 1828 the same fault was committed, as the Guards could not reach Varna before the end of August, and the 2nd Corps could not arrive at the Danube until September, when the time for operations was over. . . .

' Another fault was that three months after the commencement of hostilities the battering train had not yet reached the army, drawn up before a fortress on the sea, and that the same park of artillery was intended to serve both for Varna and Anapa.'

After committing a fatal error, both as regards the time of commencing the war and the strength of the forces employed to carry it out, Marshal Wittgenstein seems to have been equally unfortunate in his first operation.

Tempting as were the supplies to be obtained in the principalities, nevertheless as the Russian army had the command of the sea, it appears that it was a fatal error to disperse the small army available in the occupation of Moldavia and Wallachia. The Pruth and the Danube should have been crossed simultaneously, and while one army ascended the right the other should have advanced along the left bank of the latter river. Brailow and Silistria should at once have been invested, and after both had been reduced the main army might have marched on. Probably Wittgenstein did not expect to meet with so much resistance at Brailow; had this place fallen without serious resistance the 7th Corps could have at once marched on to Silistria and secured the crossing of the river at Turtukai for the 6th Corps. Thus the march of the 3rd Corps and the main body would not have been delayed and Varna would have been invested at least a month sooner than it was. Last, but not least, the Turks would not have had time to collect their forces, and probably the march of the Russians would not have been diverted from its original object by the presence of a formidable force of the enemy at Schumla.

Having thus commenced the war with a series of mistakes the Russian generals continued their course of error. The original plan of the campaign made Varna their first objective point, as being a fortified seaport it was all-important to them for the supply of their army; it also commanded the main and shortest road from the

Russian frontier to Constantinople. Unfortunately they were diverted from their original intention, and marched on Schumla, a strategical error of the most fatal description.

In the first place, the capture of that place was almost an impossibility, being an entrenched camp of great strength and occupied by a force almost twice as numerous as that which they could bring against it, and secondly, even if they had captured Schumla its possession would have been of but little use to them—they would still have had to reduce Varna if they wished to supply their army and to be in possession of the best and shortest road to the capital of the enemy. Varna once occupied, a corps of observation might have been left opposite Schumla and the remainder of the army, if strong enough, might have continued its march southwards. It was also very desirable to entice the Turkish commander out into the open, where the superior quality of the Russian troops might counterbalance the superior numbers of their enemies—but to undertake a war of mutual entrenchments—of, as it was termed, 'circumvallation and contravallation,' was an unaccountable error of a flagrant description; by it the Russians exposed themselves to imminent danger with but small hope of success. As remarked by Count Moltke: 'Forty thousand Turks with everything they wanted were posted in a central and almost unassailable position; opposite to them lay a Russian corps, little more than half their number, on the circumference of a circle twenty miles long, which the

Turks could cut through at every point by short and covered marches. The Seraskier could everywhere attack them with superior forces, and a concentration of the Russian forces at any threatened point was impossible, not only from the distance, but because in defending one point some other parts of the lines of investment would be left bare of men. The whole Russian army was stretched out in a cordon before Schumla; there was no reserve, and, had there been one, place it where you would, it must always have arrived too late, as on such ground it was impossible to discriminate beforehand between a real and a false attack.

'But putting aside the immediate danger that threatened them, the Russians were in an awkward predicament. They were without light cavalry, one may almost say without any cavalry at all, in the face of a swarm of Turkish horsemen, while they might easily have drawn from the numerous hordes of Cossacks under the Russian sway an analogous body of horsemen invaluable for the protection of the army and for collecting provisions. They had not a single point within 160 miles in the rear whither they could transport their sick and wounded; nor had they any retreat open to them in case the strong garrisons of Rustchuk, Silistria, and Varna should break through the few troops that invested them, and bring together 30,000 in the rear of the Russians.'

After once committing the error of besieging Schumla in place of Varna, according to Count Moltke they should have continued in the course they had chosen, as it was nothing but the extraordinary apathy of Hussein Pacha which saved the portion of Wittgenstein's army remaining before Schumla from utter destruction, as Generals Rudiger and Durnowo's corps were cut off from all support and communication. Even supposing Schumla had been captured, the real difficulty of passing the Balkans was by no means overcome, as the local position of defence lies beyond the Kamtchik.

We have thus far dealt with the strategy of the Russian commanders in their offensive operations, which practically ceased after the appearance of the main Turkish army in the field. Let us now turn to the Ottomans and consider how they conducted the defence of their territory. In the first place we must concede that exceptional difficulties stood in the way of the generals of the Sultan and absolutely precluded them from the possibility of conducting an active defence, such as with a more disciplined and mobile army would have been their best and safest course to pursue. Possessing, as they did, all the strongholds of the Danube and the *têtes-de-pont* opposite them, a tolerably efficient army by pivoting on the river, and threatening the Russian communications, might have effectually checked any further advance of a hostile army of the strength which was actually opposed to them; just as Radetzky in 1848 and 1849 in Italy checked, and ultimately defeated the Sardinians under Charles Albert: we will, however, suppose that such a course was not within the powers of the Ottoman commanders, and was rendered wholly impossible by the condition of the forces at their disposal. In such a case they undoubtedly did right to abandon territory which they could not effectually defend, just as the Prussians in 1870 had prepared to abandon the Rhenish provinces and retire behind the Rhine if they had not been able to forestall the French and take the initiative. Schumla and Varna were undoubtedly, under these circumstances, the first line of defence by which Constantinople might be defended, and an active field army should have pivoted between the two to assist the garrison of either. Here, however, as too often the case in Turkish war, the execution was by no means equal to the design. The dilatory movements of the Grand Vizier and of his commander-in-chief are simply unaccountable. Count Moltke concludes his observations on the campaign in the following words:—'The whole strategy of the Turks had up to the attempted relief of Varna consisted in passive resistance: by this system, favoured by natural advantages of the ground, they had succeeded in driving their foe to the brink of destruction. It required only one last effort to hurl him over, but they were incapable of it.

'Neither was it in the least owing to the combination of Russian strategy that matters had come to a tolerable issue. The preparations were insufficient, the campaign began too late, and the direction of the main army was not likely to ensure a successful result.

'But all these faults were atoned for by the innate excellence of the Russian troops. The self-sacrificing obedience of their commanders, the steadiness of the common soldiers, their power of endurance, and unshaken bravery in time of danger, were qualities that enabled them to avert the dangers of their position before Schumla, and to hold the Seraskier in check; to make up for all deficiencies and overcome all resistance in Varna, and to strike such terror into Omar Vrione that even after defeating the Russians he remained ten days in his camp, as it were thunderstruck, doing nothing, while Varna, the bulwark of the kingdom, fell before his eyes. We cannot say much for the skill of the Turkish commander, but the conduct of the Turks from the highest officer to the last soldier, at the storming of Brailow, their courage at Kurt-Tepe, their steadiness in the mines and trenches before Varna, are far above all praises.

'The fall of Varna was most fortunate for the Russians. It decided the campaign. Had Schumla fallen into their hands in place of Varna, on October 11th—and it was against the latter place that all their efforts had been directed—they might indeed have destroyed all the weak works of that position, but, with Varna and Silistria in their rear, and cut off from the sea, it would have been impossible for them to take up their winter quarters in Bulgaria. The strategical importance of Schumla is equally great to the Turks with or without earthworks, and the Russians would have had to take the position again in the next campaign.

'If we consider the enormous sacrifices that the war cost the Russians in the year 1828, it is difficult to say whether they or the Turks won or lost it. It remained for a second campaign to decide the value of the first.'

Thus does Count Moltke sum up and conclude his criticisms on the campaign, and on the measures adopted by the military leaders on both sides to carry it out. His remarks are certainly not favourable, either as regards Wittgenstein or his opponents, nor, strange to say, does he make any exception when thus reflecting generally on the incapacity of the Russian generals. It seems, however, that in this instance there has been an omission, since in another part of his work, when speaking of the operations in Wallachia, he says:—'The task entrusted to General Geismar was a thankless one, inasmuch as the greatest success could lead to no important victory, nor could it influence the issue of the campaign. Considering, however, the small means at his disposal, General Geismar accomplished the difficult mission intrusted to him with equal courage and prudence.'

It may be remarked that the above was written before the year 1853, when Omar Pacha, by occupying precisely the same position as the Pacha of Widdin in 1828, and not having met a Geismar, entirely paralysed the operations of the Russian army. Therefore it seems evident that, although a great *success* on the part of General

Geismar could not influence the result of the contests going on before Varna and Schumla, or decide the fate of the campaign, still a great *defeat* would have inevitably proved of enormous detriment, the communications of the main army would have been most seriously imperilled, and probably all advantages gained in the south thrown away. That this defeat was only prevented by the ability and boldness of the Russian general is undoubted, and hence he is apparently deserving of far more credit than either his own contemporaries or subsequent history have accorded him. It is by no means improbable that the example of what occurred in Wallachia at the close of 1828 induced Omar Pacha twenty-five years afterwards to take up his admirable strategic position at Kalafat, by which, as before stated, he obtained great material advantage.

CHAPTER V.

THE CAMPAIGN OF 1829 IN EUROPE.

Situation at commencement of year -Resources of Russians—Diebitsch—Resources of Turks—Commencement of hostilities—Capture of Sizeboli—Naval exploit of Turks—Siege of Silistria—Diebitsch's march on Schumla and subsequent operations—Battle of Kulewtscha—March across the Balkans—Capture of Adrianople—Position of Russian army at peace of Adrianople— Signature of peace.

THE political and military situations at the commencement of the year 1829 are equally interesting and deserving of attention. In the first place there was every reason why Turkey should be left to continue the contest single-handed. The English and French ambassadors had both withdrawn from Constantinople to Corfu, in consequence of the refusal of the Sultan Mahmoud to sign the treaty of July 6th, 1827. So long as the Sultan held out on this point, and he continued obdurate almost to the last, there was no reason to expect help from England, and even had the Cabinet of St. James, overcome by jealousy of Russia, waived the important matter of the treaty and despatched its fleet to aid the Turks in the Black Sea, as pointed out by Count Moltke, in consequence of the small force then possessed by Great Britain, 'notwithstanding the acknowledged superiority of the English navy,' it is more than doubtful, in face of the large Muscovite fleet in those waters, whether any reinforcement that could have reached the Ottomans from Malta would have sufficed to give them the command of the Euxine. France was bound, if not to hostility, at least to a hostile neutrality. General Schneider's brigade was then in the Morea for the protection of the Greeks, and the Algerian expedition was being fitted out; hence, as this was sufficient to occupy the attention of the French public, so serious a thing as a European war, which assistance to the Turks would have entailed, was not to be thought of. Lastly, Austria was in firm pursuit of her traditional policy—that of allowing other people to do disagreeable work, while she reaped any benefit to herself that might accrue from it. Had the Russians been very successful in the previous year, and had it appeared that the safety of Constantinople was seriously jeopardised, then possibly the Court of Vienna might have assumed a warlike attitude and have adopted a definite line of policy; but as this was not the case, as in fact both combatants were much exhausted, the Russians more especially having suffered enormous losses, and having achieved only a doubtful success, there was apparently no occasion for immediate or decided action; on the contrary, it was better to wait and act as mediator, possibly also exacting some favourable conditions for the performance of that office. Prussia alone, according to Count Moltke, acted in a manner to be commended, and was mainly responsible for the fact that the war was localised, although, of course, under no circumstances would her interests have necessitated her taking part in it. On the whole, therefore, it was evident that the two combatants would have to fight it out by themselves. Let us now consider how far they were respectively prepared for the encounter.

First, as regards Russia, we have seen that at the close of 1828 she occupied Varna, had reduced all the fortresses in the Dobrudscha, but had failed to capture either Silistria or Schumla. The Russians had also command of the sea—an all-important advantage. Count Moltke gives their naval strength as follows: in the Black Sea, eleven ships of the line, two of which were three-deckers; eight frigates, two of which carried sixty guns; and twelve corvettes and brigs of war; the squadron altogether had 1,800 guns and had Sebastopol to fall back upon. In addition to this force there was the squadron of Admiral Heyden, which blockaded the Dardanelles and consisted of eight ships of the line, seven frigates, and twenty smaller vessels, carrying altogether about 1,500 guns. To oppose this formidable force the Turks had only eight ships of the line, three of which were three-deckers, frigates, five corvettes, and three brigs, altogether about 1,000 guns. During the entire winter of 1828-1829—a very severe one, as so often happens when there is a war—the Muscovites made every effort to repair the losses of the previous year. Marshal Wittgenstein was replaced by the chief of his staff, Diebitsch, who started in his command with special advantages, inasmuch as he was not hampered by the presence of the Emperor Nicholas on his diplomatic following. He was alike general and negotiator, he was not forced to make military considerations subservient to those of politics, and, as there was no telegraph in those days to St. Petersburg, he had the entire fate of the campaign in his hands—a great responsibility, but one that principally contributed to his eventual success. The new commander-in-chief joined his army on February 24th, 1829, and Count Moltke gives the following account, derived probably from personal observation, of the measures taken to improve the Russian forces :—

'General Diebitsch immediately devoted the greatest attention to the reorganisation of his army. The treatment of the soldier was much improved, the intolerable restraint and the unnatural stiff carriage somewhat abated. Nevertheless, much still remained to be done; for instance, skirmishers were always forced to keep step and rank; for this reason they were only of use on level ground. The men's dress and accoutrements were changed for others better suited to the climate. The commissariat, a most important matter for the coming campaign, was put on a different footing; an immense baggage-train was unavoidable over uncultivated or wasted provinces. Long columns were composed of thousands of waggons drawn by oxen, which served a double purpose—for draught and for food. The parties covering the columns were armed, and had two guns, so as to be able to defend themselves if necessary; but as these waggons could not be used on the other side of the Balkan, thousands of camels had been bought on the steppes of Asia for the use of the army. This useful, patient, and strong animal, which can carry a heavy burden even through snow and on the smallest amount of food, is especially fitted to follow the movements of an army. In spite, however, of all the measures taken, provisions were scant. Each soldier received one pound of meat and a glass of brandy three times a week, besides twelve biscuits and some oatmeal daily.

'The cavalry made a splendid appearance at starting—they were entirely remounted. The front rank of the hussar regiments was provided with lances, so as to keep out of the reach of the Spahis' sabres, and the number of Cossacks was much increased. The infantry bore traces of the hardships they had undergone in their bad winter quarters. According to the testimony of an eye-witness the men's faces wore an expression of sadness and pain. After all that they had suffered in the former campaign, they looked upon themselves as martyrs to their religion and their emperor. Nowhere in the Russian quarters were to be seen or heard the jokes that never fail among German soldiers when in tolerable plight. Singing was the only expression of joy that was heard, but the songs had the melancholy character peculiar to the Sclavonian race. The soldiers were much given to religious ceremonies, and crossed themselves at every meal; in every camp a tent was fitted up as a church, and mass celebrated daily.'

As regards the actual force at the disposal of the Russian generalissimo, it was, if anything, smaller than that which had taken the field in the previous year. The Guard Corps did not participate in the campaign, nor yet the mounted Chasseurs; these were the same corps as before. General Palden commanded the 2nd Army Corps, General Krassowsky the 3rd Corps, General Roth the 6th, and Lieutenant-General Rudiger the 7th. There were also 22 regiments of Cossacks, each regiment consisting of about 200 or 250 men, but some were weaker than this. Count Moltke gives the following estimate of the strength of the entire army:—

'The cavalry consisted of 2 divisions of Hussars, 2 of Lancers, and 1 of Dragoons:—

	men	men
Altogether about 88 squadrons, or	10,500	
Of Cossacks there were about	5,500	
Altogether		16,000
'The infantry consisted of 10 divisions, making up 120 battalions at most		48,000

	guns	
The artillery of 7 horse batteries, or	60	
And 30 foot batteries, or	240	
Altogether	300	4,000
Or of actual combatants		68,000

' The army, taken altogether, was just as strong as it had been during the previous campaign until the Guards and the 2nd Corps-d'armée joined it: it was, however, somewhat stronger in artillery and light cavalry.'

When we turn to the Turks, there is much difficulty in forming even an approximate idea of the numbers that they brought into the field. Colonel Chesney estimates their forces at 150,000, including all those eventually collected for the campaign. Of these, he says, '100,000 were irregulars distributed in Rustchuk under Hussein Pacha, and in the other fortresses. A part of the remainder, or Nizam, was employed in Asia, and 12,000 men were in the lines thrown up at Ramid Tchifflik to cover the capital; thus there remained about 36,000 infantry, and 10,000 cavalry, with nearly 100 guns drawn by bullocks, to oppose the enemy in the field. But if such a number of men actually joined the Sultan's standard, which is not impossible, it could only be made out by taking into account the levies which arrived at successive periods; for there is no reason to believe that anything like 150,000 men were under arms at the same time. The effective force, however, may have equalled that of 1828.'

In one point, however, the Ottoman Government were in a better position than during the previous year—their people were, as a rule, more united, and in some instances were even enthusiastic in their wish to repel the Russian invasion. In order to please the population of Constantinople the Russian prisoners were frequently displayed, also a Russian ship, which accidentally fell a prize to the Ottoman squadron.

It is also related that less civilised trophies were exhibited—previously Russian heads were invariably forwarded to Constantinople as presents for the Sultan after any engagement. It being found, however, that these tokens of respect were somewhat cumbersome, a more portable form of present was resorted to—salted ears took the place of heads, and were, it is said, regarded with much interest and favour by patriotic Mussulmans.

But little was done during the spring, both sides being occupied in preparations. The Grand Vizier went to Schumla on March 28th, and found only 10,000 men there; the regular army, which was raised to 50,000 men, was afterwards principally despatched to Schumla. The quality of this army, however, is stated to have been of the worst—none but the poorest class of Osmanli would enlist this year, and all old soldiers were excluded, as being disaffected and attached to the Janissaries; the greater number of the recruits came from Asia, and were dragged thence by force. There was also a change in the superior officers of the Turkish army. Reschid Mohammed Pacha was named to the chief command in place of Hussein Pacha, who was very justly considered too much of a Fabian commander. Omar Vrione disappeared entirely from the scene. In some respects, however, the Porte was even worse off than previously—the Bosniaks refused entirely to serve, and the Arnauts, a most valuable and warlike tribe, held back until they saw some chance of obtaining the pay for which they bargained. On the whole it would be difficult to say which side at the outset had the advantage--the Russians started from a base comparatively near their objective, Constantinople, and had it not been for the plague, there is no doubt that they would have eventually reached the capital of the enemy.

The first object of the Russians in entering on their new campaign was to establish a proper base of operations south of the Balkans. This, of course, must be a fortified seaport, on which their onward march to Adrianople might be based, just as the advance to Varna was based on Kostendji and Mangalia, and the siege of that place on Kavarna and Baltjih. Sizeboli was selected as the most desirable spot, and as affording the best and safest harbour on the whole of the western coast of the Black Sea. On February 15th this place was taken by a *coup-de-main*—a thousand Albanians, who were the garrison, having surrendered after a mere cannonade.

The Sultan was very indignant at such boldness on the part of his enemy so near Constantinople, and he ordered the admiral of the fleet, Capitan Pacha, and Hussein Pacha, his commander-in-chief, then at Aidos, at once to retake the place. Although Aidos is only three days' march from Sizeboli, Hussein did not appear before the fort until April 9th, seven weeks after he got the order. Then a vigorous attack was made on some works that the Russians during this time had been busily erecting, but it signally failed. After this the Russians were left in undisputed possession of their important conquest to the end of the war. As regards the naval expedition against Sizeboli

Count Moltke gives the following graphic description of it:—

'Nothing could be more unexpected than the appearance of a Turkish fleet in the Black Sea. The captain of the Russian ship Raphael, forty-five guns, which was cruising in company with another vessel on the coast of Anatolia, fell in during the night with several ships which he took for his own squadron. He accordingly joined company with them without making any signal. Great was the amazement of the Turks next morning when they found the number of their ships increased by two, and still greater the alarm of the Russian captain, who found himself in the very midst of the enemy's ships. Such was the inexperience of the Turkish sailors that they would have remained in doubt which was the friend and which the foe, if the Raphael had but hoisted the red flag; but the captain lost his head, and lowered the blue cross at the first shot from the admiral's vessel. The brig Mercury, on the other hand, which was leeward, set every stitch of canvas, her gallant commander, Lieutenant Kasarski, nailed his flag to the mast, and the officers swore that the last of them left alive would fire a pistol into the powder-magazine, and blow the brig into pieces rather than let her fall into the hands of the Turks. The Mercury succeeded in escaping from the awkward pursuit and ill-directed fire of the Capitan Bey.

'The Turkish admiral had made a prize, he himself knew not how or why. Allah had literally sent it to him in his sleep. It was none the less a subject of pride and exultation; St. Raphael was replaced by a fir cone, and the vessel taken to Constantinople in triumph.'

In the year 1829 the commencement of operations by the Russians was again postponed till the month of May. The corps that had wintered in the principalities crossed the Danube at two places, Hirsova and Kalaratch, a little below Silistria. Those that effected the passage at Hirsova joined the 6th and 7th Corps between Pravadi and Varna, the others were delayed by the Danube. The first task, which General Diebitsch undertook was the reduction of Silistria; the siege was commenced on May 17th and lasted until July 1st. On that day, after a most brilliant defence, the fortress capitulated, and 9,000 men surrendered themselves as prisoners; the capture of this place cost the Russians about 2,600 men and 115 officers, and the losses of the besieged were between 3,000 and 4,000.

The particulars of this siege are given in great detail by Count Moltke, but it is scarcely our task here to recapitulate them; suffice it to say that on this occasion, as on many others, the Ottomans exhibited extraordinary determination and bravery in the manner in which they fought behind entrenchments; they also betrayed great ignorance and incapacity. Strange to say, during the entire winter, although they had been subject to a siege during the previous campaign, and knew for certain that it would be renewed as soon as weather permitted, they took no steps whatever to strengthen the very insufficient fortifications that existed at Silistria. Had the Turks been commanded by scientific and energetic officers, it is more than doubful whether either Brailow, Varna, or Silistria would ever have succumbed. Count Moltke points out that, as it was, these three places occupied 50,000 Russians during a period of from two to three months, and that this number was 'scarcely sufficient to meet the pressing exigencies of the case.' Let us now turn to the main army, and see what was going on while Silistria was being besieged.

As before stated, the Grand Vizier Reschid Pacha had collected an army at Schumla, and by the middle of May he had so far organised it as to be capable of assuming the offensive. Had he been somewhat less dilatory in his movements, he might have attacked General Roth with the 6th and 7th Corps before reinforcements had reached him from the north. As it happened he did not move at all till May 17th, nor commence his principal movement until the beginning of June. Then, having arranged, as he thought, with Hussein Pacha to make a simultaneous advance from Rustchuk, an arrangement, it may be remarked, which was not carried out, the Turkish commander-in-chief sallied forth from Schumla with all his available force to attack Pravadi. On arriving there he posted himself on the neighbouring heights and commenced an irregular siege. No sooner did General Diebitsch hear of the movement of the Grand Vizier, than trusting to the well-known carelessness of the Turks in the matter of reconnoitring, he conceived the brilliant idea of making a rapid march from Silistria, of throwing himself on the communications of the Ottoman army, and occupying the only road which led back to their refuge, Schumla. By this means he forced the Grand Vizier either to fight in the open, and probably at a great disadvantage, or else to abandon his communications, the camp of Schumla, and to retreat the best way he could. In order to cooperate with this movement, the corps of Roth and Rudiger, together with the garrison of Pravadi, were ordered to occupy the defiles in rear of that place until the Muscovite army had accomplished its intended détour. The details of this operation, which Count Moltke remarks decided the fate of the campaign, are of so interesting and important a nature that they are worthy of being recounted at length. The following account is extracted from the work of Colonel Chesney, who was intimately acquainted with the nature of the ground, and visited it soon after these events occurred; he says:—

'Count Pahlen, with the advance of the army, reached Kuchuk Kaïnardji on June 5th, and on the 8th a communication was opened by General Matadoff with General Roth at Molatch. General Kreutz, whose advance was at Kizil Childir, in front of the valley of Newtscha, formed the main body near Koargou, an elevated and strongly entrenched position. Continuing to advance, the main body was joined on the 8th at Alexjat by parts of the 6th and 7th Corps, bringing the intelligence that the Grand Vizier still continued on the plateau of Rowno, with Roth opposite to him at Eski Arnauthar. Favoured by a dense fog, and by the ignorance of the Turks, the Russian army reached Tauchan Kosluche during the night of the 9th, and the advance under Count Pahlen was pushed onward at the same time to Yeni-Bazar, where his Cossacks encountered some Turkish cavalry. These proved to be the advance of a force under Veli Pacha, which had quitted Schumla by order of the Grand Vizier, to threaten the rear of Roth and Rudiger. Count Pahlen having driven the Pacha back almost into that fortress, turned to the left and established himself at Madara, on the direct road between Pravadi and Schumla.

'On the following day another important movement took place, when General Roth, leaving two regiments to watch the Grand Vizier, effected his junction with General Diebitsch by a daring flank march. This was the more hazardous, since it was parallel to the line by which the Grand Vizier might have been returning to Schumla at that very moment, and he could, in this case, have crossed the hill to overwhelm him.

'Towards the evening of the same day, the 10th, the capture of two Tartars informed the Russian General that the Grand Vizier's army was in motion. Uncertainty as to the direction of his march caused some alarm in the camp; since from a position near Markowtscha, which is midway between Schumla and Pravadi, the concentrated force of the enemy might overwhelm any part of the exposed line of the Russians, extending as it did from

Boulanik, by Matara, Yeni-Bazar, and Tauchan Kosluche, to Pravadi, a distance of twenty-five miles. There was, however, but little occasion for uneasiness; for the various posts which had been occupied with reference to the siege of Silistria had so completely cut off the Grand Vizier's communications with that fortress, that he was still entirely ignorant of General Diebitsch's march.

'Under the impression that the demonstration against Veli Pacha was the precursor of an attack upon Schumla, Ibrahim Pacha, who was in that place, had summoned the Grand Vizier to his aid. He marched accordingly in that direction, with the full expectation of being able to overpower the forces of Roth and Rudiger, which, as he supposed, threatened his rear. Instead, therefore, of proceeding southward by Marash, or more northerly by way of Eski Arnanthar and Tauchan Kosluche, he chose the direct central line. The first part of his march was parallel to that of the Russians, from whom the Turks were separated by a mountain chain, whence their movement was watched by Russian vedettes.

'On reaching Markowtscha early on the morning of the 11th, the Grand Vizier found a strong body of cavalry posted in his front, with six guns, and supported by infantry in the rear. This force had been rapidly brought from Pravadi by General Kuprianoff, in the full expectation that his very strong position would enable him to prevent the passage of the Turkish army, which now suddenly appeared in his front.

'Kara Djehennem, the general of the Ottoman artillery,

immediately planned the following attack upon the supposed corps of Roth and Rudiger. The cavalry advanced, masking five field-pieces which eventually opened upon the enemy at a suitable distance; and the charge which took place under cover of their fire was completely successful, for the Russian cavalry was routed, with the loss of five guns, and 400 killed. The infantry, however, was more fortunate, for by rapidly changing front they gained the protection of a neighbouring wood.

' Having thus opened a road across the mountain, the Turks continued to advance, till, on reaching the other side, they discovered the advance of the Russian army; which under General Ostrochenko, had in the interim occupied the defiles between Tschirkowna and Kulewtscha; while behind the latter place other divisions of the enemy's army had been successively forming.

' The position of General Diebitsch was particularly strong, comprising as it did a succession of wooded hills separated by deep ravines. The principal of these ravines is about 1,600 yards long, with a breadth varying from between 100 to 200 yards. The narrowest part is that touching the mountain near the village of Tochirkowna, and this necessarily became the first position of the Turks; who had, consequently, very little room for either their cavalry or infantry. The Russian position was much more favourable, for at the other extremity of the defile the hills are rather lower, and terminate at the village of Kulewtscha in an open plateau.

'On this advantageous ground five battalions were posted in chequered squares, supported by two pieces of artillery, with orders to maintain their position at all risks, until the expected support, which was in full march, could arrive from the direction of Kalugvi and Matara. On the other side of this position there is a succession of gentle hills crossing the Schumla road in the shape of a crescent, which at once encloses, and most advantageously commands, the valley of Pravadi.

'The Turkish army is said to have numbered 33,000 men; including the siege artillery they had fifty-six guns. The Russians, including the force with the baggage, had about the same number; but their 146 guns gave them a decided superiority, independently of the fact that the greater part of the Turkish force was composed of militia.

'By changing front and making a rapid flank movement by way of Marash, the Grand Vizier might still have reached Schumla without a battle; but, nothing daunted by finding the whole instead of a part of the Russian army in his front, he determined to attack General Diebitsch forthwith. With this object a battery opened its fire from the commanding ground against the plateau occupied by the enemy, and at eight A.M. the loud hurrahs of the Turks were heard as they advanced through the smoke of the artillery.

'Notwithstanding the extreme difficulty caused by broken ground, a mixed body of cavalry and infantry charged the Russians with such impetuosity that, according to the account given to the author on the spot by a Russian officer, two of the squares were broken, and one of them, 1,600 in number of Múrom's regiment, was entirely cut to pieces as the men stood in their ranks. Six guns were also taken; the villages of Kulewtscha and Tschirkowna were carried; the plateau was nearly cleared, and the remainder of the Russians were actually giving way, and about to be exposed to the sabres of the victorious Turks, when the hussars under Count Pahlen arrived most opportunely to save them from their impending fate. Had the Grand Vizier followed up his victory by bringing up his reserve to attack the enemy's right wing, the day must have been completely his; but he contented himself with driving the hussars back and then resumed his former position, which gave the enemy time to bring up more troops and attack in his turn.

'General Arnoldi, with the Hulan division and a twelve-gun horse battery, came up from Matara, and, assisted by Count Pahlen with fourteen battalions and thirty-five guns, made an attack on the left of the Turks, which was led by General Budberg. Although the Turks suffered severely from the fire of the enemy's guns, which their artillery, consisting chiefly of battering guns slowly drawn by buffaloes and oxen, could not adequately return, they yet succeeded in repulsing this attack.

'During the progress of these two affairs, the main body of the Russian army continued to arrive, and formed on the crescent-shaped hills already mentioned, which outflanked the Schumla road, as well as the Turkish position on both sides. Towards noon Reschid Pacha, with a view of throwing back the Russian right wing on the main body, and thus opening a road to Schumla, made a grand attack with his infantry, which advanced by the valley from the left of their position. In carrying out this movement they got beyond the plateau, and the latter would have been turned and the passage of Schumla opened, had it not been for some Russian troops and guns strongly posted to defend that road: the corps of Roth and Rudiger, which had just advanced from Matara, were among the number.

'General Diebitsch, having now his whole force in hand, prepared a decisive attack upon the Grand Vizier, who had resumed his original position at the edge of the wood behind Tschirkowna. For this purpose the Jägers were formed under Ostrochenko near this village, and five divisions under Count Pahlen still further to the right. Two of Roth's divisions were posted, under General Zoll, the chief of the staff, so as to outflank the left of the Turks, having in reserve twenty-four battalions and some hussars. The second division, under Kuletza, was detached to Marash, to operate against the rear of the Grand Vizier.

'These arrangements being made, General Arnoldi, with four battalions and a twelve-gun horse battery, supported by two battalions with another twelve-gun horse battery and some hussars, led the attack. The ground narrowed as they advanced; but, as the Turks remained firm, it became necessary to resort to a cannonade on both sides. This was of course greatly to the disadvantage of the Ottomans, owing to the limited space occupied by them, and the battery of General Arnoldi did fearful execution with case shot.

'Notwithstanding this the contest was maintained without losing ground up to four P.M., when the fire of the Russian battery caused the explosion of two caissons in the very centre of the Turkish army. A similar mischance occurred to two other tumbrils, which had a disheartening effect. According to Lieutenant Schaufuss, the officer already mentioned as having been present, this gave the turn to the battle—confusion ensued, and was succeeded by flight. The Grand Vizier endeavoured to rally the fugitives, and for this purpose posted the fourteen regiments of the Nizam most advantageously on strong ground, that might have been defended without difficulty sufficiently long to effect this object. But these troops abandoned their post without resistance, and the flight of the Turkish army became general; it fled through the wood of Markowtscha, leaving the six Russian guns which had been taken, together with the rest of the artillery and baggage, in the hands of the enemy. The fugitives being met near the village of Markowtscha by the garrison of Pravadi, turned to the right and crossed the wooded mountains towards Kamtchik; thus, by a considerable détour, they succeeded in reaching Schumla.

'It has been already mentioned that the Grand Vizier, on breaking up his camp near Pravadi, had despatched orders to the garrison of Schumla to make a diversion in his favour by attacking the rear of the Russians. This was accordingly attempted, and with some success; but it was not sufficiently followed up. On meeting a slight check, Veli Pacha retired within the lines of Schumla; and in so doing he committed the second mistake, by abandoning entirely some of those exterior redoubts which had been such serious impediments to the enemy in 1828. If, therefore, General Diebitsch had instantly pursued the retreating garrison, he might, and probably would, have carried the important entrenchment of Schumla on the evening of the 11th, or even on the morning of June 12th, for on the former day the Russian army was only a few miles from the place, and under the most favourable circumstances, it having already acomplished the double object of cutting off and defeating the Turkish army.'

Had Diebitsch been aware of the extent of his success, he might probably have at once taken Schumla, just as the Allies might have marched into Sebastopol after the battle of the Alma; he contented himself, however, with sending a force on the 12th, under General Roth, to intercept the enemy, who nevertheless managed by a circuitous route to regain the camp. It is stated that at the expiration of ten days there were about 30,000 men assembled there under the Grand Vizier—the remnants of his beaten army. This victory practically placed Turkey at the feet of Russia; it and the campaign were lost, as Von Moltke remarks, in consequence of the adventurous spirit of the Grand Vizier, just as the previous campaign had been lost by the inactivity and lethargy of Hussein Pacha, his predecessor.

Nothing now remained to place the crown on General Diebitsch's success but to march at once across the Balkans on Constantinople. There was every reason why this course should be adopted: the Turks were demoralised and would have no time to collect their forces or fortify Aidos; the season was favourable, the heat not yet being excessive; Silistria was completely invested; supplies were to be had from the sea; and there was nothing to bar the way in the shape of a formidable hostile force or formidable fortifications. Moreover the plague had broken out among the Russian troops, and a change of scene and air was of vast importance. There was only one thing to stop the Russians, and that was want of men. Diebitsch had but 25,000; if only 10,000 were detached to watch the 30,000 men in Schumla, but 15,000 remained to cross the Balkans and penetrate into the heart of the enemy's country. It was therefore determined to wait for the fall of Silistria, when the 3rd and 4th Corps would be set free, and in the meantime to negotiate and watch Schumla. Four weeks passed in this way. At last the 3rd Corps arrived from Silistria on July 13th; and preparations were at once made for crossing the Balkans.

The details of this operation are given at some length by Von Moltke, but it seems sufficient here to indicate the routes by which the various columns marched. There is no trustworthy or distinct account of the exact strength of the Russian army at this time. Colonel Chesney puts it at about 40,000 men, 10,000 being left at Schumla and 30,000 forming the main body. Probably, when we come to consider the amount of sickness that prevailed in the Russian army, the real effective force did not exceed 35,000 in all.

The first care of Diebitsch was to deceive the Ottomans as to his intentions; in this he succeeded perfectly by marching as if in retreat to Silistria as far as Yeni-Bazar, when he directed his columns to the right. One under General Roth moved on Devna,—another under General Rudiger on Kupriquoi,—a third being left temporarily at Yeni-Bazar,—where head-quarters were fixed on the 18th. The Russians pushed on as fast as possible, and before the Grand Vizier had divined their object, had succeeded in crossing the Kamtchik river, which runs past Kupriquoi, without encountering much opposition; each man, it is stated, carried four days' provisions, and ten days' more followed in the company carts. After reaching Kupriquoi the columns turned westward to the sea-coast and by the 20th the head-quarters of the army were established at a village called Dervish-jowan, a little to the south of the mouth of the Kamtchik. While General Roth moved along the sea-coast to Missivri, the main body advanced on Aidos (both places fell with but little resistance), and on the 27th—nine days after the departure from Schumla—the columns had united south of the Balkans, prepared to move onwards to Constantinople. Burghas and the towns on the sea-coast yielded, and nothing remained but to march on Adrianople. Jamboli was reached on July 31st; here a minor affair occurred with the usual result—the flight of the Turks. At this place enormous stores fell into the hands of the Russians, who thereby were much aided in their onward march. At last, on August 19th, the Muscovite army encamped before Adrianople; at one time there was an appearance of danger, and General Diebitsch concentrated his troops and turned aside to Selimno; it was found, however, that this town was only occupied by a small force, who were easily routed.

As remarked by Count Moltke, 'the exertions of two campaigns, the expenditure of 100,000 millions of roubles, and the sacrifice of over 50,000 men, had brought 20,000 Russians to the gates of Adrianople'—great as had been the sacrifices the triumph was also great. Fortunately for the Russian general and his army their actual strength was unknown to the Turks; an officer sent by Osman Pacha to reconnoitre had reported that 'it was easier to count the leaves of a forest than the heads of the enemy.' Thanks to this ignorance the town of Adrianople, containing 80,000 inhabitants with many fugitives from the army, at once capitulated, while Halil Pacha, in place of defending the town marched out to Constantinople, with a force of about 12,000 men, on the very day that Diebitsch appeared from the northwards. Fortune seemed most certainly to smile so far on the arms of the Czar. Had a defence a quarter as determined been offered at Adrianople as was offered at Varna, Brailow, Silistria, and other places, the weak Russian army could scarcely have carried it, and once their strength was known their ruin was practically sealed.

Having got so far, it has been said that General Diebitsch should have at once moved on, and that the time he spent in Adrianople, besides being the destruction of his army in a sanitary point of view, was a gross strategic mistake. Count Moltke reviews his position at this juncture as follows:—

'General Diebitsch still had 150 miles between him and the capital of Turkey. Between Adrianople and Karistiran, the ancient Justinian way, is intersected by tributaries of the Ergineh, which afford positions of defence at every two or three miles, supposing any Turkish corps had been disposed to occupy them. The ruins of the wall of Athanasius, extending right across the isthmus, form a fresh entrenchment; and the positions on the main road at Büjuk, and especially at Kütchuk-Chekmedgè, are absolutely impregnable. They may, however, be avoided by a circuit on the north, as the so-called Strandscha mountains are, in fact, a mere chain of wooded hills from 600 to 800 feet high, and passable for infantry in every part. Two practicable roads from

Kara-Burnu on the Black Sea by Boghaskoi likewise lead to the capital. Although all these roads offer excellent positions for entrenchments, their capabilities of defence mattered little under existing circumstances. But it was impossible for the Russians to march upon Constantinople without leaving at least a few thousand men in so considerable a town as Adrianople, were it only to maintain order and protect the sick; it was, moreover, quite out of the question to advance while such an army as that commanded by the Pacha of Scodra remained in the rear unwatched. If only 6,000 or 8,000 men were appointed for this duty the Russian army would not number above 10,000 by the time it reached Constantinople.' It may be mentioned that Mustapha Pacha of Scodra in Albania, an old Janissary, had held back hitherto, with his 40,000 men, Arnauts; but now that the capital was in danger he appeared on the scene—or rather made his appearance when it was too late, since having refused to fight during the war, after peace had been proclaimed, he absolutely refused to be quiet, and for a time caused much uneasiness at the Russian head-quarters by his warlike demonstrations.

Between August 20th and 28th there was neither a movement forward nor an attempt at negotiation at Adrianople. On the latter day, however, envoys from the Porte arrived, and at the same time Russian plenipotentiaries made their appearance at Burghas. In fact, the position of the Russian army was so critical as to cause the greatest uneasiness at St. Petersburg, so much so that the Emperor Nicholas ordered a fresh levy of 90,000 men and pressed forward overtures for peace with the greatest vigour. In order to hasten this much-desired arrangement and to overcome the notorious procrastination of the Turk, General Diebitsch adopted a course equal in brilliancy and wisdom to his march from Silistria on the Vizier's communications at Schumla. He gave the orders for an advance on Constantinople. Three columns moved forwards: one on the left opened communications with Admiral Greig in command of the Black Sea fleet on September 7th. At the same time the right wing reached Enos on the Mediterranean, and the centre column advanced to Karistiran on the direct road to Constantinople. As the magnanimity of the Russians in not going farther has recently been lauded it is well to quote Count Moltke's own words as to their position at this time; he says:

'Thus on the day when the Turkish plenipotentiaries broke off the negotiations, the advanced troops of the Russian army stood with their right wing at Midia on the Black Sea, and their left at Enos on the Ægean, covering a space of 110 miles. The two corps at Visa and Luleh Burgass amounted in all to about 8,000 men, and might therefore pass for the advanced corps of a considerable army. As they had already marched half-way from Adrianople to Constantinople it was time that the main body should make its appearance. This consisted of the 7th Corps at

Adrianople: from this corps one detachment with two guns had been sent to Hermanly in the direction of Philippopoli; the 37th Regiment of Chasseurs had remained at Slivno, and one regiment of Bug-lancers had been sent to Enos. Thus, then, the so-called "Gros" consisted of ten battalions and fifteen squadrons; in all, after deducting the numerous sick, about 4,000 or 5,000 men. Such was the army which was to make head against 30,000 Arnauts, to keep in subjection a town of 80,000 inhabitants, and finally to conquer another city containing 500,000 souls.'

When speaking also of the possibility of General Diebitsch marching on Constantinople direct from Adrianople, he says: 'It is pretty clear that the time of action was over for General Diebitsch; he could only make demonstrations which might overawe the Turks; this he accordingly did. The Russians at Adrianople were estimated, even by the European ambassadors at Pera, at 60,000 men: if he had marched upon Constantinople this delusion would have been dispelled. At St. Petersburg the war was by no means looked upon as ended because the Balkans had been crossed, as is shown by the ukase of August 10th ordering a levy of three souls upon every 500, which in Russia amounts to about 90,000 men. A few reserve regiments and companies of invalids were now directed upon Adrianople, Admiral Heyden's fleet was strengthened by three ships of the line and several frigates from the Baltic, and the second half of the loan of

42,000,000 florins negotiated with Holland was now raised. The position of General Diebitsch with 20,000 men in a hostile town of 80,000 inhabitants, half-way between 30,000 Turks at Constantinople and 30,000 Albanians at Sophia, while his own corps was exhausted by exertion and disease, must have given rise to very serious uneasiness at St. Petersburg. General Krassowski had endeavoured to make himself master of Schumla, but had failed. He had commenced a regular siege, opened trenches, and had several skirmishes without taking one of the Turkish works; Prince Madatof had been mortally wounded, and General Kisselef found great difficulty in keeping the Turks out of Wallachia. Widdin, Nicopolis, Sistoro, Rustchuk, and Giurgevo still held out, and the communication between these places by the Danube was restored. General Geismar, it is true, had crossed the river, but only in order to follow and observe the menacing movements of the Pacha of Scodra.

However, it matters little how critical was the position of Diebitsch and his army: neither the Sultan, nor yet the European diplomatists who were the advisers of the Ottoman Government, knew it. Accordingly, yielding to the panic which prevailed at Constantinople, and to the representations of the foreign ambassadors, more especially the ambassador of England, Mahmoud gave way, and on August 28th, 1829, the Peace of Adrianople was signed. The conditions of this treaty were by no means very onerous or humiliating to the Porte. In accordance with his previously declared intentions the Czar gained no increase of territory in Europe—what he acquired in Asia will hereafter be noticed. The fortresses held by Turkey on the left bank of the Danube—Turnau, Kaleh, and Giurgevo—were relinquished and their fortifications razed; the principalities, Servia and Montenegro, though nominally still vassals of the Sultan, were placed under the protection of Russia; and last, but by no means least, no Turkish garrisons were to be allowed to occupy them. These conditions were in reality more advantageous to Russia than they appeared—but nevertheless they cannot be regarded as severe. And thus ended the war of 1829.

CHAPTER VI.

REMARKS ON THE CAMPAIGN IN EUROPE OF 1829.

The character of the Russian operations—Remarks thereon—Extract from Appendix to Count Moltke's book on sickness in the Russian army—Field-marshal Diebitsch.

MANY who read the history of the campaigns of 1828 and 1829 in a cursory manner and regard the military results, rather than the causes that produced them, have arrived at conclusions which on closer study are found to be mistaken, and which are calculated rather to mislead than to guide those who would wish to gain an insight into the future from the history of the past.

Let us first consider the manner in which the operations of the war of 1829 were conducted, taking, as before, Count Moltke's remarks for our guide. As in the previous year the campaign was delayed in its commencement until May, and the forces employed by Russia were far too small for the task they had to perform. The campaign lasted, deducting the stay at Adrianople, three months, and consisted of one siege, one battle, and a march of about 500 miles. The great advantage which the Muscovites had was the possession of Varna; without this and Sizeboli it would have been almost impossible for the army, such as it was, to obtain sufficient supplies to carry it throughout its long march.

The two movements which decided the contest were first the flank march from Silistria and consequent successful battle of Kulewtscha, which destroyed the Ottoman army, and secondly the bold movement across the Balkans, leaving Schumla in the rear. The passage of these mountains was effected practically by only one road, which was for all effective purposes undefended; this fact, however, in no way lessens the credit due to the boldness of General Diebitsch, who had no reason to know that he would be thus unopposed. Reschid Pacha, although energetic and venturesome, appears to have made two mistakes, the one venturing out to attack Pravadi, thereby allowing himself to be surprised on the flank and rear, and the other remaining at Schumla after Diebitsch had broken up his camp. Instead of remaining there for fourteen days, he ought at once to have issued out with 20,000 men, leaving 10,000 behind, who were amply enough to protect the fortress; he should have marched viâ Kotesch Eski, Stamboul and Kasan to Selimno,—there he might have united with the Arnauts, and appearing on Diebitsch's flank must have hindered his further advance. If, however, the Vizier could not or did not choose to act as suggested, he should have kept his forces together, and not squandered them in weak detachments as at Aidos, &c. On the whole it may be said that as, in the campaign of the previous year, it was not the ability of Wittgenstein, but the incapacity of Hussein Pacha that caused the defeat of the Turks, so in the present one it was the genius of Diebitsch and not the folly of Reschid Pacha that gave victory to the Russians.

In reading the remarks of the great strategist of the age on these operations, it is impossible to avoid perceiving the analogy between the movements which he criticises and those which he himself years afterwards directed with such brilliant success. One might almost say that the battle of Sedan was won, not on the playing-fields of Eton, but on the hills before Schumla. Diebitsch's flank march bears a striking resemblance to the movement of the German armies, which ended in MacMahon's ruin; and the masking of Schumla with the bold advance onwards to the blockade of Metz and the forward movement on Paris. There can be little doubt that the lessons learnt by the Prussian Captain attached to the Staff of the Russian head-quarters in 1828 and 1829 bore fruit in the knowledge that raised the Prussian Monarchy to the Empire of Germany.

We have seen the weakness of Diebitsch's army and its critical condition when the peace of Adrianople put an end to hostilities. From this it has been argued that no Russian army has a chance of reaching Constantinople, and that the Turks are perfectly able to take care of themselves. Before arriving at this conclusion, which appears to be entirely a false one, it is well to consider what were the causes of such extraordinary weakness on the part of the Muscovites. Those who read the following pages extracted from the Appendix of Count Moltke's book will wonder—not that Diebitsch performed so little, having got so far,—but that he ever reached the Balkans. Certainly the horrors here described are a warning to all armies whose fate it may be to campaign in the same regions.

Extracts from Appendix.

'No sooner, indeed, had the Russian army entered the Principalities than a vast number of the soldiers fell ill. The surgeons were unanimous in considering the disease to be of a very malignant character, but they differed as to whether it were a low gastric fever or a putrid fever— whether typhus or the plague. The name, it is true, did not matter much, as the plague is closely related to those diseases, and indeed is perhaps merely another form of them, aggravated by the influence of soil and climate. The characteristic symptoms, such as buboes, carbuncles, and boils, made their appearance, but no one liked to utter the dreaded name, or to resort to quarantine regulations, which were hardly compatible with a campaign.

'Some measures of the kind were, however, indispensable; for though a few recent experiments have appeared to prove the contrary, long and frequent experience has shown that infection may be communicated by the touch of plague-stricken persons, and still more by that of their clothes.

'Before the breaking out of the war there were in Russia two lines of quarantine—on the Dnieper and the Pruth; the former had been taken off at the beginning of the campaign in order to facilitate communication. But before the entrance of the Russian troops, scattered cases of plague had appeared in Wallachia, and the Hospodar had established a plague-hospital at Dudeshteh. The cases became more numerous in the spring, and by the middle of May four convents were filled with the sick. Now the quarantine on the Pruth was taken off, and that on the Dnieper reimposed with a duration of sixteen days, and boards of inspection were organised at Bucharest and Jassy. A little later the main army before Schumla had to be protected by quarantine regulations, not only against Turkish deserters, but also against Wallachia. Unfortunately, the plague broke out in Hirsova, the principal point of communication between the army and Russia, and it became necessary to establish a quarantine at Bazardchik. At Varna the troops were inspected every week, and these precautionary measures were so successful that the main corps in Bulgaria remained free from the plague all through the year 1828. As the inhabitants had foretold, the character of the disease in the Principalities changed when the hot weather set in; it did not, however, die out, as the communication could not entirely be stopped; at one time the Russians were infected by the natives, at another the natives by the Russians; it was in vain that the sick soldiers were lodged in separate huts of brushwood, that the clothes, linen, and even the munitions of whole battalions were cleansed, and a number of suspected houses burnt. Spite of all these precautions, the sickness continued to spread in the Principalities throughout the autumn, and by the middle of November 1840 villages were infected. It was not until the severe cold set in in December that the plague entirely ceased among the troops that were besieging Giurgevo and Kalarash, and in the hospitals at Bucharest it still continued. What made the matter worse was that those hospitals were only calculated for the reception of 500 sick, whereas thousands were brought thither from all directions, of whom a great number proved to be infected with the plague. On February 11th, 1829, sixty-one villages were purified by order of General Roth.

'Hitherto we have spoken only of the plague, but nervous intermittent and putrid fevers, dysentery, scurvy, and inflammatory disorders, prevailed everywhere, and destroyed ten times as many soldiers as the plague, which had hitherto been confined within narrow limits. Meanwhile the opening of the new campaign drew near; the cycle of diseases of the first campaign was closed, and in February 1829 the number of sick and dead was at its miminum between the two campaigns. The diseases had reached their acme in September and October; during the latter month alone 20,000 sick had been received in the hospitals without counting the field hospitals. The greatest number of deaths had occurred in January 1829; for in this month, during which there was an armistice,

6,000 men died; but the relative mortality of the first campaign did not reach its highest point until February, 1829, when one out of four sick died.

'The intensity of the disease is shown in the following table.

'The number of deaths per cent. were—

	1828								1829	
	May	June	July	Aug.	Sept.	Oct.	Nov.	Dec.	Jan.	Feb.
In the regimental hospitals . .	1·8	2·7	2·0	2·7	5·6	7·2	10·9	10·5	...	...
In the hospitals .	7·4	7·2	10·2	16·6	18·9	22·3	23·4	23·3	25·5	28·8

'The vast amount of illness is shown by the fact that during the ten months from May 1828 to February 1829 no less than 75,226 of the less serious cases were treated in the field hospitals, and 134,882 serious cases in the hospitals, making altogether 210,108 sick.

'Reckoning the whole strength of the Russian army, including non-combatants, at 100,000 men, which is a very liberal calculation, every man had on an average, therefore, been twice in hospital. From this positive information, and the rates of percentage given in the table, it appears that during the first campaign, and the subsequent winter quarters, the Russians lost at least 82,000 men in the hospitals. This number does not, of course, include those who were killed on the field of battle, and therefore were not brought into hospital at all. It may therefore be said, without exaggeration, that this first campaign cost the Russians nearly one half of their actual effective force.

'In the middle of May 1829 symptoms of plague broke out for the first time on the right bank of the Danube, at Czernavoda, Babandagh, Kostendje, Mongolia, Bazardchik, Kavarna, and at last in Varna, the most important point of all, at which were the reserves, magazines, and arsenals of the whole army, and a depôt of 4,000 invalids. The infection was supposed to have been spread by the distribution of the munitions which had belonged to the deceased soldiers of the 16th division of infantry, and which had been shut up for a long time in a magazine. At all events the guardians of the arsenal were the first who died with positive symptoms of plague. However, the close quarters of the troops, the bad food, and the exhalations from so many dead bodies, generated scurvy, and the most malignant forms of fevers. In the middle of June the numbers daily admitted into the hospital at Varna amounted to from fifty to eighty, and the death of eight surgeons deprived the sick of almost all assistance.

'A few battalions were removed to an encampment outside the town; the men were made to bathe in the sea; the tents were fumigated with vinegar; the munitions were aired, the clothes of the dead burnt; and a space enclosed with ditches set apart for plague-stricken patients.

'The appearance of this plague hospital, if such it can be called, was frightful. The sick staggered about, gasping beneath the burning sun, among dying and dead. In June the plague reached such a height, that about 1,000 men a week were brought into the plague hospital. By August 26th, 5,509 sick had been received here; of these 3,959 died.

'One day, June 25th, there were 300 deaths, the corpses were heaped up like dogs and carted away. Out of forty-one surgeons twenty-eight were infected, and of these twenty died. Out of seven apothecaries four died, besides thirty dressers, hospital attendants, &c.

'As the surgeons only arrived a few at a time, intervals occurred during which there was only one doctor to take care of all these sick. The enormous mortality among the surgeons was the more unfortunate, as they were replaced, for the most part, by inexperienced young men, generally foreigners and unable to speak the language. Not only in the hospitals but on every road into the town, in every field, and behind every hedge, were found dead and dying men, while drinking and riot was going on in the tents of the cantiniers. The state of things was no better in other places. Brailow was completely deserted; even the posting-house was removed out of the town so that travellers might not be forced to enter it; 1,200 men were treated there for plague in June, of these 774 died; almost all the surgeons and hospital officers were dead.

'In Slobodjeh the entire management of the plague hospital was left in the hands of one single non-commissioned officer. The plague had broken out in Bessarabia. At this time the main corps of the Russian army lay before Schumla, and it was of course of vital importance to protect it from a fearful pestilence. The corps was surrounded by a cordon of outposts. The large convoys which had been despatched with proper precautions were suffered to pass free, but the carts of the cantiniers which were to supply the head-quarters were stopped here in crowds, while the greatest scarcity prevailed in the camp. Spite of all, the infection crept through, but the cases of plague were scattered, and on the whole the state of health of the main army was good; what the troops chiefly suffered from was dysentery.

'As soon as the army had begun to cross the Balkans, all the sick in the ambulances of head-quarters were transported to Balchik. The troops which had to pass through suspected places marched between cordons of outposts, to prevent all communication with the inhabitants. All the convoys from Varna were purified before starting, and re-examined on their arrival. A strict quarantine was introduced along the course of the Kamtchik, and the seaports in the Bay of Burgass were provided with lazarettos.

'A great number of the men sunk under the fatigue during the first few days' march. By the time they had reached Devno the number of sick in the ambulance had reached 400, who were suffering from diarrhœa, jaundice, and scurvy. Many of the men threw away their ten days' provisions of oatmeal and biscuit, unable to bear the weight. The corps reached the first ascent of the mountain with sadly thinned ranks, and even at Derwash-Jowann a hospital had to be established under temporary huts for the accommodation of 600 sick.

'At the southern foot of the mountain the troops rested from their long fatigues and privations, beneath the shade of fine oaks and beeches, and amid gardens affording vegetables and half-ripe grapes. The soldiers were rejoiced and encouraged by their successful passage of the Balkans, and were filled with fresh life and hope. Only about fifty men had been wounded at the taking of Aidos, and there were not a hundred sick in the town. In Aidos the streets had to be cleared of the dead bodies of the besieged, and the houses to be cleansed from dirt. No symptom of plague showed itself here, but the army was now attacked with intermittent fevers. In a very few days both officers and men complained of inconceivable languor and fatigue, insomuch that many of them could scarcely walk. Besides the intermittent, they were attacked by continued fever, accompanied by delirium, and such relaxation of the capillaries, that the slightest blow, or even touch, caused blue marks in the skin; the bite of the flies, which attacked these patients with especial avidity, produced purple spots half an inch in diameter in a few moments. On the fifth or sixth day the patients died in a state of unconsciousness, and their bodies immediately began to decompose like those of hunted animals. The intermittent fevers, with redoubled paroxysms, rendered the patients weary of life, and were worse than the plague. Very few had been wounded, but these were attacked by tetanus; more than half the number of deaths, however, were caused by dysentery.

'Every day hundreds left the ranks of the army already so much enfeebled; some lost their senses for thirty-six hours in the paroxysms of fever, others were perishing of thirst. The hospitals on the farther side of the Balkans filled so fast that there was neither room to receive the sick nor clothes and linen for their use. Most of the necessaries had been left behind in Bulgaria, where, during the month of July alone, 19,000 sick had been added to the 18,000 who had been left there. Thus during the month of July no less than 40,000 men, more than half the active force of the army, lay in hospital. As yet the plague had not followed the main army, but it hung like a black cloud over the northern horizon of Bulgaria. The quarantine establishment on the Kamtchik was filled with persons suspected of plague, and the character of the continued fevers became so malignant that it threatened to turn to plague.

'During the month of September 2,096 men lay sick at Burgass, 6 of whom had buboes. In October, out of 2,117 sick, 53 had the plague, and in November one-half the whole number of sick were plague-stricken. The quarantine had been kept up with the utmost rigour, and it seems probable that the plague had developed itself from the fever without contagion. . . . .

. . . .

'By the time the army had been in Adrianople a week, 1,616 sick were taken there; by September 1st it contained 3,666, and by the middle of the month 4,641, one-fourth of the whole remaining disposable force. After the conclusion of the war the plague broke out in the hospital in its most fearful shape, and in the midst of peace carried off those who had withstood the sword, fatigue, and disease until the end of the campaign.

'To these immense numbers of sick nothing could be afforded but a bare shelter. Adrianople did not contain a supply of stores sufficient to last any length of time; the most ordinary food was wanting; there was not even hay or straw to litter down the sick upon the wooden pallets of the barracks; they were laid upon torn-up Turkish tents with knapsacks as pillows and no covering but their cloaks. The winter set in with fearful severity; most of the windows were unglazed, and the doors would not shut. In a short time the beautiful grove of plane trees had disappeared, for even the healthy troops wanted firewood, and the very bones of the dead out of the cemeteries were used as fuel. At first there was no lack of surgeons, but the work they had to do was beyond human powers: there were no dressers to be found at all and scarcely any hospital attendants. The doctors were forced to prepare and administer their remedies themselves, and when the plague broke out they nearly all fell victims to it, as was the case wherever it prevailed. . . . . .

. . . .

'During the month of October 1,300 men died at Adrianople alone of diarrhœa; 1,500 were sent thither from Kirklissa, suffering under the same disease, and scarcely able to reach the hospital from exhaustion. The diarrhœa patients, whose vital powers were completely exhausted, perished with cold like flies in autumn, with the thermometer at about 41°. In order to protect their feet against cold they kept on their boots until they complained of violent pains in their feet, and upon their feet being examined, about October 16th, they were found to have mortification in the toes, arising from want of external and vital heat.

'According to the terms of the treaty of peace, the Russian army was to go into winter quarters at Burgass, but it was absolutely impossible to transport such a number of sick people along such roads; 4,700 sick, with 300 or 400 men commanded to serve as attendants, had to remain at Adrianople under cover of the 36th Regiment of Chasseurs, making altogether about 6,000 men.

'Before the departure of the corps on October 29th, the first case of plague occurred in the hospital, and soon afterwards the disease spread with irresistible violence until not one of the 800 wards was free from it.

'The external symptoms of the plague are described by the Russian physicians as follows. The outbreak of the disorder soon become rigor, and change towards midnight into violent heat with delirium, resembling an inflammatory fever. In this stage the patient is very talkative, and maintains that his illness is no case of consequence. If anyone approaches him, he jumps up, but immediately staggers backwards, or falls as if struck by lightning: the face is swollen, the expression altered, and the eyes fixed and covered with a white film. The patient sees and hears imperfectly and speaks thick, but much and fast; his memory is so weak that he often does not know his own name or that of his regiment: on the whole his appearance is that of a drunken man. In a subsequent stage of the disease he sinks into a torpid silence and plucks his clothes; he complains of cold, crawls about on the earth, heedless of the injuries he inflicts on himself, and often dies at the very moment that he is tearing his neighbour in order to drag off his clothing for himself. The breaking out of buboes does not save him from death, which ensues at the end of forty-eight or twenty-four, and sometimes of even four hours. The only favourable crisis is violent perspiration.

'In a disease of which the course was so rapid, all internal remedies were found unavailing. At Varna, pouring cold water over the patients had sometimes cured, and always relieved them, but at Andrianople the weather was too unfavourable, and the patients too sensitive to cold, to admit of this treatment, and the only thing which afforded any relief was external friction with oil. Towards the end of September the plague reached its utmost height; from fifty to seventy men died every day, and the disease only died out in the following March from want of more victims.

'Only two transports went to Burgass at all, one in December with 300 convalescents, and one in May with 170 sick. They were escorted by 300 or 400 men in good health; all the rest had perished. Of the 6,000 who stayed behind in Adrianople 5,200 died.

* * * * *

'The number of deaths per cent. was as follows :—

	1829									
	Mar.	Apr.	May	June	July	Aug.	Sept.	Oct.	Nov.	Dec.
In the regimental hospitals .	...	...	9·3	10·7	10·0	11·1	14·3	18·8	27·3	19·6
In the hospitals .	20·4	25·6	28·2	56·6	41·1	33·7	34·6	42·0	45·6	39·1

'On an average, therefore, there died in 1828 :—In the field regimental hospitals, 5 per cent. In the hospitals, 19·2 per cent.

'And in 1829—In the field regimental hospitals, 14·6 per cent. In the hospitals 37·0 per cent.

* * * * *

'In the regular hospitals alone were—

1829	Received	Of these there died
In March	12,170 sick	$\frac{1}{5}$ = 2,434
„ April	17,625 „	$\frac{1}{4}$ = 4,406
„ May	14,419 „	$\frac{1}{3}$ = 4,806
„ June	18,000 „	Above $\frac{1}{2}$ = 9,500
„ July	19,000 „	$\frac{2}{3}$ = 7,600
That is, during 5 months	81,214	28,746

'During the following months the mortality rose from one-third to two-fifths, and even to one-half. The number of sick continued to increase in the small army at Adrianople, and the deaths during the last five months of the year were at least as numerous as during the five previous months. We know that 5,200 men more died out of the number left behind there. If to all these we add the deaths which took place in the field hospitals, and the number of those killed in battle, we shall probably fall far short of the truth if we reckon the loss sustained by the Russians during their last campaign at 60,000 men.

'This estimate, no doubt, includes part of the great body of non-combatants and of the small reinforcements which followed the main body from Sizeboli to Adrianople. We may, however, assume that not more than 10,000 or 15,000 combatants returned home across the Pruth, and that the Russian army was almost wholly destroyed during the second campaign.

'Such an extraordinary state of health or rather sickness could not have been foreseen; it far exceeded all calculation, and it is difficult to form a conception of an army engaged in offensive operations of which the larger half is lying sick in the hospitals.

'The blame which has been cast upon the higher branches of military administration in this respect appears to us unjust; it was manifestly impossible in such a country to carry the means and appliances for nursing and curing

40,000 sick, or to enforce during a campaign the quarantine regulations necessary in a time of plague. But such a state of things as that which we have just described must not be left out of our calculations in forming an opinion as to the performances of an army and its leaders.'

On reading the account of these horrors, the feeling naturally arises, What must have been the talent and determination of the general who was undeterred by them and still led his army on! As General Diebitsch was such a hero, the following description of him, given by Lord Albemarle in his 'Fifty Years of my Life,' may prove interesting; being derived from personal observation, it is undoubtedly authentic. He gives, as an extract from his diary:

'Field-Marshal Diebitsch is a little fat plethoric-looking man, scarcely five foot high, with a large head, long black hair, and a complexion of the deepest scarlet, and a countenance indicative of a certain irritability of temper, which has earned for him from the troops, in addition to his proud title of Yabalanski, or crosser of the Balkans, that of Smawar, or tea-kettle.'

CHAPTER VII.

THE CAMPAIGN IN ASIA IN 1828.

State of affairs in Asia in winter of 1827-28—Attitude of Persia—Russian preparations for invasion of Asia Minor—Resources at her disposal—Alternative methods of attack—Preparations of Turks—Commencement of campaign—Fall of Kars—Outbreak of the plague—Capture of Akhaltsikh—Defeat of Seraskier—Capture of other fortresses—Conclusion of campaign—Remarks.

THE campaign in Asia in 1828, although not on so large a scale as that in Europe, was far more successful and decisive in its conclusion. Just as the war conducted by Marshal Wittgenstein, his lieutenants, and his opponents, was little else than a succession of strategic misconceptions and tactical blunders, so that waged by General Paskewitch, the Russian commander-in-chief in Asia, was a striking example of how small means and insignificant opportunities, if turned to proper account, may produce brilliant results.

The seat of the Asiatic campaign in 1828 was the tract of land between the Caspian and the Euxine. In the previous year Russia had been engaged in a successful war with Persia, and had forced the latter power to conclude peace. The Shah, however, on the publication of the Turkish Hatti-scheriff in December 1827, refused to ratify the treaty which he had previously signed, in hopes that, in view of the impending war with Turkey, he might obtain better terms. Orders were consequently sent from St. Petersburg to Count Paskewitch to prosecute a winter campaign against Persia with all vigour. He therefore advanced in the snow as far as the range named Kaftan-ku, and thereby so struck terror into the heart of the Persian court that, almost without a shot having been fired, they sent envoys to sue for peace. The treaty of Turkman-chai, signed on February 10th, 1829, was the result—by it Russia acquired the Khanates of Erivan and Nak-nihchevan, the fortress of Abbas-Abad, a large indemnity, and the sole right to maintain vessels of war in the Caspian Sea. The conclusion of this treaty was a great advantage to Russia, since not only was a certain enemy thereby neutralised, but also a large tract of territory was acquired, which formed a valuable base of operations for the coming campaign.

Although the frontier of Asia Minor after the conquest of the Caucasus by Russia had no natural defensive boundaries, and with their usual apathy the Turks had almost entirely neglected the fortifications of all the frontier fortresses, nevertheless the invasion of Asiatic Turkey presented many difficulties and many dangers. In the first place the distances to march were enormous, and neither the resources of the country nor the quality of the roads were such as to permit a force of any size to advance far, still less to manœuvre with rapidity. The population were, as a rule, hostile and warlike, and if the generals of the Sultan had taken the trouble to organise their forces with sufficient energy, and in good time, they might have brought into the field an army that would have entirely enveloped the small force which was all that Paskewitch could array against them. As usual, accounts differ as to the numbers of the Russian army. M. Felix Fonton, in his work 'La Russie dans l'Asie Mineure,' puts it at 23,393 infantry, 6,192 cavalry, and 130 guns, while 13,860 infantry, 2,391 cavalry, and 42 guns remained in reserve in Russia; others have estimated the entire force at some thousands less. There is, however, no doubt whatever that the column under the immediate command of the Russian general, which did the real work of the campaign, only numbered about 8,000 infantry, about 3,000 cavalry, and 70 guns. In addition to these land forces, there was the fleet under Admiral Greig of eight sail of the line, five frigates, and eleven smaller vessels, and a contingent of about 6,000 men, which was sent in May from the 7th Corps to take Anapa.

It may be said that three separate and distinct lines of operation were open to Count Paskewitch. The first is the road which coasts along the shore of the Black Sea to Trebizonde, the second runs from Tiflis to Kars and Erzeroum, by the pass of Saganlugh over the Allaghery mountains, the third and last is by Ararat. Not only is the centre road by far the best, being the main communication from Asia to Constantinople, but it leads to those towns which it was particularly necessary to subdue, hence it was selected by Paskewitch for his main advance; while two other columns were also despatched to the flanks, one under General Hesse, consisting of six battalions, a regiment of Cossacks and sixteen light guns, to the Black Sea, the other on the left under General Tchevtchevade to Armenia. With that secrecy and prudence which Jomini declares to be essential to great and successful operations, Paskewitch concealed his intentions so well during the winter of '27 and '28, that the Turkish rulers made no preparations whatever to oppose the coming invasion; it is stated that the Pacha of Kars even permitted the inhabitants to sell their grain in the Georgian markets, thereby materially contributing to the provisioning of the Russian army.

The war commenced with a descent on Anapa, which took place about May 14th with the force before mentioned. The fortress was attacked with all vigour, and on June 23rd surrendered with its garrison of 85 guns and 3,000 men. The main Russian land force commenced its operations almost simultaneously with the attack on Anapa. On May 25th about 12,000 were assembled at Gumri, reserves of guns and ammunition being established at Tiflis, Redut-Kalà, Baku, and Dervent, and proceeded at once to advance on Kars. As usual the Turks were taken unprepared and Paskewitch encountered no opposition until he reached that town, which he proceeded to attack on the southern side. Had the Ottoman commanders been less dilatory in their arrangements, not improbably the Muscovite army might have encountered a serious disaster, since the Pacha of Erizerum was collecting 60,000 men to relieve Kars and the Pacha of Akhaltsikh was engaged in concentrating forces on their right. Fortunately, however, for Paskewitch both Pachas were late, and Kars capitulated on June 23rd with 129 cannon, 22 mortars, 33 standards, and about 17,000 men. On the whole the defence was fair, but by no means equalled the attack either in skill or determination. Kars was at this time supposed to be impregnable and was certainly one of the most formidable fortresses in Asia. It had been built by Amurath III. between the years of 1578 and 1589. In addition to a position of great natural strength, being on one side inaccessible, it had more fortifications than are usually accorded by Turks to their fortresses, and thereby was enabled to make a successful resistance to Nadir Shah in 1735 and again to the Russians in 1807. Hence its capture in so short a time had a great moral effect throughout Asia. Just as the Russian flag was hoisted on the battlements of Kars the Turkish force intended to relieve the town appeared on the neighbouring heights, and was obliged to retrace its steps to the mountains.

Immediately after this brilliant success a new enemy to the Russian army appeared on the scene: the plague broke out and before its course could be averted by the

ATTACK ON AKHALTSIKH.

vigorous measures adopted by Paskewitch, it carried off several hundred people. This outbreak of disease somewhat delayed Paskewitch and enabled the Seraskier to collect 35,000 men whom he placed at Ardagun on the right rear of the Muscovite army. The Russian general, however, did not tarry long; he made a demonstration as if he were about to attack Erzeroum, thereby causing the Seraskier to retreat; he then retraced his steps and suddenly appeared before Akhalkalaki. This little fortress was defended to the last, but being of insignificant strength it soon succumbed, as also the post of Hertviz, which was taken by a detached force of about 3,000 men.

The next operation was the attack on Akhaltkish, or Akhaltsikh as it is also called, which was reached about August 12th after a march of many difficulties and dangers. Almost simultaneously with the arrival of the Russian army the Seraskier also appeared, this time again too late to prevent his enemies occupying a strong position on the west side of the town. Both armies entrenched themselves and both endeavoured to assume the offensive, the Turks being in the proportion of more than two to one. The Ottoman general, however, had committed the fatal mistake of separating his forces into four bodies. Paskewitch profited by the error, and in a brilliant night attack entirely defeated the Turkish field force, capturing ten of their guns. After this catastrophe the fortress of Akhaltkish was left to its fate, and the army intended for its relief retired towards Ardagun. The Akhaltsikheans, however, manfully refused to yield, and mindful of the boast that 'they had never been subdued' held out to the last. As the town was entirely commanded by adjoining heights the defence could not be a very long one, more especially as the Jews and Christians of the place were by no means so desirous as the Turks of being killed or burnt amid their houses. Finally, after a succession of assaults and struggles almost without precedent in history, the stronghold was taken on August 27th. It is stated that the defenders lost no fewer than 4,000 men, and the attackers, according to their own account, about 6,000, but probably far more.

The defence of this fortress has not inappropriately been compared to that of Saragossa: in both the principal resistance was made by the inhabitants from house to house; if anything, the Asiatic town was more desperately defended than the European. Every inch was obstinately contested, and the town was only captured by the defenders being burnt out. Even then the remnant that remained retreated to the citadel, whence they were allowed to march out for Erzeroum with all the honours of war.

The fall of Akhaltsikh was followed by that of Atskhur and Ardagun; as is often the case when a strong fortress is captured after a desperate resistance, the actual capture of the place itself is but the smallest portion of the results. The moral effect caused by such a capture induces the garrisons of neighbouring places to lose heart, and to yield almost without striking a blow. This appears to be more especially the case with the Turks. After the fall of Brailow one after another the strongholds of the Dobrudscha yielded as soon as they were attacked,—in the same way after the fall of Akhaltsikh every place before which the Russians appeared capitulated at once and the invaders were left masters of the territory as far as the Saganlugh. Prince Tchertzevadze had been almost equally successful in Armenia, and an advance of the Pacha of Mush having been checked by the Russian garrison of Kars, at the end of September the invaders had finished the campaign and were unmolested. The results of these brilliant exploits of Paskewitch, effected though they were with so small an army, were by no means unimportant—5 fortresses, 313 pieces of cannon, 195 standards, and 8,000 prisoners had fallen into his hands within five months. He was master of the whole of the territory from the Georgian frontier as far as Saganlugh; in fact, when the winter set in, a small Russian army of about 15,000 men, with 34 guns, occupied a triangle of which Kars was the apex, and thus were in an admirable and secure position for an advance in the following spring.

It may be remarked that in addition to the movements of the centre column, which we have followed, there were also minor operations on the flanks, as before mentioned, on the coast of the Black Sea and in Armenia. These were just as successful as the movements of the main body, so that Count Paskewitch, while Persia remained neutral, had no reason to feel anxiety either respecting his actual position or as to his base of operations for the campaign of the following year.

CHAPTER VIII.

ASIATIC CAMPAIGN OF 1829.

Preparations of Turks for campaign—Threatening attitude of Persia—Consequent precautions of Paskewitch—Turkish attempt on Akhaltsikh—Successful defence and results—Letter of Paskewitch—Defeat of Hadgi Pacha—Defeat of the Seraskier near Kainly—Retreat of Hadgi Pacha—Fall of Erzeroum—Check of the Russians at Khart—Final defeat of the Seraskier—Retreat of Russians—Conclusion of war—Remarks on campaign—Conditions of peace.

THE Asiatic campaign of 1829 commenced almost with the new year. So alarmed was the Sultan by the advance and successes of Paskewitch that he lost no time in putting forth all his energies to regain his lost territory and to re-establish the prestige of the Ottoman armies in Asia. His first step was to disgrace the leaders who had been defeated, '*pour encourager les autres.*' The Seraskier, Halil Pacha, and his lieutenant, Kiossa Mahomet Pacha, alike shared this fate, and were replaced by Hadgi-Saleh, Pacha of Maidan, and Hagkhi Pacha of Sivaz, both of whom were supposed to be men of ability and energy.

These leaders at once commenced their preparations for the coming campaign; large depôts of provisions and ammunition were stored at Erzeroum and elsewhere; all believers were summoned to the defence of the Crescent, their religious fanaticism and loyalty to the Sultan were appealed to with the most fervid proclamations, while at the same time—an unusual occurrence in Turkey—the sinews of war were not wanting, large sums of money being sent to the commanders from Constantinople, still further to intensify the sacred devotion of the Faithful to their supreme Leader. It was hoped that these preparations would enable two large armies to be set on foot by the commencement of spring. One of these, 80,000 strong, with 66 guns, was to assemble at the base of the Saganlugh and march on Kars and Akhaltsikh, while another, numbering 50,000 men and 50 guns, under the Pachas of Mush and Vann, was to attack the left flank of the Russians and penetrate into Armenia.

Before, however, these preparations could be carried out or perfected, an event occurred which precipitated matters. On February 12th, 1829, the Russian minister at the Persian Court was assassinated. It was supposed by both parties that this event, accidental although it might be, probably would be the forerunner of a Persian and Russian war; hence General Paskewitch had to dispose his troops so as to resist, if necessary, the advance of a Persian army on the left bank of the Araxes, while the Seraskier deemed that he might commence operations without further hesitation.

The first operation of the Mussulman army was directed against Akhaltsikh. This place was selected for attack not only on account of the moral effect which the recapture of so important and renowned a fortress would produce on wavering allies, but also because it seemed more open to attack than Kars or some of the less important strongholds. Accordingly, Ahmed Bey with 15,000 men appeared before Akhaltsikh on February 18th, while simultaneously the Seraskier threatened Kars in order to distract the attention of Paskewitch. The latter, however, was not deceived; he not only reinforced the garrison of Akhaltsikh, but despatched as large a body of troops as he could spare to assist in relieving it. Notwithstanding this reinforcement the defenders only numbered 2,000 men, being commanded by Prince Bebutoff, whose name has ever since been handed down with honour throughout the annals of Russian history. The attack and defence of the fortress were equally determined and brilliant. The outer town was carried at once, and the citadel was nearly lost owing to the presence of some houses near its walls which had not been levelled, and which the Turks occupied. Finally, on the morning of March 16th, when the besieged were at the last extremity, signs were seen of a retreat on the part of the investing army. Prince Bebutoff immediately sallied out to pursue them, and about two o'clock in the afternoon was met by the head of the Russian columns under General Burtsdorff, who had been sent to raise the siege. Akhaltsikh was saved, and with it the hardly-won results of the last campaign.

The successful defence of this fortress had an immense

moral effect favourable to the armies of the Czar throughout Asia, just as its fall would probably have been the first cause of their ultimate defeat and ruin. The Shah, on hearing the news of the Muscovite success, immediately changed his policy, suspended his warlike preparations, and forwarded to St. Petersburg the assurances of his devoted attachment to the Emperor Nicholas. A letter of exhortation addressed at this time by Paskewitch to Abbas Mirza, and quoted by Fonton, is peculiarly interesting to Englishmen, as indicating that, although nominally allies, even in those days there existed between the Russian and English Governments that antagonism of interests and feelings which of late years has unhappily been so strongly developed. He says, 'Ne comptez pas ni sur les promesses des Anglais ni sur les assertions des Turcs. Les Anglais ne vous défendront pas ; leur politique n'a en vue que les intérêts de leurs possessions dans les Indes. Nous pouvons conquérir en Asie un royaume et personne ne s'en inquiètera. En Europe chaque pouce de terrain peut donner lieu á des guerres sanglantes : la Turquie est nécessaire à l'équilibre européen ; mais les puissances de l'Europe ne regardent pas qui gouverne la Perse.'

The events of the last fifty years have proved most forcibly the truth of Paskewitch's remarks. Russia has acquired ranges of territory in Asia equal in extent to half-a-dozen European kingdoms, and except an accidental protest—the result of the extreme inquisitiveness of some troublesome traveller—she has met with no opposition beyond what the inhabitants of the country she annexed could offer her, whereas the least advance or encroachment in Europe has at once raised an Eastern question and twenty years ago involved her in a calamitous war which threw her back a century.

Eastern and semi-independent potentates have never been remarkable for fidelity to their nominal ruler; the chieftains of Asia Minor in 1829 were by no means bright exceptions to the usual rule. The Pacha of Mush, when he found the Russian arms still triumphant, promptly gave in his adherence to what he believed to be the winning side, and thereby deprived the Sultan of the services of about 12,000 Kurdish cavalry, who were much needed. The Seraskier also found much difficulty in collecting troops, although, had time been allowed him, probably he would have eventually assembled a most respectable army. Paskewitch, however, was not one of those who allow golden moments to pass by unheeded. As he was enormously outnumbered, his only chance was to take his enemy in detail, and he selected for his first point of attack that frontier which was nearest and weakest. Accordingly when the Seraskier's lieutenant or 'Kaia,' Hadgi Pacha, was still preparing for another assault on Akhaltsikh, General Burtsdorff was ordered to attack him in front while General Mouraieff, was detached from Ardagun to threaten his left flank. The two Russian columns united on June 2nd at a village called Dighor, and although only about 7,000 against 15,000, they succeeded in defeating the Kaia with the loss of 1,200 men, and drove his army back on the mountains in a thoroughly disorganised condition.

By this success the Russian general was enabled to join his right wing to his centre; he concentrated a force of about 12,000 infantry, 5,700 cavalry, and 7 guns on June 9th at Kotanly, and proceeded to attack the Seraskier, who was threatening Kars. The Turkish army was strongly posted; it was very numerous, and, unless outmanœuvred, could not be attacked with any prospect of success. With the true inspiration of a great commander, Paskewitch at once determined to execute a movement apparently most hazardous, but whose brilliant success was its complete justification. On June 13th the Seraskier, Salegh Pacha, with no less than 30,000 men, was moving up to occupy a strong position on the road to Erzeroum at Zermi, while Hadgi Pacha, having collected his routed forces, amounting to about 20,000, chiefly irregulars, had posted himself on the flank of the road near Milli-Dux. If these forces were permitted to effect a junction, Paskewitch had but a poor chance of success; accordingly while he distracted the attention of the Kaia in front with one small column, with another, comprising the main body, he made a circuitous march and interposed himself between the two forces of the enemy, thereby abandoning his communication with Kars, and in case of defeat making his ruin almost certain. It is stated that the Russian column which effected this turning movement marched thirty-two miles over two snowy ridges without making a halt, and only just reached the desired pass in time to prevent its occupation by the Seraskier.

As soon as the Kaia discovered that the attack on his own camp was nothing but a feint, he at once detached a small force under Osman Pacha to occupy the Zermi road and endeavour to prevent any further advance of the enemy until the arrival of reinforcements. Osman Pacha performed his task well, but was overwhelmed by the superior numbers of the Russians, and thus the separation of the Turkish army was completed. It cannot, however, be said that Paskewitch's position was in any way secure. Notwithstanding his first success, he found himself at Kainly between two forces both infinitely superior in numbers to his own. The question was, which should he attack first: he wisely selected the most formidable, and threw himself on the Seraskier with all his army. The attack was just made in time; had it been delayed even a day the Russian army might have been attacked in flank or rear by Hadgi Pacha, while it was engaged with the Seraskier in front. As it was the main body of the Ottoman army was defeated with great loss, and by the night of June 19th was in full retreat.

It may be remarked that all accounts agree in stating that this battle, although in results favourable to the Russians, was by no means easily won—in fact, it was perhaps the hardest fought and the most critical contest of the two campaigns. However, it was won, and now Paskewitch was able to turn on the Kaia, whose irregular troops, demoralised by the defeat of their comrades, gave but little trouble. The entrenched camp at Milli-Dux was taken without difficulty, and with it Hadgi Pacha and staff. 3,000 prisoners, nineteen cannon, and nineteen standards fell into the hands of the Muscovites—in fact, the rout of the Ottomans was complete. The performances of Paskewitch's army on this occasion, if all accounts are true, have seldom been equalled, either in ancient or modern warfare. In less than twenty-five hours they had marched thirty-five miles, had beaten two armies, both more numerous than themselves—they had captured two camps, two Pachas, one general-in-chief, besides prisoners, guns, standards, and were in a condition to follow up their successes without delay or hindrance.

The Russian general did not fall into the error of Hannibal and halt after his victory, thereby losing its fruits. He pressed on without delay, captured the fortress of Hassan-Kale, on the road to Erzeroum, by June 23rd, and four days afterwards was in possession of the capital itself. The surrender of this town was the immediate result of the defeat of the field army; although not elaborately fortified, it might have opposed a serious resistance if properly defended. The Asiatic militia were wholly unable to follow Horace's maxim of 'æquam memento rebus in arduis servare mentem.' They became utterly demoralised by defeat, and those who did not disperse to their homes but remained in the field were an encumbrance rather than an assistance to the general who commanded them.

After the fall of Erzeroum the campaign practically came to an end, although various operations of minor importance took place before peace was actually declared. It may be mentioned that, while the main body of the Russian army was operating against Erzeroum, the Pacha of Vann took advantage of the weakness of the Muscovite left and attacked Bazarjid; the town fell, but the citadel held out until the news of the surrender of the capital caused the Pacha to retire.

As soon as Paskewitch was established in Erzeroum he pushed on some troops to Kniss and Baiburt, both of which places were easily captured. He then directed General Burtsdorff on Khart; there the Russian army encountered, on July 19th, its first reverse: the Lazians, who occupied the town, fought desperately, and repulsed the invaders with the loss of their general. This check, however, was soon avenged by Paskewitch himself; he marched out and by a rapid turning movement intercepted a force coming to relieve Khart, and reduced the town itself. But little now remained between the Russian army and Trebizonde. The capture of this place would have been of enormous importance if only on account of the communication thereby opened with the fleet in the Black Sea—accordingly, the army advanced, and on August 14th had reached Karakaban and Ghurnish Khana, only forty-six miles from

Trebizonde. Here the difficulties in the way of a further advance were found insurmountable. The population, in place of their being friendly as in Armenia, were hostile, and threatened the communications. The army itself, never very strong, had been so weakened by detachments at the various points on its route, that now it was almost insufficient for its own protection; in addition to this the roads were found to be impracticable for artillery. Finally, in face of these drawbacks, the Russian general was reluctantly compelled to order a retreat. Baiburt was evacuated, the works blown up, and on August 29th the invading army was concentrated at Erzeroum; while the main body had been thus occupied, various operations had likewise taken place on the flanks. General Pankzatieff had been most successful in Guriet and on the shores of the Black Sea, where he had defeated 8,000 Turks in the defiles of Mukha-Estatt, and had captured sixty-eight guns. An expedition undertaken by General Sachen, governor of Akhaltsikh, to subdue the Adjars was not so fortunate.

At the beginning of September heavy autumnal rains set in, and Paskewitch made preparations to withdraw his troops to Georgia, leaving only garrisons in the captured towns. On hearing of the retreat of the Russians, the Ottoman militia again reassembled. the Pacha of Vann again moved out of his Pashalik, and the Seraskier concentrated about 1,000 men at Baiburt, with 6,000 at Tchifflick. Paskewitch apparently continued his preparations for retreat; in reality he collected his troops and turning back with about 6,000 men again separated the two forces of the enemy, and utterly routed that which was at Baiburt. Twelve hundred prisoners, six guns, and twelve standards remained in his hands. The Seraskier who again had come up too late, retreated to Balakhor, when he heard of the armistice which preceded the treaty of Adrianople and the conclusion of peace. Thus ended this most brilliant and successful campaign. Paskewitch left garrisons in the conquered towns and marched back to Georgia. As he passed over the Saganlugh he was met by the bâton of Field Marshal despatched to him by his Imperial master—never was a reward more deserved or better earned.

These campaigns of Paskewitch in Asia bear a striking resemblance to some of the wars which mark the early history of the British empire in India. In both we see a small force advancing, as it were, with extraordinary rashness, into the heart of an enemy's country, fighting battle after battle against extraordinary odds, taking fortress after fortress by the most desperate assaults, and, in fact, securing victory when by all the ordinary rules of war it ought to be beaten. Paskewitch, like Clive, displayed his great genius by his correct appreciation of the quality and capabilities of his enemy. He took liberties which, in the face of an European army, must have caused his ruin, but which, as events proved, were his only chance of securing victory.

In the 1828 campaign, at once grasping the point which he should make his first objective, he marched straight on Kars, and, unlike Wittgenstein, did not permit himself to be deterred or diverted from his object by a threatening but not really serious danger on his flank. He thoroughly understood the Asiatic character, and the effect which a bold offensive, coupled with great rapidity of movements, invariably produces on it. He struck sharply and quickly, giving his enemy no time to think or recover from his first astonishment. Rather than cause a delay, which would raise the *morale* of his adversary, he would run the risk of moving with insufficient preparations, and even thereby in some degree imperil the certainty of his success—thus armies melted before him like snow, and the capital of Asia Minor surrendered almost from the very terror of his name. Undoubtedly the most brilliant and likewise the most hazardous of all his operations was when he placed himself between the two Turkish armies at Milli-Dux; any hesitation would then have been his destruction, nothing saved him but his boldness and the fighting qualities of his soldiers.

While, however, we give Paskewitch all the credit which he so fully deserves, it must not be forgotten that the quality of the troops with whom he had to contend was of the worst description. The Turkish soldiers fighting against Wittgenstein and Diebitsch were bad, but those opposing Paskewitch were far worse; being chiefly composed of militia and irregulars, they had neither the discipline nor the stability required to rally after a defeat, although in case of success they would probably have fought well and might have exhibited great qualities.

Similarly we do not find in Paskewitch's campaigns either that determination or persistence on the part of his adversaries which was so frequently opposed to the British troops in India,—none of those battles fought from dawn to eve and renewed on the following day, such as are not unknown in our history. Paskewitch also seems to have avoided allowing his men to engage in those cavalry skirmishes, which were so frequent in the war in Europe, and which so tended to demoralise the Russian and encourage the Turkish cavalry. Perhaps the Ottoman horsemen that fought in Asia were less formidable than those who rallied round the Sultan in Europe, most certainly they were far less successful. When speaking of these skirmishes, in which during the '28 campaign the Mussulmans almost invariably had the best of it, Count Moltke makes some remarks on the Turkish method of warfare which are worth repeating. He says: 'The remark that whenever you see one turban you may be sure there are a thousand more, is in the main correct. The Turks know nothing of advanced guards, outposts, and other military precautions, but always remain together in large bodies. They forced their adversaries to do the same if they did not wish to encounter the same checks as heretofore. The Turkish way of fighting is like that of the wild boar, which does not seek his foe, but awaits his approach in the thicket and then rushes blindly upon him. An impetuous attack may be expected from the Turks, but not a lasting or obstinate defence. Against Orientals it is no use keeping troops in reserve. The best cards should be played out at once. A few hours always decide the fate of the engagement; and Turkish history affords no example of battles fought from sunrise to sunset, like those in the west of Europe.'

As far as can be gathered from the accounts of the various combats that took place in Asia Minor during these two years the characteristics thus indicated by Count Moltke were almost always displayed by the Turks. On one or two occasions they fought well and even desperately, but were wholly unable to maintain a long or doubtful battle. Their marching power seems also either to have been very indifferent or not to have been turned to proper account. Although the operations of the second campaign were on the Turkish side far better conducted than those of the first year, still in both the commanders invariably appeared on the scene of action too late to be of any use. The Seraskier arrived just after Kars had been taken—similarly he was too late at Akhaltsikh. In the following year the new generals, although warned by the fate of their predecessors, were scarcely less dilatory, but their plans were better conceived, and had they remembered Napoleon's maxim that 'victories are more often won with the legs than the arms of soldiers,' they might not improbably have achieved considerable success.

On the whole, considering the vast amount of territory and the number of fortresses which his armies had subdued, more especially in Asia, it cannot be said that the terms which the Emperor Nicholas exacted at the Peace of Adrianople were excessive or severe. He had, it is true, loudly proclaimed to all Europe that in making war he desired not an increase of territory—not personal or national aggrandisement, but that he was solely actuated by a desire to improve the condition of the Christian subjects of the Porte, hence it was expected that he would be reasonable in his demands: but assurances and manifestoes before the commencement of a war are not always binding at its successful conclusion. 'Might is right' may too often be considered the motto of philanthropic monarchs. We must therefore certainly accord the praise of moderation to Nicholas and to his government on this occasion. We have already seen that he exacted a large indemnity and occupied some provinces till it was paid—also that he acquired Brailow and a small amount of territory on the Danube, but this was all in Europe. In Asia, however, the fortress and Pashalik of Akhaltsikh were ceded to him; not indeed a very large but nevertheless a very important tract of country, both from its possessing a considerable portion of coast on the Black Sea and from the facilities it afforded for an invasion of Asia Minor in the event of a future war.

CHAPTER IX.

WAR ON THE DANUBE OF 1853 AND 1854 AND PREVIOUS EVENTS FROM PEACE OF ADRIANOPLE.

Relations that existed between Russia and Turkey after 1829—Revolt of Mehemet Ali—Victories of Ibrahim Pacha in Syria—Assistance given to Turkey by Russia in 1833—Russian forces quit Constantinople—Second Revolt of Mehemet Ali in 1839—Intervention of Allies—Danger of an European War—Strategical Position of Jaffa and Acre—Bombardment of Beyrout and Acre—Convention of 1840—Occupation of Principalities by Russia in 1849—Events that occasioned Crimean War—Assurances of Nicholas—War on the Danube in 1853; success of Omar Pacha—Siege of Silistria—Retreat of Russian Army—Landing in the Crimea—War in Asia and fall of Kars—Peace signed—The Treaty of Paris.

AFTER the signature of the Peace of Adrianople in 1829, twenty-four years elapsed before Russia and Turkey were again opposed to each other. Then there occurred the great conflict called the Crimean War, which threw the Muscovite empire back for a century, and shook the whole of Europe to its foundations.

It is beside our task here to enter into the latter period of this war, when the allies were the principal combatants and the Turks played but a most insignificant part. It even seems unnecessary to refer to the various actions after the invasion of the Crimea, although in some of these the

Ottoman troops engaged the Russians, both as auxiliaries and single-handed, with more or less success. It is in the highest degree improbable that an invasion of the Crimea or any portion of the Russian territory in the Black Sea will be again attempted, except as a diversion. Certainly the Porte single-handed would hesitate before engaging in such an undertaking, and any future allies that she may possess, would scarcely be so foolish as to repeat the Crimean experiment. Hence the events that took place in the latter end of 1854 and in 1855 can scarcely be said to afford any indication as to what may occur in any possible contest of the future between these hereditary and national enemies. It is, however, different with respect to the earlier portion of the war, and the campaign on the Danube in 1853 and 1854 is in the highest degree interesting and instructive to those who would wish to study the strategical and with it the political bearing of the entire question.

Before entering into the actual events which were the commencement of the Crimean War, it is necessary to review shortly the relations which existed between the Russian and the Ottoman empires during the twenty-four years which immediately succeeded the Peace of Adrianople.

Scarcely had Turkey been delivered from the great peril which menaced it in 1829 before another and even still more serious danger appeared to threaten its existence. Mehemet Ali, the Pacha of Egypt, was a man of remarkable ability and insatiable ambition ; born, strange to say, in the same year as both Napoleon and Wellington, he had spent the greater portion of his eventful life in preparing for the one great stroke which should place him and his family for ever on the throne of Egypt, not as vassals of the Divan, but as independent monarchs,—which should make him possessed of the fertile lands of Syria ; and, if fortune favoured, might even enable him to supplant the family of Othman in the leadership of the Faithful. At last there appeared to be a favourable opportunity for the accomplishment of all his designs, and his army was admirably drilled and well officered ; he had a fleet of seven sail of the line, and twelve frigates, a force superior to what now remained of the Turkish fleet after Navarino. Above all he had a son Ibrahim Pacha, who had studied the art of war, and who, as events proved, could turn his study to the best possible account. And while his preparations were thus completed, the condition of the armies which he would have to encounter was such as would seem in every way to favour the chances of their defeat. While the material and numbers of the Ottoman troops had not yet had time to recover from the drain and exhaustion consequent on the campaigns of 1828 and 1829, their leaders and the Imperial government, with the usual apathy of the Turk, had done nothing whatever to remedy the deficiencies which those wars had made so evident. The discipline of the rank and file was in no way improved ; the officers were not better selected, nor were they more zealous in the study of their profession; the arsenals were still exhausted, and the exchequer still empty; in truth the opportunity was well chosen and the measures which so long had been prepared for profiting by it, were on the whole admirably carried out.

The pretext for a war was soon found. In the autumn of 1831 the Pacha of Acre had received and sheltered some thousands of 'fellahs,' or peasants belonging to the delta of Egypt, who had fled to Syria to escape from the exactions of their own government, and to obtain employment during the harvest. Mehemet Ali demanded the surrender of the fugitives, and when this was refused, he fitted out an army of about 30,000 infantry and 8,000 cavalry, and despatched it under the command of Ibrahim Pacha to enforce his demands.

It is not our task here to follow out the campaign of 1832 between the Turks and Egyptians, highly interesting though it is; but for those who regard Syria as a future and not improbable battlefield, where the British road to India may one day be defended, a study of this war will be by no means thrown away. The physical characteristics of this country are peculiarly adapted for defence, and thus may be explained the vast number of wars that have from the earliest days been fought on its soil. The only practicable line by which Asia Minor can be reached from Egypt is the coast road, on which Acre and Jaffa lie, and which they command; hence nearly all the contests which have taken place in Syria have centred round these strongholds from the pre-historic days of Troy down to those of Napoleon. The defence of Acre by Sir Sidney Smith is still more than famous; by it Napoleon declared that he missed his destiny, since, had he taken it, 'he would have changed the face of the world.'

As soon as the Egyptian forces appeared on his frontier Abdallah Pacha, the Pacha of Syria, at once threw himself into Acre with 2,500 men, which was all the force that he could muster. The siege of the place was at once undertaken with great vigour by Ibrahim Pacha, but his own talent as a general in the field was not equalled by the skill of his engineers, and the besiegers made but slow progress. From the middle of December 1831 to the end of March 1832, the fortress was still unreduced, and by this time the Divan had been able to collect some forces for its relief. Three armies were set on foot—one of about 18,000 men, under Hussein Pacha, the celebrated general of the '28 campaign, formerly the aga and destroyer of the Janissaries, was directed through Anatolia; another of about the same strength advanced towards Homs on the Orontes, while a third, of about 10,000 men, seized Tripoli and occupied the sea-coast. Ibrahim Pacha was by no means taken aback by these dangers, great as they appeared; he at once raised the siege of Acre, as Napoleon, when General Bonaparte, raised the siege of Mantua in 1796; and following the example of his great predecessor the Egyptian general took up a central position between his enemies and at once boldly attacked them. The force at Tripoli was easily routed, and the others paused in their onward march. Ibrahim was thus enabled to return to Acre, and on May 27th he carried it by assault. The fall of this fortress gave him a base of operations on the sea-coast and enabled him to act independently of his communications by land, giving a freedom of action which he turned to the best possible account. The Turkish armies suffered a series of crushing defeats at Homs, at Beylau, and at Konieh. So decisive was this last-named engagement that, had Ibrahim known the extent of his success, he might have marched direct on the Bosphorus, but, as remarked by Allison, the empire of Constantinople was protected by the shadow of its former renown, and most fortunately for the house of Othman, Ibrahim fell into the error of Hannibal, and remained inactive for a month. Then on Jan. 20, 1833, he marched on, and by Feb. 1st had reached Kutchieh, near Scutari, too late to achieve the brilliant results which his great success might have won for him.

Among the many miraculous escapes from destruction, which in the last hundred and fifty years have been recorded in the history of the Ottoman empire, there was none more extraordinary or miraculous than this; although in truth it is a page in history which for the honour of Mussulmans and for the dignity of their religion had better never have been written. The danger, indeed, was one that appeared to involve the entire disruption of the Turkish power. The fame of Ibrahim's victories had spread far and wide from the Euphrates to the Danube; from the Caspian to the Mediterranean; the wild tribes of Asia, and the down-trodden Greeks of Europe were alike moved by them, and both equally desired to escape the tyrannic rule which for centuries had oppressed them. In the hour of his need the Sultan turned his eyes to Great Britain, and implored her assistance against his rebellious vassal. At that time England was in no condition to defend even her most vital interests, still less to protect an ally. Her forces reduced to a minimum, were otherwise occupied, and France, who was next appealed to, was equally disinclined to despatch any force to the East. There was no resource left for the Porte but to throw itself into the arms of Russia, and this time the appeal was not disregarded. With a promptness, only equalled by its timeliness, a Russian army and fleet appeared at Constantinople, and the onward march of the Egyptians was stayed.

At Constantinople a peace was soon afterwards proclaimed with Egypt. Mehemet Ali, finding that he had to face the power of Russia, willingly acceded to terms, and accepted the government of his various conquests, which were confirmed to him by a *firman of amnesty* issued by the Sultan. The Russians were now masters of the situation, but agreeable as their position at Constantinople might be to themselves, it was by no means so pleasant to the Western Powers, who at last were roused from their indifference. Diplomacy became most active, and at last it was arranged, at the demand of England and France, that the Russian troops and fleet should retire from the Bosphorus as soon as the Egyptian army had recrossed the Taurus. This arrangement was carried out, and apparently the Emperor Nicholas had derived no advantage whatever from his kind and philanthropic action in rescuing his neighbour, except a treaty of alliance, which was a mutual compliment rather than a mutual advantage. To this treaty, however, named that of Unkiaz-Skelessi, there was added a secret clause, which gave to Russian ships of war alone the right to enter the Dardanelles. The importance of this concession can scarcely be over-estimated; the material power of Russia in the Black Sea was thereby enormously increased, and her influence became predominant. Eventually, perhaps, this secret treaty was the cause of all her misfortunes in 1854 and 1855, since its discovery first caused France and England to unite in their action regarding the Eastern Question, and was the primary cause of the Crimean War.

After this it might have been hoped that affairs in the East would, for a time at least, have remained tranquil, and that the peace of Europe would not again have been disturbed by them. Such, however, was not the case. So soon as the year 1839 there was a complication, which brought France and England to the verge of war, and which was only settled by the force of arms. Mehemet Ali, encouraged by a French alliance, again was the cause of war, but this time he can sincerely be called the aggressor. Sultan Mahmoud, feeling certain of English support, precipitated matters, and brought to blows the enmity which had long existed between himself and his vassal. As in 1833, he was signally defeated both by land and sea, but fortunately for himself was carried off by death before he had had time to see the extent of his discomfiture.

The boy who succeeded Mahmoud, Abdul-Medjid by name, fortunately did not possess the iron will of his predecessor, and was no obstacle to peace. It is, however, probable that the complications would have had even more serious results than attended them had not Servia at this juncture revolted. This and other indications of approaching decay proved to the Great Powers that active intervention was indispensable in the affairs of Turkey. Each Power being more or less jealous of the others, vied with the others in offers of assistance; finally, in July 1840, a treaty was signed between Russia, Austria, England, Prussia, and Turkey, by which the differences between the Porte and Mehemet Ali were finally settled. France, however, was not included in this convention, and had Louis Philippe then listened to the counsels of his Prime Minister of the day, M. Thiers, or had Lord Palmerston been less bold and resolute, the excitement of the French nation at the slight supposed to have been offered them must have had a vent in war. As it was, probably mutual jealousy of the designs of Russia had some effect in causing the counsels of peace to prevail, as they were urged by M. Guizot, who succeeded M. Thiers, and was a devoted friend of England. As it happened, it was indeed fortunate for this country that Louis Philippe did not yield to the popular clamour of his people, since never was England more defenceless—a cry for economy had reduced her armaments by sea and land to the lowest ebb, and she had only nine sail of the line in the Mediterranean to meet twenty sail that the French and Egyptians could muster. Boldness, however, made up for want of material strength, and the naval campaign that followed is alike honourable to the gallantry and skill of English sailors, as it was to the courage and decision of the government that directed them.

A few words only are required to explain this maritime war, which is important if only to show the importance of naval superiority and prompt action in campaigns that have their theatre in Syria. The characteristics of this country are thus described by Allison:—' It results from its peculiar physical conformation that the possession of the coast-line is indispensable for any military operations, either of Egypt against Asia, or of Asia against Egypt. All conquerors on either side, from the earliest times, have gone by this route. By it, on the one hand, Sesostris led his invincible hosts to the conquest of Persia, and Saladin brought his fiery squadrons to combat the Crusaders, and Napoleon advanced from the banks of the Nile to revolutionise Asia. By it, on the other, Cambyses passed when on his march to Thebes, and Darius led the Persians to avenge the victories of the conquering queen, and Alexander marched from vanquished Thebes to the shrine of Jupiter Ammon. An army advancing from Egypt to Syria must bring up all its supplies by this line; its whole communications lie through the seaport towns. Thence their vital importance in war. An enemy who, from the sea, succeeds in interrupting the possession of the line, has achieved the greatest feat in strategy; he has thrown himself on his adversaries' communications without compromising his own. A blow at Acre or Jaffa is like a severe stroke on the spinal marrow; it paralyses all below the wound.'

At this time the Egyptian troops were occupying Syria, and any unaided attempts of the Turks to dislodge them would have been hopeless; hence the allies determined to strike a decided blow before the French had time to interpose. A British fleet under Admiral Stopford bombarded Beyrout in August 1840, and soon destroyed the town. A few weeks later Acre was similarly attacked and also captured, while an allied force numbering 12,000 men landed and reduced Sidon. After these reverses, more especially after the loss of Acre, the key of Syria, the Egyptian troops could only retire, and their government soon after came to terms. In 1841 a convention was signed by all the Great Powers, including France. As this treaty remained in force until the Crimean War, and is of great importance as regards the strategic and political bearing of the Eastern Question at the present day, it is well to note its conditions. They were as follow :—

'1. That the straits of the Bosphorus and the Dardanelles, in conformity with the ancient usages of the Ottoman empire, shall remain permanently closed against all foreign vessels of war as long as the Ottoman Porte shall enjoy peace. 2. The Sultan declares, on his side, that he is firmly resolved to maintain immovably the ancient rule of the empire, in virtue of which it is forbidden to vessels of war of all nations to enter the Dardanelles or the Bosphorus, and in virtue of which these straits remain for ever closed, as long as the Ottoman Porte shall be at peace. 3. His Majesty the Emperor of Austria, and their Majesties the King of the French, the Queen of Great Britain, the King of Prussia, and the Emperor of Russia, on their part engage to respect that resolution of the Sultan, and to act in conformity with the principle there expressed. 4. The ancient rule of the Ottoman empire being thus established and recognised, the Sultan reserves to himself the right to grant firmans of passage to small vessels of war, which, in conformity with usage, are employed in the service of ambassadors of friendly Powers. 5. The Sultan reserves to himself the right to notify the terms of this treaty to all the Powers with which he is on terms of amity, and to invite their accession to it.'

For the next twelve years there was apparent peace and tranquillity in the East; once, it is true, there was a difference between the courts of St. Petersburg and the Porte, but this was readjusted by the intervention of

England, and up to the commencement of the year 1853 there was no reason whatever to imagine that this ever-igniting Eastern Question would again disturb the peace of Europe. Then came the Crimean War, which is still fresh in the recollection of the present generation. The causes of this war were precisely the same as the causes of all the numerous Russo-Turkish wars that have occurred in the last century and a half—ambition on the one side, misgovernment of her subjects and helpless weakness on the other. The pretexts, however, for the contest were numerous and complex, while the manner in which it was eventually brought about and the various negotiations that preceded it would fill a volume if they were faithfully recorded. It will suffice for our present purpose merely to summarise the events as they occurred, and to call attention to the salient points in the military operations.

It may be remarked that only on one occasion between the Convention of 1841 and the events immediately preceding the Crimean War, was there any serious difference between the Courts of St. Petersburg and Constantinople. In 1848 the revolutionary fever which pervaded Europe extended also to Wallachia, and this afforded a pretext to Russia to occupy the Principalities. In consequence of this step diplomatic relations were suspended between the Czar and the Porte, but were renewed by the interposition of England in 1849; and the Russian troops were withdrawn. Also by the treaty of May 1st in the same year, signed at Balta Liman, the protective duties imposed on the Principalities by Russian influence were withdrawn, and great commercial prosperity was the result. It is stated that before the end of the year no less than 1,400,000 quarters of wheat were sent to England from the port of Galatz alone.

We now come to the events which brought about the war of 1853. On February 20th of that year Prince Menchikoff appeared at Constantinople charged with a special mission to the Divan. Neither his own conduct nor that of his followers was conciliatory, and on March 22nd he delivered an imperative demand for a Sened or Convention for a protectorate over the Greek Christians of Turkey. Negotiations of various descriptions continued until May 21st, when Prince Menchikoff and his mission quitted Constantinople, his demands having been refused by the Porte, who in the meantime, however, had issued, as is its custom, many firmans, circulars, and hatti-scheriffs, and had set on foot active warlike preparations for the approaching appeal to arms. In all the negotiations that were thus going on now and subsequently in the Turkish capital, the French, and more especially the English ambassador, Lord Stratford de Redcliffe, took an active part; they both supported the Divan in its refusal to grant the Russian demands, and further gave proof of their intention to afford material as well as moral support by summoning the fleets on June 15th to Besika Bay.

After the departure of Prince Menchikoff from Constantinople there was still an interchange of the accustomed diplomatic notes and despatches. On May 31st Count Nesselrode, the minister of the Czar, announced in a letter to Reschid Pacha that, as the demands of the Russian government had not been acceded to, in a few weeks the Imperial troops would receive orders to cross the Pruth—' Not to make war upon a sovereign who has always been considered as a faithful ally, but in order to secure a material guarantee until the Ottoman Government should give ·those proofs of equity which had hitherto been sought for in vain.' Subsequently, in a despatch dated June 11th, addressed to the ministers and agents of Russia at foreign courts it was stated that ' His Majesty does not aim at the ruin and destruction of the Ottoman empire, which he himself on two occasions has saved from dissolution. On the contrary, he has always regarded the existing *status quo* as the best possible combination to interpose between European interests, which would necessarily clash in the East if a void were actually declared; and that, as far as regards the Russo-Greek religion in Turkey, we have no necessity, in order to secure its interests, of any other rights than those which are already secured to us by our treaties, our position, and the religious sympathy which exists between 50,000,000 Russians of the Greek persuasion and the great majority of the Christian subjects of the Sultan.' . . . Also : ' After three months of laborious negotiations, and after having exhausted even the last possible concessions, the Emperor is now compelled peremptorily to insist on the unconditional (*pur et simple*) acceptation of the draft of the note. But still influenced by those considerations of patience and forbearance which have hitherto guided him, he has granted the Porte a fresh reprieve of eight days, in which it has to take its decision. That period passed, painful though it may be to his conciliatory disposition, he will be compelled to think of the means of obtaining, by a more decisive attitude, the satisfaction which he has in vain sought by peaceful means.'

Finally, on July 3rd, three Russian army-corps crossed the Pruth and occupied the Principalities, and now, practically, the war commenced, although the formal declaration was not issued by Turkey before October 23rd, and not until every effort had been made by the usual diplomatic expedients to bring matters to a peaceful issue. While war had been thus threatening, every preparation had been made by the Porte to render itself capable of meeting the approaching storm. Affairs, as has been remarked, afforded a remarkable contrast to their condition in the year 1828. While in the days of Sultan Mahmoud half the Mussulman population were disaffected or lukewarm; now they vied with each other in sacrifices to display their loyalty and to assist their government to the utmost of their power. The support of the Western Powers gave an additional stimulus to Turkish confidence and enthusiasm; in fact of the many wars in which, as has been related in the foregoing pages, the Ottoman empire has been engaged with Russia, in none would she have had a better chance of contending successfully than in 1853, even supposing she had entered the contest single-handed.

It has been suggested that probably, had not the Western Powers interfered and by urging moderation and caution on the Divan caused it to lose time, a defence of the Principalities would have been attempted: this appears unlikely, both from the precedents of former wars and from considerations of actual military expediency at the time. Colonel Chesney, who brings forward this view, points out the advantage which, possessing the resources of Moldavia and Wallachia, was conferred on Russia, and the manner in which the finances of the Ottoman Government and the spirit of its subjects suffered by the delay. He acknowledges, however, that not improbably the Turkish troops might have had very soon to abandon the line of the Pruth altogether and retire on the Danube; under these circumstances the policy of ever occupying an untenable position and squandering an army by useless detachments may well be questioned. While Colonel Chesney thus argues that the allies conferred a great advantage on Russia by indirectly being the cause of her occupying the Principalities without resistance, Mr. Kinglake, on the other hand, in his 'History of the Crimean War,' declares that the Emperor Nicholas committed a gross strategic error by occupying Moldavia or Wallachia at all, as thereby the communications of his army were exposed to a flank attack, and as he had imposed the Danube as a boundary on himself he was at a disadvantage, for there was no reason whatever why the Turks should in any way limit themselves to the right bank of the river.

Omar Pacha was appointed commander-in-chief of the Ottoman army, and his subsequent exploits fully justified the wisdom of the choice. Since the beginning of the period when war seemed inevitable, he had been collecting his forces on the right bank of the Danube; in all, there was a nominal and fairly appointed force of 100,000 men, but from all accounts scarcely more than 70,000 effectives—the main portion of these were posted at Widdin. Prince Gortchakoff, on the other hand, the generalissimo of the Russians, had about 80,000 men in Wallachia and Moldavia; but these, as appears always to be the case with Russian armies in the field, were suffering terribly from sickness. On October 23rd active hostilities commenced by a Russian flotilla attempting to force a passage up the Danube; a few days later Omar Pacha crossed the river, and by November 4th had established himself on the left bank at Kalafat on the Upper, and at Turtukai on the Lower Danube; a similar attempt to sieze Giurgevo had failed. The check which the Muscovites received in opposing the passage of the Ottoman troops on these occasions had its influence in many ways. It inspirited the Turks to a remarkable degree, and probably was to some extent the cause of their making a better stand against their traditional enemies in the actions of this war than in those of the many that preceded it. Omar Pacha also thereby acquired a position of great strategic importance; it will be seen on referring to the map that while holding Kalafat and Widdin, he entirely outflanked the Russians, and could seriously molest their communications; also that his occupation of Turtukai gave him a similar advantage lower down the stream. He could cross the Danube himself without hindrance, and make incursions on the enemy, while on the other hand he was protected from similar reprisals by the obstacle of the river itself, and by the self-imposed boundary which the Czar had made of it for the action of the Muscovite troops. In these said incursions Omar Pacha freely indulged during the course of the winter, with more or less success, and also he repelled, after a four days' struggle, an attack that was made early in January on the entrenched camp at Kalafat.

At last the Emperor Nicholas began to understand that he had committed one of the most fatal errors which can be committed in war; he had lent himself to half-measures, and had thereby incurred all the consequences without deriving any of the advantages of a vigorous offensive. In his difficulties the Czar called the celebrated Paskewitch to his aid, now named Erivanski from his Asiatic conquest of the province of Erivak. This renowned warrior pointed out that the boldest course was likewise the safest, and that the only hope of success lay in a vigorous offensive. The Lower Danube was to be crossed early in the spring, Silistria was to fall by May 1st, and Lesser Wallachia being abandoned, the main army was to press forward, as in '28 and '29, on Schumla and the Balkans, thence to Adrianople, and thence farther, if it could, to the Bosphorus. Before, however, speaking of the events that occurred in the attempted Russian invasion of 1854, the affair of Sinope on November 30th, 1853, must be recounted.

It must be remarked that, although the Porte had formally declared war against Russia on October 23rd, the Czar by announcing that he in no way desired to injure the Turks, but only required 'material guarantees,' had to a certain extent debarred himself from hostile operations; at least this apparently was the view which the Western Powers took of his position, hence their indignation when on the date before named a squadron consisting of seven frigates, and two corvettes was attacked in the bay of Sinope by a Russian fleet consisting of six line-of-battle ships, two frigates, and four steamers, and was destroyed. The indignation which this action excited in Europe far counterbalanced the material advantage it gave to the Russians by the destruction of the Turkish vessels, and exemplifies still further the false position in which the Czar had placed himself by his self-imposed restrictions.

The Russian operations in the spring of 1854 did not commence as early as intended, and in place of having reduced Silistria by May 1st, it was already the 19th of that month before Paskewitch appeared before the town. This fortress, stated by Count Moltke to be the worst on the Danube, has nevertheless almost always played an important part in Russo-Turkish wars. In 1854 the defences had been planned and renewed by an able Prussian engineer and, as is their custom, the Turks turned these defences to the best possible account by the determination and brilliancy of their individual prowess when they were led and commanded by English officers. Notwithstanding that the siege was pressed with great vigour and that Omar Pacha, from some reason hitherto unexplained, did not march from Schumla where his troops were concentrated, to its relief, nevertheless the Russians were unsuccessful, and on June 22nd, barely more than a month after the cutting of their first parallel, they raised the siege and recrossed the Danube. A few days later, on July 7th, the Ottomans had another triumph at Giurgevo; here, as at Silistria, they were so fortunate as to receive the assistance of British officers. About twelve battalions of Russian infantry, some squadrons of cavalry, and some guns were encamped at Giurgevo, and opposite them at Rustchuk there was a large Turkish force under Hassan Pacha. Apparently the Turkish general had as little intention of making an attack as the Russian had expectation of receiving one. General Cannon, however, and some other English officers, who arrived in the Ottoman camp, persuaded the commander to allow some portions of his force to cross the Danube in various places, and to execute what

Hassan believed to be a reconnaissance, but which in effect turned out to be a bold and skilful offensive movement. In the encounter that followed the Muscovites were worsted, and had to retire, leaving the Turks in possession of the field. Three days later Prince Gortchakoff appeared on the scene with his whole army set free from the siege of Silistria; but in the meantime some British gunboats had ascended the Danube, under Lieutenant Glyn, and had established a bridge of boats across the river. Probably over-estimating the force before him, the Russian generalissimo abstained from an attack and retired to Bucharest. A short time afterwards, in compliance with a peremptory demand from Vienna, the Principalities were evacuated by the troops of the Czar and replaced by those of the Austrian Emperor, and thus ended the occupation of Moldavia and Wallachia and the campaign on the Danube of 1853 and 1854.

In the beginning of September the allied armies, which previously had been concentrated in the neighbourhood of Varna, set sail for the Crimea. On the 14th and four subsequent days they landed, and on the 20th the battle of the Alma was fought. From henceforth until the close of the war in 1856 the contest became one of the Western Powers against Russia, and no longer continued to be a Turkish war. The details of the campaign in all its phases have been fully and ably recounted elsewhere, and it is no way part of our present task to enter into them. As before remarked, it is improbable that the Crimean experiment will be again repeated. If a landing is at any future time attempted on the Russian coast of the Black Sea it will be only as a diversion, and will be distinct from the main and decisive operations of the campaign.

It only now remains to notice shortly the campaign in Asia, which ended in the capture of Kars by the Russians. In July 1854 Lieutenant-Colonel Williams, now Sir Fenwick Williams, was appointed by the British Government to accompany the Turkish forces in Asia Minor. He joined the army at Kars on September 14th; it then had a nominal strength of 28,000 men—some of whom were twenty-two months in arrears of pay. The Russians had previously been preparing an invasion of Turkish territory, and a powerful army under General Mouravieff appeared before Kars in the summer of 1855. On June 16th the first attack was made on the fortress but was repulsed; by the middle of July the place was invested, and on September 21st an attempt was made to carry the place by assault: this also failed; and notwithstanding fearful sufferings and hardships the heroic garrison held out until November 26th, when they were allowed to march out with all the honours of war. While the siege of Kars was proceeding, an army had been despatched under Omar Pacha to effect its relief. Unfortunately the delay in assembling this army was so great and apparently its movements were so unnecessarily slow, that it arrived too late to effect the object for which it had been intended. About 20,000 men were landed at Redoute-Kaleh in September, and by October 28th the Turkish commander had got together altogether about 30,000 men; 20,000 of these were available for field operations, and proceeded to move on the Russian communications. On November 6th, they had reached the river Ingoun, where they met a force of Russians of greatly inferior numbers, and succeeded in repelling them. After this successful action, Omar Pacha apparently rested on his laurels, and we hear no more of him or his army of relief during the remainder of the war.

Early in 1856 negotiations were set on foot for peace between Russia and the Allied Powers. On March 30th the treaty of Paris was signed; by it Russia relinquished a small portion of territory in Bessarabia, thus abandoning all control over the Danube. She likewise subscribed to various other conditions, by far the most important of which were the neutralisation of the Black Sea. As these articles were repudiated in 1870, they are given *in extenso* as follows:—

'*Art.* 11.—La mer Noire est neutralisée; ouverts à la marine marchande de toutes les nations, ses eaux et ses ports sont, formellement et à perpétuité, interdits au pavillon de guerre, soit des puissances riveraines, soit de toute autre puissance, sauf les exceptions mentionnées aux articles 14 et 19 du présent traité.

'*Art.* 12.—Libre de toute entrave, le commerce, dans les ports et dans les eaux de la mer Noire, ne sera assujetti qu'à des règlements de santé, de douane, de police, conçus dans un esprit favorable au développement des transactions commerciales.

'Pour donner aux intérêts commerciaux et maritimes de toutes les nations la sécurité désirable, la Russie et la Sublime Porte admettront des consuls dans leurs ports situés sur le littoral de la mer Noire, conformément aux principes du droit international.

'*Art.* 13.—La mer Noire étant neutralisée, aux termes de l'article 11, le maintien ou l'établissement sur son littoral d'arsenaux militaires-maritimes devient sans nécessité comme sans objet. En conséquence, Sa Majesté l'Empereur de toutes les Russies et Sa Majesté impériale le Sultan s'engagent à n'élever et à ne conserver sur ce littoral aucun arsenal militaire-maritime.'

CHAPTER X.

THE RESOURCES AND ARMED STRENGTH OF RUSSIA AND TURKEY AT THE PRESENT TIME.

Events connected with Eastern Question from Treaty of Paris up to Present Time—The Russian Army—Russian Railroads—Roumania, Servia, Montenegro, and Greece—Resources of Turkey—Turkish Army

WE have carried the history of the various and many wars between Russia and Turkey up to the close of the great contest in the Crimea, which resulted in the treaty of Paris. From the date on which this was signed up to 1870 affairs in the East wore a most tranquil aspect. Russia, deprived of the power of organising hostile armaments in the Black Sea, devoted herself to internal reforms and to the construction of railways, which unhappily for the country through which they run, and for those who advanced money to further their development, were laid down solely on strategic principles without any regard to their commercial utility, or to the convenience of the inhabitants for whose use they were nominally intended. It must, however, be mentioned that before Russia had had time to recover from the exhaustion consequent on the struggle she maintained for two years against the

Western Powers, she had to undergo a trial which, if anything, tested her strength and paralysed her resources even more than, or certainly as much as, almost any of the external wars in which during the course of her history she has so frequently been engaged.

In 1863 there was a Polish insurrection, or rebellion it might more properly be termed. So serious was this outbreak, and so strong and even savage were the measures taken to repress it, that intervention was meditated and even proposed by some of the other European Powers. The Emperor Napoleon suggested a conference to settle the affairs of Russia, just as a conference was recently proposed to settle the affairs of Turkey. Eventually he was not supported, the idea of the conference fell through, and the Polish rebellion was crushed with a high hand; probably the stories of Russian atrocities at the time were in a great measure fabricated or exaggerated, but that they were fully credited in this country is proved by the indignation meetings that were held throughout the country to protest with that warmth of heart that characterises the English people against oppression and barbarous cruelty. It may be added that in 1865 there was a Druse and Maronite war in Syria, which was suppressed by a temporary occupation of French troops.

During this period the Turk was indulging in the, to him novel, amusement of borrowing money from other nations, and of wasting it on himself; not indeed that the waste was novel, but the power of borrowing was one of the many advantages which he derived from the Crimean War. Had the money thus freely lent him been fairly or profitably expended, the Turkish empire might now be in a flourishing condition, and its inhabitants might be contented and well-doing. As it is, there are nothing but some ironclads, some big guns, and a number of imperial palaces to show for the vast sums of which foreign bondholders have been robbed.

Thus fourteen years passed away almost without incident, so far as the Eastern Question was concerned. In 1870, however, as soon as the fall of Metz was announced, Russia, without further warning, gave notice to her representatives at foreign courts that there were some clauses in the treaty of Paris which she must decline to consider any longer binding. The clauses referred to were those given above, and which relate to the neutralisation of the Black Sea. After some negotiations, her demands were acceded to; at the time England and perhaps Austria were the only two Powers who were in a position to offer even a protest at this sudden and high-handed announcement. Both Germany and France were far too busily engaged to enter into such matters; Austria pursued her accustomed policy of a masterly inactivity, and the Government of the day in England, which was the power above all others affected by the proposed concession, apparently did not realise the magnitude of the point they then without difficulty yielded. As it happens, the finances of Russia have lately been too embarrassed, and the time has been too short to enable her to profit by the great privilege which she then gained without effort or danger. She is still comparatively powerless in the Black Sea, and as yet there is no great arsenal, like Sebastopol, either to menace Constantinople or to shelter the fleet which doubtless in the course of a few years she will not fail to create. In considering, therefore, the resources of the two ancient and traditional combatants, should they again come to blows, we have only to consider the land forces of Russia; her fleet is now so inferior in point of numbers to that of Turkey, that it may be left out of the question.

In estimating the forces of Russia, it must be remembered that there is much on paper that does not exist in reality, and that her military system is now in a transition state. The following extracts from some articles that recently appeared in the *Times* give in a concise form an account of her army, and of the methods in which it is raised. The author is not responsible for these articles himself, nor does he know who wrote them; as, however, they appear to be specially valuable, he ventures to make some extracts.

There are at present at work in Russia two different systems. The old one was in use up to 1874; the new one is not yet, and will not for a long time be in working order. Both systems are complicated, and we must endeavour to avoid confusing the reader with too many details. Let us begin with the old system. Though we have marked the division between the two systems in force by the year 1874, the reform, or re-organisation, was projected several years back, and to prepare for it many changes had been made. The Russian soldier was always a conscript, but before the reign of the present Emperor he was generally a conscript for the term of his working life. By degrees modifications were made. Service was reduced step by step as to its duration; therefore to keep up the same number of men in the ranks more recruits had to be taken, in proportion to the reduction in length of service. At last, in 1870, under the administration of the very clever and liberal-minded Minister of War, General Milutine, the principle of general service prevailing in Germany was adopted, except for the Cossacks, a force more or less irregular and very tenacious of its privileges. Since then an attempt has been made to apply the law to them, and even out of the depths of the Czar's dominions have come reports of resistance to the execution of the decree. To give a notion of what such a step means, we can only fancy the result of a general conscription of Sikhs and Ghoorkas in India, or of the Scotch Highlanders 200 years ago. The organisation of the Cossacks will be described hereafter; for the present it must suffice to say that they have always been considered as irregular troops, having their own officers, manners and customs. The new law for recruiting may possibly have affected the strength of the army between 1870 and 1874, but to avoid confusion we will take as the old system that which prevailed up to 1870, and continued to be in force nominally until the new one was introduced.

Up to the beginning of the year 1874 the military forces of Russia were divided into three distinct parts:—1. The Regular Army; 2. The Irregular Army; 3. The Imperial Militia, or General Levy.

The Regular Army was further divided into:—A. The Field Troops, or Active Army; B. The Reserve Troops; C. The Sedentary, or Local Troops.

(*a*). The Field Troops, or Active Army, consisted of 188 regiments of infantry, 32 battalions of rifles, and 48 frontier battalions, 56 regiments of cavalry, 310 batteries of artillery, 3 of which were mountain artillery and 47 mitrailleuse batteries, 11 battalions of sappers, 6 half-battalions of pontoniers (or bridge equipage), 6 parks of military telegraphs, 28 half-parks of field artillery (doubled in time of war), 7 half-parks of horse artillery, 2 parks of siege artillery, and 47 divisional ambulances.

(*b*). The Reserve Troops.—These we find variously estimated by different general staffs; the latest gives one *cadre* per regiment of infantry, 56 squadrons of cavalry, 7 batteries of artillery, and 4 battalions of sappers.

(*c*). The Sedentary, or Local Troops.—These consisted of fortress troops, including 25 battalions of infantry, 59 companies of artillery, increased to 91 on a war footing; troops for interior duty, including 72 Government battalions and about 600 district detachments which were charged with etappen duties, the maintenance of order, &c.; troops of instruction, including one battalion, one squadron, two batteries, and one company of electricians.

This is a sufficiently elaborate organisation for the military forces of a nation which desires to be early in the field, and a few explanations are necessary before it can be understood. First, with regard to the Active Army. Some of the regiments consisted of three battalions, others of four. Each cavalry regiment had four squadrons besides the one squadron counted in the Reserve. The frontier battalions garrisoned the military districts of Orenburg and Western and Eastern Siberia, constituting, with the Cossacks, the military force of those districts. Others, quartered in the Caucasus or Turkistan, garrisoned the fortresses and, if called upon, had to take the field with the rest of the Active Army. Twenty-four were in the Caucasus, two in Orenburg, four in Western Siberia, six in Eastern Siberia, and twelve in Turkistan. They had four companies each, and one company of rifles. Each battery of field artillery had in peace four guns horsed, and in war eight guns. Horse artillery batteries had all their eight guns horsed in peace, but had only two waggons and reduced detachments. The battalion of Sappers had each four companies, and consisted on a war footing of 900 rank and file per battalion. The pontoniers were for bridge-making, and each half-battalion had 240 pontoniers on a war footing, made up to a total of 424 by officers, drivers, &c. It carried 26 iron pontoons and 12 trestles, so that it could build a military bridge 700 feet in length. The field and horse artillery parks are for the supply of ammunition, both for artillery and infantry, and for the refitment of the batteries. The use of siege artillery and ambulance parks is too well known to need explanation. The organisation of transport for the Intendance was left to be organised in time of war according to the circumstances of the case, and this was clearly a defect.

The Reserve Troops were employed to train recruits and horses and supply the losses of the army in peace and war. They were distributed throughout the various military districts.

The Sedentary Troops were used for garrisons and for keeping order in the districts. For the latter purpose the Government battalions, Circle detachments, and others act as police guards, &c.

Let us now glance at that extraordinary and peculiarly Russian force—the Cossacks, or Irregular troops. These wild horsemen—for though there are some Cossack Infantry they are quite subordinate in interest to the great force of Cavalry—possess certain privileges which they hold by tenure of military service. With the exception of an insignificant portion, they provide their own equipment for war. They have not been subjected to the ordinary military organisation of the empire, nor obliged to fight in other than their old wild way. They have even a different system of outpost duty from that of the regular troops. Their dress is different, they ride horses which would almost be called ponies in England, and are but little dependent on supplies carried by trains labouring in the rear of the army. Unencumbered by baggage, unless it be the spoils taken from the enemy, and going home to their savage wives and children, they can march almost incredible distances, hang round the front, flanks, and rear of an enemy's army like flies buzzing about the head of a trotting horse. They can intercept convoys and keep troops guarding the communications of an army always on the alert. Woe betide the stragglers of an army which invades Russian territory! The Cossacks are of various tribes and cannot all be sent away from their homes even in war. Those of the Caucasus were used against the Circassians, and, frequently mating themselves with stolen beauties who seem equally at home in a Sultan's harem or a Cossack's hut, produced by far the handsomest race in Russia. In 1812–14 these strange horsemen formed a chain of posts from the Seine to the Don to carry off systematically works of art and other booty from Paris. Their horses are as intelligent as dogs. Their pace is the gallop, and they will go on for many miles over rough country with noses lowered almost to the ground, picking their way like packs of hounds; or they will remain perfectly quiet while their masters stand erect on the saddle to survey the surrounding country. If our Heavy Cavalry are called big men on big horses, the Cossacks are essentially little, but strong men on little horses. But where the horse of a Scots

Grey or Inniskilling would starve, the Cossack pony flourishes. Of little use for a charge, they are wonderful as light cavalry, and obey orders with submission and alacrity. Only they will execute the commands in their own way, and we have previously remarked that reports of resistance to the imposition of a new law of service have reached this country.

They are divided into several tribes, the Cossacks of the Don, who alone are liable to general service everywhere, the Kuban Cossacks, the Cossacks of the Terek, the Astrakan Cossacks, the Orenburg Cossacks, the Cossacks of the Ural and of Siberia, the Siemiryechensk and Transbaikal Cossacks, and the Cossacks of the Amur. The Cossacks of the Don, the Kuban Cossacks, the Ural Cossacks, and the Cossacks of the Terek furnish detachments for the guard of the Czar, and have a certain proportion always ready for service in time of peace; the rest are only available in war, and then only for local and frontier defence. Among irregular troops must be included a militia of about 5,000 men formed in the provinces of the Caucasus, who also furnish three squadrons for the Czar's guard.

The Cossacks are all formed in *polks* or regiments, and each *polk* is divided into different numbers of *sotnias* or hundreds, usually either six or four. Since the greatest interest attaches to the Cossacks of the Don, we will pay particular attention to them.

The Cossacks of the Don include the regiment of Cossacks of the Guard and the Ataman Regiment of the Guard, which together number about 2,320 men and very nearly the same number of horses, and are each formed in six squadrons; the Hereditary Grand Duke Regiment, which has also six squadrons; besides 64 *polks* of Don Cossacks having six *sotnias* each, numbering each 924 men and 894 horses when mobilised; and an Instruction *polk*. They have their own artillery, which consists of one horse battery of the Guard and 13 field batteries, numbered from 1 to 13. The horse battery of the Guard has four guns in peace, but when ready for war has 12 guns, and is divided in two half-batteries for the field and one half-battery for reserve. Nor are the ordinary field batteries of the Don Cossacks complete in peace. They have only two guns till they are called out for war, when they receive the rest of their guns and equipments from store at Kiev, being made up to eight guns per battery, with their ammunition waggons and stores. But it must not be supposed that the 64 *sotnias* of Don Cossacks, or even the Guard, are continually in a state of readiness for war. About a third only are employed in Finland and in the districts of Warsaw, Vilna, Odessa, and Kiev. At St. Petersburg there are only a division from each Guard regiment and one half-battery of the Guard. The remainder are at home on furlough, ready to take their turn of duty. When war comes, not the 64 *polks* only can be called out and mobilised, the whole of the *polks* are ordered to the war, and such men as are not caused to fight in the ranks are yet armed and considered available at least for home defence, because every Don Cossack is liable to do military duty at any time. This seems a severe tax on their time and lives, yet they bear it cheerfully as an ancient custom, though they object to the modern form of general service. Their dress is a tunic, loose baggy trousers, a cloak, and a sheepskin cap. Other Cossacks have fur caps. The arms of the Don Cossacks and several other tribes consist of pikes, Circassian swords, and rifled carbines. Curiously enough, only the Cossacks of the Guard wear spurs, but, perhaps, they would find it difficult to use them, for they have a peculiar seat on horseback with their legs tucked up very high. The artillery wear the same dress as the cavalry, and are armed with Circassian sword and pistol. The sword is worn in the belt.

The horse equipments consist of blanket, wooden saddle-tree, horse-rug, *chabraque*, two leathern wallets, and a forage rope. The Ural Cossacks of the Guard indulge in the luxury of a valise. The usual regimental train of most nations is represented among the Cossacks by only one waggon per regiment, but a pack animal is allowed for every ten men in war, and we are much mistaken if it is not sometimes pretty well laden with booty.

It would hardly repay the trouble of the reader if we were to enter into a description of the rest of these wild feudal soldiers, especially because they do not appear in war, though their watch over the home country frees forces which would otherwise have to do duty in districts or garrisons. The main point to be remembered is that on the outbreak of war Russia can always flood an enemy's country with almost savage horsemen, who have none of the mild traditions of civilised warfare, and would act according to their untamed nature. They could never stand against moderately good regular cavalry; but they can move so far and so fast, galloping over slippery stony paths, appearing and disappearing without any sense of shame at retreating, that they would be as unmanageable by regular cavalry as little boys are by a policeman. If England were ever in collision with Russia, the best answer to the Cossacks could be given by bringing over some of the corresponding cavalry which exists under her hand or that of her great feudatories in India. The Turkomans, also from Central Asia, are horsemen of much the same character. It is impossible to give the exact strength of the Don Cossacks for war, since it is governed, not by any special organisation, but by the number of men who can actually be taken. During the Crimean war 84 *polks* were called out, and if we take the strength of a *polk* at 900 men, this would give more than 75,000 men, besides the regular cavalry. We do not know the actual state of the controversy as to change of organisation, but it is probable that the arrangements which prevailed up to quite lately would hardly be overthrown on the eve of a campaign. What there is of Cossack Infantry belongs to tribes which do not march with the field army in time of war, and they have no special reputation.

Having thus spoken of the Cossacks and irregular troops, who have always played such a great part in Russian wars, we will turn to the regular army and see how far the system on which it is raised coincides with that now adopted by other Continental Powers. One of the results of the 1870 campaign in France was to cause all European nations to reorganise their armies. Russia was no exception to this rule. Universal military service was at once introduced, and committees were appointed to draw up a law for regulating it; to quote the words of the same writer in the *Times* :—

This law, known to be drawn up in 1873, and published everywhere in 1874, did not come into actual operation till January 1, 1875.

It was based upon the compulsion of every Russian subject to form part of the military system, without power to furnish a substitute for his personal service. What did this mean? The population of Russia is said to reach the enormous figure of 82,000,000 souls, of whom about 76,000,000 are in Europe. When the men suitable by their age for military service came to be reckoned, it was found that there were 6,000,000 of them. Estimating that one-third would have to be exempted on account of physical incapacity or other valid reasons, there still remained 4,000,000 sturdy men able to fight at the bidding of the Czar. But no country, least of all Russia, could face the expense of training so vast a body of soldiers, nor could they be taken from their homes without greater pressure than even now exists upon the labour of the country. The number to be taken is terrible enough, amounting as it does on paper to nearly 2,000,000, without including the militia; but that number will not be even partially trained for several years to come, and it is very doubtful whether the Imperial finances could stand the strain. If the men are ever provided, they cannot be armed, clothed, trained, and put in the field without an expenditure of which Russia is not likely to be capable in our time. The very effort to do so will cripple her and add to the general difficulty of the task she has set before her. However, the organisation has been decreed, and is being carried out as far as it can be, and we will now give the principal facts concerning it.

Personal military service is compulsory on every Russian from the age of twenty; but this provision did not apply to the Cossacks, who were to have a special organisation little different from their former irregular and half-voluntary service. The number of men actually taken as soldiers in each year—the 'contingent,' as it is called—may vary according to circumstances, and this is in itself a hardship. But whatever it be for a particular year, it is divided into two unequal parts, 25 per cent. of the recruits being taken for the field army, and 75 per cent. for the local troops, which are destined to form the reserves. The 25 per cent. taken for the field army have to give fifteen years of service, six of which are supposed to be passed with the colours, though in reality the men are on furlough during the fifth and sixth years. Up to the end of the eighth year they belong to the 1st Reserve, and for the next four years to the 2nd Reserve, which is intended to form battalions ready to supply losses in the field, and thus feed the active army. The remaining three years of service are to be passed in another portion of the Reserve liable to be used as circumstances may direct. The 1st Reserve fills up the regiments when mobilisation is ordered; the 2nd Reserve supplies losses in the field or hospital; the remainder may either be used like the 2nd Reserve, or form new divisions if required. But the 75 per cent. do not escape scot free. They also serve for fifteen years, but only in their own districts, where they undergo a certain amount of instruction, and in case of war are called up to form local reserves. When the fifteen years of service are past, all the men of the contingent fall for the next five years into the Reichswehr, which also includes all Russians not forming part of any of the annual contingents. These also owe service to the Czar from their twentieth to fortieth year of age, only they will not be called upon to take the field unless the crisis requires their services. Volunteers, as in Germany and France, may join the service earlier than their twenty-first year, and will only be kept in the ranks for a period varying from three months to two years, according to their education and military aptitude. A lad may volunteer when he is seventeen years old, and go home before he is eighteen. This institution of short service volunteers is a sort of safety-valve, guarding against the pressure of universal liability upon the well-to-do classes. It takes the place of the old system of substitutes, and, while allowing none of the contingent to escape personal service, makes that service as easy as possible. The Reserves, after their first training, may be called up twice to attend manœuvres, but cannot be kept longer than six weeks for each manœuvre. The Reichswehr cannot be called out at all in time of peace. If the new organisation were in full working order, which it cannot be for some years to come, and if all expectations are verified by facts, the Russian army would stand about as follows, including Cossacks :—

Field Army	755,000 men.
First Reserve	110,000 ,,
Second and last Reserve	900,000 ,,
Cossacks	180,000 ,,
Total	1,945,000 ,,

The Reichswehr is expected to reach the figure of about 1,500,000 men (250,000 being old soldiers), which would bring the Russian military forces to a total of nearly three millions and a half of armed men, or nearly two millions more than were available for war according to the old organisation. If we count only the 250,000 old soldiers of the Reichswehr as being really effective, there would still remain the terrible incubus of nearly 2,200,000 strong men destined for the trade of war.

At present the numbers do not nearly reach this enormous figure. The war strength of Russia was on paper, in 1874, 1,579,268 men, out of whom the cavalry formed no less than 1,217 squadrons, and the artillery possessed 2,728 guns. Of these about 1,150,000 were in Europe, more than 200,000 in the Caucasus, nearly 125,000 in Asia. The general services of the army accounted for the rest. Omitting the sedentary troops from the calculation, the European Army was supposed to have of field troops and reserves about 755,000 and 250,000 respectively; in the Caucasus there were about 170,000 field troops and 23,300 reserves. The new organisation has given even a higher proportionate number for the army intended to act in Europe. We find that the original estimate was, without counting either non-combatants or last reserve, or garrison troops or Reichswehr :—For Europe, about 27,500 officers and 1,025,000 men; Caucasus, 3,600 officers and 13,600 men; Turkestan and Orenburg, 1,000 officers and 42,000 men; Siberia, 850 officers and 45,000 men.

These numbers are given roughly, and do not even include the combatant Staff. They are, however, merely imaginary as far as the present crisis is concerned, and we should probably exaggerate Russia's military power if we were to take the estimate of the old organisation as our guide, and give her 755,000 field troops with reserve of 250,000 as the army in Europe was supposed to stand in 1874. The Austrians study Russia very carefully. A book on the strength of her army, published by the Austrian General Staff in 1871, and translated for the English War Office, gave a strength of 534,960 infantry, 92,474 cavalry, and 1,572 guns as the movable army for offensive operations in Europe, with a strategical reserve of 83,440 combatants.

The same writer in the *Times*, from whose articles the above extracts are made, gives the following information regarding the quality and *personnel* of the troops that form the *cadres* already described:—

Of all the European states Russia is the best supplied with horses. No less than 16,000,000 of one sort or another exist within the dominions of the Czar, and, exportation being difficult, their price is low, averaging about 20*l*. They are for the most part small and rough in appearance, but extremely hardy, and capable of picking up a subsistence where most troopers would starve. This fact makes mobilisation easier than it is among more civilised communities, and the same remark applies to almost all the necessaries of an army. Russia is also well provided with artillery of a modern type, breechloaders of a system superior to that of the Germans in the late war, and closely resembling the new German model. The pieces bear a high proportion to the numbers of infantry and cavalry—namely, about 3½ per thousand. One of the most striking measures adopted by the Czar in view of the tactics in 1866 and 1870–71 was the increase of cavalry and field artillery, and there exists a school of tacticians who believe that horsemen and guns will play a greater part in future wars than has yet been generally supposed. But cavalry are of comparatively little use in hilly countries, and, supposing Bulgaria occupied by the Northern army, the chain of the Balkans would have to be passed before further progress could be made towards Constantinople. Guns do not constitute the whole value of an artillery force; and unless the Russian artillery—removed as it is from the quickening influence of competition with other nations—has improved vastly since we last saw it about seven years ago, it is extremely slow in movement, and altogether inferior to the infantry. It has never yet achieved a reputation comparable with that of Germany, Austria, England, or France in her old days. We are, however, anxious to insist on the fact that while the enormous paper forces of Russia cannot for the present be put in the field, she has ample means of all kinds, both in men and weapons, for a campaign against Turkey. The infantry are armed with breech-loaders, the last and best pattern being the Berdan rifle, of which there are sufficient for her present purpose, even if that purpose be beyond a mere occupation of Bulgaria. The same may be said of engineers' bridge equipage and train, and the new organisation provides for a full supply of these. It is probable that these services are not at present all on the spot where they are needed, but we must again remember that Russia is mobilising her army at leisure, and is under no pressure such as ruined the French in 1870. She has also for some time been organising railway battalions, to which, besides their own officers, will be attached both officers and men from the engineers and the rest of the army. Telegraph parks have been established, each of which will have 306 men in time of war. Each park is divided into three sections. The first section will move with the army of operation, taking with it thirteen carriages laden with materials for their marvellous work. The second section will constitute a reserve with ten carriages, and the third section will have the duty of keeping up the communication between these active sections and the State telegraph lines. All this is very different from the dull Russian army of the Crimean war.

The Cossacks of the Don, who used to be entirely irregular, but alone of all the Cossacks were available for general service in war, are now supposed to be on a more regular footing and are intended to be formed in regiments. They used to supply their own horses and equipment in time of war. The Russian Government now offers to take either the whole or a part of this expense off their hands; but, as we mentioned in a previous article, there are rumours that these wild horsemen object to be caught and tamed, even though the hook be golden. The Cossacks of Asia will remain, as formerly, irregular troops.

The whole territory of Russia is divided into fourteen great military circumscriptions, ten of which are in Europe and four in Asia; the Cossacks of the Don form a special circumscription. Each of the circumscriptions is divided into four divisional districts, which comprise several governments, and these again are subdivided into recruiting circles. The whole of this arrangement has been based upon the distribution of the field and local troops, the condition of the communications, and also upon geographical considerations. A general officer commands each circumscription and administers its military as well as its political affairs. Each division of the army, when mobilised, is to receive one regiment of Don Cossacks, and each army corps will have one division of cavalry. But the army corps have no organisation in time of peace; they have to be formed freshly with all their special trains and equipments when war is determined upon. Hence arises a necessity to mobilise long before the armies are to march. In this respect Russia is on a very different footing from Germany, which would put off mobilisation to the last moment, certain to be in time at last, whereas it is very improbable that Russia could mobilise a large force under at least a month, and we cannot but believe that her preparations are not yet on so great a scale as would be necessary if the words of the Czar were untrue, and he had formed the deliberate intention of marching his army to Constantinople.

We have now given all the leading facts which seem necessary for a general comprehension of Russian organisations for war. To enter into further details would be confusing to the general reader and might mislead the student, for the greatest of all facts to be had in remembrance is that the present events find her in such a state of change as must hamper her own movements, and leave uncertain whether any particular part of the organisation will be worked on the new or the old system. But before quitting the subject of the Russian army we must say a few words as to the flesh and blood of which it is composed.

In the first place the law of general service cannot possibly have leavened the mass of the army with men of superior intelligence. Education is behindhand in Russia, and the mass of the old recruits were dull and heavy, incapable of fighting in any other formation than that of the column, whereby every man was supported in spirit by the comrades round him. It remains to be seen whether the tactics rendered necessary by modern firearms can be practised with success by the Russian troops in war. The few intelligent men who may find themselves in the ranks must be swallowed up among the mass of ignorance. It is impossible that there can be many of them yet, for the best of them will be volunteers who have had only three to six months' training, and there can be little doubt that, behind the veil of her exclusiveness, Russia conceals a system by which her educated sons take care to escape among those who are either not included in the annual contingent, or, at least, slip out of the net, which has meshes big enough to favour the escape of 75 per cent. of those named. Still the Muscovite soldier is not to be despised. If he is intemperate and of a dogged temper, he is at least hardy for the first few years of his life, and learns to shift for himself without the constant supervision held to be wiser in Western armies. There is, however, a wrong side to this picture. As his officer is no special Providence to him and the use of the stick is not unusual, the goodwill that exists in the English army between officers and men is unknown in Russia. Again, recent changes and increases of the army have tended to lower the position of the officer more than the attempt at higher education has raised it. Up to 1866 the position of officer in the army was an appanage of nobility; the new law has thrown open the commissioned ranks of the Army to all Russian subjects who are capable of passing certain educational tests. Now, we by no means side with that influential party in Russia which has for years insisted that the Czar, by adopting the reforms suggested by General Miliutine, has been playing into the hands of the immense democratic forces known to exist in spite of general service, a wealthy aristocracy, and an army of secret police. But it may be doubted whether a country and an army which have recently undergone such vast and organic changes are in a position to sustain with equanimity and steadiness anything like a defeat, or even a severe check. The average Russian soldier never sees a great town, never learns what civilisation and mental training really mean. Unfortunately the same fate befalls the bulk of the officers, most of whom pass nearly the whole of their lives in barbarous regions, where society, as we know it, hardly exists, and where the cravings raised by a certain amount of education cannot be fed with their proper food, but strive to quench themselves in strong drink and gross forms of sensuality. We are far from saying that this is a universal picture, but all who know the Russian army insist that it is not uncommon. As the superstition with which nobility used to be regarded dies out of the nature of the Russian soldier, he is likely to be critical upon such so-called education as leaves his officer only better than himself in that he can afford a greater amount of sensual pleasures. Officers are promoted by seniority up to and including the rank of Lieutenant-Colonel. The Czar then selects for the higher ranks until the officer becomes a General, when seniority again comes into play. The rank of Field-Marshal is, as usual, reserved for those who have rendered the highest services at the head of armies in the field. The officers of the Old Guard count two grades higher than their comrades of the Line. Officers of the other Guard regiments take rank with the Staff—namely, one grade higher than regimental officers of the same standing. To become eligible for the Staff, an officer must have passed through a certain course of training in the military schools, and most praiseworthy efforts are being made by the Czar to spread a higher education throughout all the ranks of the army.

The above gives a fair idea of the Russian army in its normal condition; when, however, we attempt to discover the actual amount of forces which she could bring into action for offensive purposes we are almost entirely in the dark. So much secrecy is used in connection with all state matters in the Muscovite empire; newspapers are so quickly and relentlessly suspended for publishing information regarding the army, and moreover there is so much corruption and mismanagement among officials, that any statements regarding actual effective numbers must be almost entirely derived from conjecture. There are, however, some essential points connected with the means she possesses for putting her vast forces into motion, such as must not be overlooked, and regarding which we have tolerably full information.

The great defect and weakness of Russia is the absence of proper communications throughout her vast and, as a rule, sterile territories. It was hoped that railways would remedy these deficiencies, and they have hitherto always been regarded as the means by which the Muscovite empire would attain a power and importance unequalled since the days of the Romans. Unfortunately, the bane of many countries—military despotism—has made its hurtful influence visible in the matter of railways, as in many other affairs.

We learn from an article published by the 'Gazette of the German Railway Association' that the lines now existing in Russia are of the most inconvenient and unsatisfactory description. All those in the south and south-west, with the exception of the portion between Odessa and Razdelnaia, a distance of seventy kilometres, are only single lines, and have stations at great distances from each other. Thus the number of trains that can travel on them is necessarily most limited. Sixteen kilometres is the least distance between stations on the line from Kharkow to Nikolaiew, and eighteen kilometres on the lines from Kiew to Best and from Landvarovo-Romuy, twenty kilometres on the Loyovo-Sebastopol line, while the maximum distance sometimes attains twenty-five kilometres. The inconvenience of these long distances is self-evident, more especially as there is but a small supply of rolling-stock; and it is calculated that it would be quite impossible to despatch more than twelve trains per day, and this number only if all went well and worked without mistake or miscarriage. The general manner, moreover, in which the lines are laid out is most unfortunate and mistaken; they avoid all the large towns as being difficult to protect, and pass through forests and steppes, which contain often neither water, food, nor shelter. The celebrated line from Moscow to St. Petersburg and the line of the Crimea are cited as examples of this.

In addition, moreover, to mistaken designing in the first instance, the railways themselves are badly laid down, the permanent way is infamous, and the curves very sharp, so as to preclude the possibility of very long trains or a rapid rate of speed. Also the entire system is now only partially developed; for instance, the whole region between the towns of Kiew, Brest-Setowski, Minsk, and Kowotoff, a tract larger than Belgium and Holland combined, has not a single line through it. There is also another serious objection—the absence of a proper supply of water, which is indispensable for the supply of the locomotives and for the use of passengers, whether human beings or animals. Aqueducts and reservoirs have been constructed, but these require to be kept perpetually full, and their failure at any point might cause an enormous amount of obstruction and delay. The stations, moreover, are of the most meagre description, and there are no sheds, accommodation, or shelter for troops, such as they would of necessity require in the long journeys to be made through Russia in the event of a concentration on the southern frontier. The last point noted is the absence of an efficient railway staff, which in case of an emergency could not hastily be supplied.

The moral that we draw from the above information is that the Russian Government, if they intend war, acted wisely in allowing full time for mobilisation, since the precedent of Germany, in the 1870 campaign, in their case by no means holds good.

Having spoken of the resources and strength of Russia, let us now turn to consider her possible allies, and how far they are in a position to assist her. It may be here remarked that while trying to examine the forces that Russia could bring into the field, we have only dealt with the European part of the question, as undoubtedly in Europe the decisive conflict would be fought. In Asia the Muscovite superiority is probably beyond question, as hereafter will be noticed; and although the Turkish fortresses of Erzeroum, Bajaret, Kars, and Batoum are reported to be in a good state of defence, and to have been recently strengthened, still there is but little effectually to check a Russian advance into Asia Minor.

The first possible European ally of Russia is Roumania. This kingdom was incorporated as such from the provinces of Moldavia and Wallachia in 1859, and is now governed by a prince of the Hohenzollern family. Although nominally subject to Turkey, and paying an annual tribute of 4,000,000 piastres, it is practically independent, and could no more refuse to join with Russia in case of a war than Hesse-Cassel could decline to assist Germany in 1870, that is to say, unless its neutrality was guaranteed and insisted on by the Great Powers. The history of this country is a curious study, and illustrates the danger that inevitably must attend those lands which lie between two powerful nations. At one time protected by Russia, at another subject to the Porte, it has been for centuries the bone of contention, and not unfrequently the battle-ground, of neighbouring powers. The two Principalities, as they are termed, in some respects resemble Holland and Belgium; and for the peace and balance of power in Europe, they ought to be as sacredly protected from the rapacity and ambition of their powerful neighbours.

It is unnecessary here to enter into the physical peculiarities of the kingdom except so far as they affect the military and political situation. On the whole, the country is decidedly favourable both for the passage and the maintenance of an army on the march from Bessarabia to the

Danube. The railways are marked on the map, and are of the same gauge as those in Turkey, namely, 4 ft. 8½ in., Russia, with a most wise prescience and regard to strategic considerations, having made a break of gauge on all her frontiers, so that in the event of invasion, by simply removing the rolling-stock, she might render her lines of rail useless to an invader. The gauge of the Russian railways is 5 ft. Moldavia possesses some good and well-planned roads, in most cases paved and admirable lines of communication; the bye roads are as a rule unmetalled, but in hard weather would be available for the use of waggons and artillery. Wallachia, although it possesses few if any metalled roads, is also fairly provided with means of communication. The following are the lines of railway in actual working :—

a. Giurgevo—Bukarest.
b. Bukarest—Pitesti.
c. Bukarest—Ploesti—Buzeo—Braila—Galatz.
d. Galatz—Tecuci—Adsiud—Baceu—Roman-Pascani—Vereschti.
e. Vereschti—Suezava—Itcani.
f. Vereschti—Botosani.
g. Pascani—Jassy.
h. Tecuci—Berlad.

The following lines are projected :—

a. Pitesti—Slatina—Crajova—Turn—Severin—Vercerova.
b. Buzeo—Kronstadt (in Transylvania).

c. Jassy—Sculeni—Kiseneff (in Bessarabia).

d. Galatz—Reni—Odessa.

The following roads are those of most importance; many are now but indifferent, but before long it is intended to have them all metalled, and their repair thoroughly carried out:—

1. From Bukarest by Plojesti and Buzeo to Focsani, joining here the existing metalled road ascending the valley of the Sereth.

2. From Bukarest by Pitesti, Slatina, Crajova, to Surn-Severin.

3. From Slatina by Kalinesti to the Rothenthumin Pass.

4. From Pitesti to Kalinesti.

5. From Pitesti by Kimpolung to La Crucea in the Sorzburg Pass.

6. From Kalafat to Crajova.

7. From Plojesti to the Predial in the Tömöser Pass.

8. From Turnul-Migureli to Slatina.

9. From Picetul to Tirgujiul.

10. From Olteniza to Bukarest.

11. From Braila to Buzeo.

12. From Galatz to Tecuci.

As regards the means of supporting an army there are few countries that contain such resources as Roumania. The soil is most fertile, the climate most favourable, and the population very industrious. There is a great amount of cattle and sheep; pigs are also bred in large numbers.

The country is well provided with country-carts and vehicles; there is also a fair amount of horses and draught animals.

As regards the army, it also presents a respectable force, and would be most valuable as a contingent. It is divided into

1. The standing army and reserve.
2. The territorial army and reserve.
3. The militia.
4. The national guard and rural levies.

It is estimated that in time of war the standing army would afford 36,000 infantry, 1,700 cavalry, and 96 guns; the territorial army about 40,000 men, 12,000 irregular cavalry, and the *personnel* of 83 batteries, which as yet are not armed. The militia would furnish about 33,000 infantry and 5,000 cavalry. This would appear a most formidable force for so small a kingdom; as, however, very frequently happens, these troops exist principally in prospective and on paper. It may, however, be safely assumed that Roumania, if allied with Russia in a war, could certainly put on foot about 50,000 men, and the proper proportion of cavalry, if not of artillery also, to co-operate in the open field, and could maintain this army in a fairly long campaign. As regards the quality of the army, but little opportunities have as yet been afforded for testing its fighting capabilities. The training and instruction both of officers and men appear to be very fair: the infantry of the regular army are armed with 'Peabody' rifles, the others still retain the needle-gun; the cavalry are mounted on light horses of the Cossack type; and the artillery have Prussian breech-loading guns. From all accounts the military stores are fairly maintained, and undoubtedly all the administrative departments are far better organised than in Turkey.

Of the other possible Russian allies among the small states, we have Servia, Montenegro, and Greece. The value and quality of the Servian troops have been so fully tested in the late war that it appears unnecessary to refer to them. Of the original army as it existed in the spring of 1876, probably very little now remains, and from all accounts it would be no easy matter to raise even a mob of 'men with muskets' out of the thoroughly wearied and disheartened population. Nevertheless we may conclude that a certain contingent would in any case be forthcoming in the event of its being demanded by the Czar. Opinions of the best informed differ as to the numbers that could be brought into the field, and probably the Servian Government are themselves in absolute ignorance of the really efficient forces at their disposal. When, however, we consider that the population of Servia numbers 1,325,437 souls, that there is a nominal army of 102,598 on a war footing, and that there is a reserve of nearly 38,000, there can be little doubt that, even after all the many losses of the recent campaign, and the demoralisation defeat has produced, a very valuable contingent would still be available as auxiliaries to the Russian army. It would be by no means an extravagant estimate to put this contingent down at 30,000 men, which, even if not of the best quality, would be most valuable in masking fortresses, in guarding communications, and in such duties, the performance of which so much reduce the strength of an invading army.

We next come to Montenegro. This province, although nominally an integral portion of the Ottoman empire, has never really formed part of it, and has been a source of weakness rather than of strength. The area of the country only covers 1,557 square miles, and the population only numbers about 130,000 Serbs, who are principally Greek Christians. In character they are warlike and turbulent, and as their country is mountainous and suited to guerilla warfare, they have from time to time given the Porte much trouble. In the event of a war they are certain to be allied with the enemy, and not unfrequently get up serious disturbances on their own account. There is no standing army, but the fighting men enrolled number about 25,000; these are of most excellent quality, but are miserably armed, which is not surprising, considering that the revenue of the country is under 5,000*l.* a-year. Still so admirable are their fighting qualities, and so great their aversion to the Turk, that if supplied with arms, money, and officers by Russia, Montenegro might furnish several thousand men, who doubtless would perform excellent service in the case of an invasion of Turkey, and from their geographical position, by uniting with the Servians, and advancing on the flank of an Ottoman army, either posted in front or in rear of the Balkans, they would seriously threaten its communications, and cause a formidable diversion.

We come lastly to Greece. This little state, which, it may be said, owes its existence to the classic traditions and sentimental philanthropy of Europe, has a population of about 1,457,894 souls, including the inhabitants of the islands. It has a nominal revenue of 1,217,964*l*., and a rapidly increasing debt of twelve millions. Unfortunately the administration of the government, either as regards ability or absence of corruption, does not present a favourable contrast, even with that of Turkey. Financial difficulties have tended to render the army a force only dangerous in name, whose energies in peace time are fully occupied in keeping down the brigandage which they have been wholly unable entirely to eradicate. All the population are liable to military service between the ages of twenty and forty, and the annual contingent is set down at 2,500. According to the official return the effective force of the Greek army capable of taking the field is as follows:—

Infantry	24,514
Artillery	1,577
Cavalry	575
Engineers	715
Gendarmes	2,346
Total	29,697

In addition to the above there are volunteer corps, about 20,000 strong, and about 80,000 National Guards available in case of invasion. It cannot, however, be said that any part of this force is in the least formidable, and it would be extremely difficult effectively to mobilise it from the want of stores, arms, and equipments. Nevertheless the diversion it might effect on the frontier of Thessaly would be by no means unimportant, if thereby it only succeeded in neutralising twenty thousand Turkish troops that probably would be sadly needed elsewhere. The navy of Greece comprises two ironclads and two or three unarmed vessels, none of much account, and armed with obsolete guns—the material of the sailors is excellent.

However, from the turn that affairs have recently taken, and the great jealousy that has arisen between the Slaves and the Greeks, it is by no means certain, or even probable, that Greece would side with Russia, even supposing that Turkey seemed to be getting the worst of the contest. In the first instance, until the fortune of war was fairly decided, we may be tolerably certain that Greece would remain neutral, or at least would take no part in active operations.

It now remains only to speak of Turkey and the forces at her disposal. Here again we are somewhat in the dark. Like her neighbour and possible antagonist, the greater portion of her army exists only on paper; and her stores and military equipments are only to be seen on the invoices presented to the Government.

The Turkish empire is stated by the most recent authorities to have an area of 1,812,048 English square miles, and a population of 35,350,000. Of this area 207,438 square miles and about 15,500,000 inhabitants are in Europe; 660,870 square miles and 16,050,000 inhabitants in Asia; and the remainder in Africa.

The various races are classified in the official return as follows; but it cannot be said that this table can be considered as accurate, even at the time when it was published; now, of course, the estimate can only be an approximate one.

	In Europe	In Asia	In Africa	Total
Ottomans	2,100,000	10,700,000	. .	12,800,000
Greeks	1,000,000	1,000,000	. .	2,000,000
Armenians	400,000	2,000,000	. .	2,400,000
Jews	70,000	80,000	. .	150,000
Slaves	6,200,000	. .	. .	6,200,000
Roumans	4,000,000	. .	. .	4,000,000
Albanians	1,500,000	. .	. .	1,500,000
Tartars	16,000	20,000	. .	36,000
Arabs	. .	885,000	3,800,000	4,685,000
Syrians and Chaddens	. .	200,000	. .	200,000
Druses	. .	81,000	. .	80,000
Kurds	. .	1,000,000	. .	1,000,000
Turcomans	. .	85,000	. .	85,000
Gipsies	214,000	. .	. .	214,000
Total	15,500,000	16,050,000	3,800,000	35,350,000

Practically, when we deduct the tributary states we find that the direct subjects of the Porte in Europe number about 9,500,000, and in Asia 16,750,000. Of the former about five millions are Christians, and four millions Mahomedans, the remainder belonging to various other sects. It is, however, stated by those best acquainted with the country, that at least two millions of the nominal followers of Islam are so from necessity, not from choice, and would in the event of a threatened disturbance of the Turkish power, at once attach themselves to the popular and national cause. We thus find about two millions of Mahomedans face to face with upwards of seven millions belonging to other creeds and races, from whom they have taken the sovereign power, and whom they rule with a government whose obstructions and oppression are only equalled by its corruption.

From the days of the Janissaries, who were of Christian parents, kidnapped in early youth and reared as Mussulmans, the Turkish army was up to 1856 entirely recruited by Mahomedans, when the impolicy of such a system becoming daily more and more evident to the Divan, the liability to military service was extended to all subjects of the empire. Formerly the Christians had to pay a sort of poll-tax as exemption; this was abolished, and in its place there was established a war-tax, which gained from about 27*l.* to 45*l.* per recruit, the nominal annual contingent to be furnished by the Christian population being 16,000 men. Practically, however, this reform only resulted in a raising of the revenue from 40,000,000 to 65,000,000 piastres, but in no way caused the Christians to have any share in the military service, and at the present time Mussulmans alone take part in it. As is the case in all the countries of Europe except our own, the military system of Turkey is modelled on that of

Prussia. The empire is divided into six corps, which have their head-quarters at the following places:—

1st Corps (Guards)	. . . .	Constantinople.
2nd „ (Danube)	. . . .	Schumla.
3rd „ (Roumelia)	. . . .	Monaster.
4th „ (Anatolia)	. . . .	Erzeroum.
5th „ (Syria)	. . . .	Damascus.
6th „ (Irak)	. . . .	Bagdad.

Each corps district furnishes a Nizam or active army, in which all those liable to service are supposed to spend four years for the infantry, and five years for the cavalry and artillery; they then pass to the Ihtiât or first reserve for two years in the case of the infantry, and one year in the case of the cavalry and artillery soldier: then the men are transferred to the Redif or second reserve for six years, three years in each class; finally, they go into the Mustafiz or territorial militia for eight years. It was calculated that by the year 1878, by which time the system would be in full working, the nominal force of the empire would be as follows:—

1. Nizam	150,000 }	210,000
Ihtiât	60,000 }	
2. Redif, 1st class . . .	96,000 }	192,000
„ 2nd „ . . .	96,000 }	
3. Mustafiz		300,000
Total . . .		702,000

The army corps, according to the latest reports obtainable, actually comprise the following troops of the Nizam (standing army) and special regular levies:—

First Corps (Guards).

Infantry:—
    Seven line regiments of three battalions . 21 battalions
    Seven rifle battalions . . . . . 7 ,,
Cavalry:—
    Five line regiments of six squadrons . . 30 squadrons
    One Cossack brigade (two regiments of four squadrons . . . . 8 ,,
Artillery:—
    One line regiment of nine field and three horse batteries . . . . . 12 batteries
    One reserve regiment (Ihtiāh) of twelve field and one mountain battery . . . . 13 ,,
Engineers:—
    One sapper company . . . . .
    One engineer brigade of four battalions each of two companies. Total eight companies.
One battalion of artificers.

        Total, exclusive of Engineers { 29 battalions / 38 squadrons / 25 batteries

Second Corps (Danube).

Infantry:—
    Six line regiments of three battalions . . 18 batalions
    Six rifle battalions . . . . . 6 ,,
    One frontier regiment on the Danube . . 3 ,,
Cavalry:—Four line regiments of six squadrons . 24 squadrons
Artillery:—One line regiment . . . . 12 batteries
Engineers:—One sapper company.

        Total . . . . . { 27 battalions / 24 squadrons / 12 batteries

Third Corps (Roumelia).

Infantry:—
    Seven line regiments . . . . . 21 battalions
    Seven rifle battalions . . . . . 7 ,,
    Bosnian brigade, two regiments . . . 6 ,,
    Frontier regiment on Greek border . . 3 ,,
    ,, ,, Bosnian border . . 4 ,,
    ,, battalion (Niksic) . . . 1 ,,
    Austro-Herzegovinian battalion . . . 1 ,,
Cavalry:—Four line regiments . . . . 24 squadrons

Artillery:—
    One line regiment . . . . . . 12 batteries
    Mountain batteries in Herzegovina . . 3 ,,
Engineers:—One sapper company.

          Total . . . . $\begin{cases} 43 \text{ battalions} \\ 24 \text{ squadrons} \\ 15 \text{ batteries} \end{cases}$

First Volunteer Corps (Anatolia).

Infantry:—
    Five line regiments of three battalions . . 15 battalions
    One regiment of one battalion, the others
      being with the Ilmen division . . . 1 ,,
    Six rifle battalions . . . . . . 6 ,,
Cavalry:—Three line regiments of six squadrons . 6 squadrons
Artillery:—One line regiment . . . . 18 ,,
Engineers:—One sapper company . . . 12 batteries

          Total . . . . $\begin{cases} 22 \text{ battalions} \\ 18 \text{ squadrons} \\ 12 \text{ batteries} \end{cases}$

Fifth Corps (Syria).

Infantry:—
    Seven line regiments . . . . . 21 battalions
    Seven rifle battalions . . . . . 7 ,,
Cavalry:—
    Four line regiments . . . . . 24 squadrons
    One dromedary corps about to be established. 6 ,,
Artillery:—One line regiment . . . . 12 batteries
One sapper company

          Total . . . $\begin{cases} 28 \text{ battalions} \\ 30 \text{ squadrons} \\ 12 \text{ batteries} \end{cases}$

Sixth Corps (Bagdad).

Infantry:—
    Six line regiments . . . . . . 18 battalions
    Six rifle battalions . . . . . . 6 ,,
Cavalry:—Two line regiments . . . . 12 squadrons
Artillery:—One regiment (incomplete) . . . 9 batteries

          Total . . . . $\begin{cases} 24 \text{ battalions} \\ 6 \text{ ,,} \\ 12 \text{ squadrons} \\ 9 \text{ batteries} \end{cases}$

It is, however, needless to say that this force, or half of it, exists only on paper, and that, even were the regulations strictly carried out, and the annual contingent of recruits regularly brought to the colours, from the great extent of the Ottoman dominions and the necessity of overawing the disaffected populations, only a comparatively small army would ever be available for action at any one particular point. It is unnecessary here to enter into the detail of either the administration or the organisation of the army; suffice it to say that the administration, if it can be called such, is of the worst description, and the systems on which it is conducted are enveloped in such hopeless confusion as to render explanation of them *impossible*.

There is no organised train or commissariat service whatever, and the method of clothing the troops is ill-regulated and wasteful; whereas the garrison of Constantinople is dressed and equipped in an unnecessarily liberal manner, the troops of the provinces are utterly neglected. The only exception to this lamentable picture of maladministration and mismanagement is the organisation of the sanitary department, which is excellent, and will in garrison bear comparison with any other in Europe; in the field, however, this service is no exception to the general rule, as, from all accounts at present, there is no regular organisation adapted to the requirements of war. As regards the fighting qualities of the troops themselves, they are probably much the same as they have always been. The material of the Turkish rank and file has always been excellent, but the officers, more especially the superior ones, are wanting both in education, ability, and interest in their profession; the infantry are drilled entirely according to the tactics of the French army, but the practical training is lamentably deficient, and extends very little beyond common parade movements, outpost duty and real essentials being entirely neglected. The infantry at present, as a rule, are armed with Sniders. It is stated, moreover, that about 40,000 Henry-Martini rifles have recently been delivered by foreign firms who previously had detained them from want of payment; but the men are little, if at all, trained in the use of firearms; still they possess many qualities most valuable in war— they fight admirably behind entrenchments, can endure great hardships, and—an important matter in Turkey— do not mutiny when they receive no pay.

The cavalry in its present state cannot be spoken of so favourably. It has a nominal strength of twenty-two line regiments, each regiment of six squadrons; and two regiments of the Cossack brigade of the guard—each of four squadrons; so that in all we have 140 squadrons of regular cavalry, each of a nominal war strength of 143 horses. The cavalry is all light, and is most indifferent, being deficient in manœuvring power, badly officered and wretchedly equipped. The horses, however, are hardy and serviceable. Two squadrons of each regiment are armed with a carbine, the remainder with a lance and revolver; the drill is also entirely of French type, and apparently is as indifferently carried out as in the case of the infantry. In fact, it may be said that the Turkish horsemen of the present time have lost all the dash and enterprise which rendered them during the last century the terror of European armies, and contributed so much to carry the Crescent to victory, while they have gained none of the solidity and steadiness of the troops on which they are modelled, and whose deficiencies only they have succeeded in copying. The entire force of regular cavalry in Turkey numbers on a war footing about 20,000 horses, exclusive of its camel corps; formerly there was also a dromedary corps that were practically mounted riflemen, but this, from all accounts, has been abolished.

We next come to the artillery, which is decidedly the best arm, both as regards organisation and instruction. According to the returns, the following is its approximate strength:—

Six line regiments of twelve batteries . .	522 officers. 7,944 combatants. 9,258 horses. 432 guns.
Reserve regiment of thirteen battalions about	1,600 horses. 78 guns.

There is also a garrison artillery of a nominal strength of 14,000 men. Although every effort has recently been made by the Turkish Government to improve the armament of its forces, for financial reasons the orders given for guns to foreign contractors have not been executed with the same readiness as they have been given.

Hence, at present, cannons of all descriptions and systems are mixed up in hopeless confusion, and we find not unfrequently muzzle-loaders and breech-loaders, rifled and smooth bores in the same battery. There is lastly an engineer corps about 2,400 strong, which is of very little account, few of the officers possess any professional or technical knowledge, and the equipment of the force is of the most meagre and insufficient description.

In addition to the regular army, which we have just described, there are also irregular forces, some of whom have been used in the Servian war and in Bulgaria with results only too fatal to the prestige and interests of the Government by whom they were employed. They are divided into

a Enlisted Bashi-Bazouks.

b Volunteer Spahis, Bedouins, &c.

The former are a badly organised and worse disciplined infantry, recruited from the scum of the Turkish towns, and allured to the military service by the hopes of plunder, in which they freely indulge on friend and foe alike. They are more an incumbrance than an assistance to an army, if engaged in regular warfare; and are only employed with any effect against unarmed or semi-armed inhabitants of a disaffected district. The Spahis, &c., are exclusively cavalry, and are mainly furnished by the Arab races; they are formed in troops under their chiefs, and are in no way to be depended upon. In the Crimean War, it is said that about 10,000 were raised, but they were never used. Nevertheless, it is probable that if properly led and organised they would perform valuable service in irregular warfare, in outpost duty, and in the pursuit of a defeated army, like the Cossacks who hung on the rear of the Grand Army in Napoleon's retreat from Moscow in 1812. It is calculated that about 60,000 irregular troops could, in the event of very pressing danger, be enlisted in defence of the Porte, and of these the greater portion would be in Asia; it is doubtful, however, whether a quarter of this force would be worth their rations.

To the above forces of the Ottoman Empire proper may be added contingents from Egypt and Tunis. Both these states have already sent some troops to Constantinople, but the exact number is not known. There can be little doubt that the former power could, under certain circumstances, contribute a most valuable auxiliary force; the Egyptian army numbers, in its normal condition, nearly 60,000 men, and the capabilities of its troops (if properly led) were fully proved in the campaigns of Ibrahim Pacha. The Egyptian officers moreover are vastly superior to the Turkish, and are properly trained and educated. At the present time, however, it is by no means probable that any force which the Khedive could send to the assistance of the Porte, would be very numerous or very valuable. Egyptian finances have recently been reorganised, the Exchequer has been drained, the army exhausted and partially demoralized by the disastrous wars with Abyssinia, and lastly it is the interest of the Egyptian Government as far as possible to dissociate itself from the falling fortunes of the Ottoman empire. Independence is doubtless the end which the Khedive is desirous of obtaining, and which probably before long the Great Powers of Europe will be only too glad to accord him. If we put down the Egyptian contingent at about 15,000, or at the most 20,000 men, we shall probably have overshot the mark.

Lastly, we come to Tunis. The armed strength of this state since the suppression of piracy has been by no means formidable, and at present would add but little to the resources of the state to which it is nominally subject. There is no means of obtaining any exact information either as to the forces which have already been sent to Constantinople from Tunis, or as to those which might eventually follow. It is however stated, on good authority, that between 4,000 and 5,000 partially drilled men, half regulars and half irregulars, are all that could be relied on.

In conclusion it may be broadly stated that the entire strength of the Ottoman empire presents now a total effective of 365,000 men; of these 203,000 men are in first line, 129,000 in the second line or reserve, and about 33,000 gendarmerie—trained soldiers who are required and mainly employed on police duties. Of this nominal force it is needless to remark that probably only about 70 per cent. could be brought into line, if indeed so many, and for actual operations to resist an invasion from Europe we may consider that 160,000 is the very maximum which, under the most favourable circumstances, could be collected. Under these circumstances it cannot be questioned that were Roumania, Servia, Montenegro, and Greece to unite and co-operate with a Russian advance from the Danube, it would be wholly impossible for the Porte permanently to retain Constantinople. The geographical conditions, the present state of the Turkish fortresses, and more especially the temper of the subject populations, all tend to this conclusion; these points, however, will be discussed hereafter.

It cannot, however, be said that the danger which in case of war with Russia threatens the Turkish empire comes only from the north of the Balkans; a danger almost as great, or according to some, even greater, threatens her in Asia. Five lines of railway are available for the concentration of Russian troops on the confines of Armenia, namely those that lead to the Volga at Nizninovgorod, Caricini, and Sarton, by means of which troops can be conveyed on the Volga and the Caspian, *via* Baku, to the South Caucasus. There are also two other lines from the interior to Noro-Cerkask, whence troops could be conveyed to the great military station of Tiflis. The army of the Caucasus is always more or less on a war footing, and has probably an effective strength of about 50,000 men, although it is considerably more on paper. This force might be easily doubled in less than a month by means of the railways named, and at least

90,000 men would be available for the invasion of Asia Minor. Even supposing that this invasion were not carried out, a simple concentration of troops on the Russian frontier would hold fast half the Turkish army on the border of Armenia, if indeed half or even a quarter of that army could be spared, which is more than doubtful, since the 6th Corps must occupy Nedschid in force, unless Arabia be relinquished; the 7th Corps could scarcely be spared from Jemen, and we may rest assured that a very large body of troops would be required throughout the interior of Asia Minor, unless the Turkish army opposing the invaders wished to have their communications cut, and themselves attacked in rear. Centuries of misgovernment have not rendered the Ottoman rule more popular in Asia than in Europe, and most certainly there would not be wanting intrigues and external encouragement to foster civil dissension in the event of a war. It seems evident that four out of the seven corps, into which the Turkish army is formed, could not be spared from Asia Minor, and they could apparently oppose but an ineffectual resistance to a well-organised and numerous Russian army advancing from the Caucasus; more especially if the latter were commanded by a Paskewitch. In any case only three corps would be available for the defence of Constantinople if threatened from the North. In fact it is difficult to say whence the greater danger might come from, Europe or Asia. Erzeroum is from all accounts now well defended, but would really be but an insignificant obstacle to an advance were there a sufficient force to mask it, and, although the distance to march is much greater, until we come near Scutari, there are no lines of defence in Asia Minor which can be compared to the Danube and the Balkans, still less to the position before mentioned at Büjuk-Checkmedgè to the north of the Bosphorus. It is true that nature apparently has done all in her power to render Constantinople fitted for the seat of empire of the world, as even on the south side there is a fair defensive position in Asia Minor; this, however, would require fortifications which do not exist. As regards the resources of the Porte on the sea, a far more favourable report may be given than of her forces on land.

The Turkish navy is by far the most formidable portion of the defences of the empire. At the end of 1874, it comprised twenty ironclads and eighty steamships, all, with one or two exceptions, constructed in the best dockyards of Europe, and on the whole fairly armed. The material of the sailors is by no means good, and they have not sufficient practice to render them really efficient. The greatest proportion of the navigating officers and engineers are foreigners, and the admiral in supreme command of the navy, Hobart Pacha, is an Englishman. It is stated to be the intention of the Porte to give the command of all their ships to English officers if they can procure them. As with all the other administrative departments in Turkey, the naval arsenal is by no means well organised or well provided with stores. Notwithstanding, however, all its defects, the Ottoman navy is that branch of its defensive force with which it has the least reason to be dissatisfied. For offence it probably would not be very formidable, but for the protection of Constantinople its value is undoubted.

Having spoken of the Turkish fleet our remarks would be incomplete were no mention to be made of that possessed by Russia, comparatively insignificant as it is. Mr. Reed, a competent authority on these matters, gives, in a letter to the *Times*, the following account of it:—

The navy of Russia consists of three floating-batteries of about 3,300 tons displacement, carrying $4\frac{1}{2}$ and in one case 6-inch armour, with no gun larger than one of $9\frac{1}{2}$ tons, and with a speed below ten knots. Next, there are ten small American type monitors, of from 1,400 to 1,600 tons displacement, carrying 5-inch armour, and two $15\frac{1}{4}$-ton guns, at a speed of seven to eight knots. Also three similar vessels, slightly larger, but no stronger, except in carrying two turrets instead of one. Next come four vessels which were built in the days when many persons believed in rigged ironclads with low freeboard, and which would have shared the fate of the 'Captain' had they ever been sent to sea. They are vessels of about 3,600 tons displacement, carrying comparatively thin armour ($5\frac{1}{2}$ and 6 inches), with guns in some cases of 27 tons weight, and steaming at $10\frac{1}{2}$ to 11 knots. The capsizing of the 'Captain' doomed these four vessels to harbour-service; then follow two wooden armour-plated frigates of large size and fair speed, but carrying very weak armour and comparatively light guns. A third frigate, built of iron, but somewhat smaller, and in no sense stronger, may be classed with these. This last vessel, the 'Prince Pojarsky,' is the only, or almost the only, ironclad that

Russia was able to send to Besika Bay when the British fleet had assembled there. All the above vessels, with the last-named exception, are in the Baltic, and will probably remain there for ever; for, although many of them would, no doubt, be more or less valuable for defensive purposes, they cannot be considered fit for operating at any great distance from Cronstadt. There remain of Russian ironclads but six, among which are the 'Peter the Great,' and the two circular ironclads, of neither of which need I say more here. Neither, indeed, need the remaining three be dwelt upon, inasmuch as they are but partially armoured vessels, having a belt of armour only, and being designed as cruising vessels, carrying, therefore, a large spread of canvas. Of these vessels only one, the 'General Admiral,' has reached approximate completion; the other two, the 'Duke of Edinburgh' and the 'Mineen,' may, however, be finished in the course of next year.

Subsequent to the above, there appeared a letter in the *Times* from an apparently well-informed correspondent, who wrote from St. Petersburg on January 3rd, 1877, and who gives some interesting information regarding the present condition of the Muscovite fleet. It is, however, only fair to add that his statements are to a certain extent questioned by Mr. Reed.

He points out that the Russian Naval Budget is now third on the list of European Powers, and that if this money had been properly laid out ' she would now be in possession of a fleet, not only stronger than the miserable Mediterranean squadron, which is now in American waters, but of one capable of coping with that of Turkey.' He maintains that 'it would have been more profitable in every way for the state, had the Russian Government spent more money in developing the ship-building capabilities of Nicolaieff, instead of going to the enormous expense of building two vessels of an untried type at St. Petersburg and sending them by rail to the Black Sea.' As regards the actual effective condition of the much-vaunted vessel 'Peter the Great,' he makes the following statements:—' She is so weak that if driven through the water at a speed greater than eight knots she shakes to such a degree as to leak in an alarming manner. Although the extent of her longest voyage is the distance between Cronstadt and Reval, her boilers are already under repair, and a Commission which was lately assembled to examine her has expressed an opinion that all the large steam pipes should be renewed. As to her present capabilities for either offensive or defensive purposes, it is sufficient to say that when her heavy guns are fired rivet-heads fly about unpleasantly. I think I have said enough about this ironclad, the pride of the Russian navy.' As regards the 'Popopkas'—the two Russian gunboats in the Black Sea—he says that 'it is literally dangerous to fire the guns on board of them. During a recent gun practice on board one of them near Otchakof, the following results were obtained:—At the first round almost every man on board was knocked down; the whole of the superstructure on deck was blown away, and the deck itself, which is iron-plated, was considerably bulged in a downward direction.'

If the above is true, the Government of the Czar need not hope to derive much assistance from their navy in any immediate war with the Turks. However strong the Russian navy might be in the Baltic or in the Mediterranean, so long as the Ottomans hold the Dardanelles it could have little, if any, influence on a campaign in Bulgaria and Roumelia. This fact appears to have been forgotten by many, who have recently discussed this question,—the naval force in the Black Sea is the important point, and as long as this is practically limited to two gunboats, as at present, the Russians would be at an enormous disadvantage. As before explained, the command of the Euxine would be useful to them for two reasons, first for the supply of their army, and secondly in order to turn the lines, which are about twenty miles to the north of Constantinople, and which, if properly fortified, would from the land side be practically impregnable.

CHAPTER XI.

THE CHANCES OF SUCCESS POSSESSED BY EACH COMBATANT IN THE EVENT OF WAR.

Divergence of Views on the Subject—To ensure success a large force required by Russia—Probable Russian system of invasion—Time required by the various Corps to reach the Danube and Schumla—Lines of defence to be occupied by the Turks—Line of the Danube—Schumla—The Balkans—Selimno Pass—Flanking column by Servia—Time required to reach Adrianople—Probable date when Constantinople would be threatened—Alternative plan of operations—Difficulties of railway transport—Importance of Schumla—Description of the position of the Chekmedgès—of that on the Dardanelles—of the position in Asia Minor—Opportunity lost by Russia in 1876—Concluding remarks.

HAVING reviewed the armed strength of the two possible combatants, Russia and Turkey, it now remains for us to consider the chances which they will respectively have in any contest that may ensue, either now or hereafter. If, at the present moment, the opinions of those best able to form a judgment on this question were collected, probably we should find an enormous divergence of views. Some are convinced the Russians have nothing whatever before them but a triumphal march on Constantinople—' there may perhaps be a few skirmishes, an insignificant siege, and possibly a considerable action, but the result of none of these, they say, can be doubtful.' The Turks have never been able to stand against the Russians in the open field, and their fortresses, not being fitted to resist modern artillery, are now worse than useless, as they only serve to paralyse a number of troops that would be far more useful in the open field. Another party, on the contrary, and in England perhaps they are in the majority, profess the greatest confidence in the Turks. They say that in previous wars the Ottoman empire has held her own, and so it will again ; they point to the condition of the Russian army at the peace of Adrianople, and to Omar Pacha's successes on the Danube in 1854 ; they lay stress on the fact that at the present time the Muscovites have not got command of the sea, and declare that consequently a large invading army would starve, while a small one would be defeated. Probably, the truth lies between these two extremes, and in any case it can only be a matter of conjecture not of certainty. Let us examine the grounds on which a correct opinion may be based.

It appears that the actual result of any campaign between these two powers—leaving Austria entirely out of the question—depends

 1st. On the condition of the Russian army.

 2nd. On the condition of the Turkish army.

 3rd. On the state of the Turkish fortresses.

At the present time, on all these points information is but meagre and by no means trustworthy. It has been shown that the Russian railways are very badly organised, and in no way fitted for the transport of troops; also that the army is now in a transition state, and that, while one system has been disarranged, the other has not yet had time to get into working order. These circumstances alone are quite sufficient to account for reports that have come from Bessarabia regarding the great difficulty experienced by the Russian authorities in mobilising and in transporting their forces to the frontier; the strength of the corps there from all accounts is considerably below the nominal establishment on a war footing, and hence the numbers of the force prepared to cross the Pruth very probably are short of the 210,000 men supposed to be assembled. This of course is a most serious consideration. We have seen that the failure of Diebitsch to reach Constantinople in 1829 was entirely owing to the insufficiency of the force under his command for the task it had to perform, and it is absolutely essential to ensure success in the invasion of Turkey that a Russian army should be sufficiently strong to mask Rustchuk, Silistria, and Schumla, as Strasburg, Metz, and the other French fortresses were masked in 1870, and still to have the power of marching upon Constantinople. General Fadéeff, in his 'Opinion on the Eastern Question,' estimates that if 250,000 men reach the Danube, 150,000 will attain Constantinople, whether the Maritime Powers oppose or not, the only obstacle to this arrangement being Austria. We have pre-supposed the neutrality of this Power and will consider her political and strategic position elsewhere.

It therefore would appear that if General Fadéeff's opinion is correct, as indeed seems likely, the nominal strength of the Russian army at present mobilised, namely, 210,000 men, is barely sufficient, even if Roumania affords a contingent, which is doubtful, and Servia adds the remnant of her beaten army, which is certain. Supposing an invading army of a strength inferior to the necessary minimum of 250,000 were to proceed to occupy Bulgaria, unless the Ottoman army is in a far worse state than usually represented, and unless the various frontier fortresses are practically useless, the invaders would have to act like Romanzoff, Potemkin, and Suwarrow in former days, and to sit down before all the fortified places halting until these were reduced; this would more especially be necessary, inasmuch as the command of the sea is lost, and the only means of supplying the army under such circumstances is by rail and road; hence the communications must be made secure. The Turkish railways are so constituted as to be of little use for an invading army in the passage of the Balkans, and in all probability the rolling stock would have been removed. This would be a most serious matter, as the gauge is different from that of the Russian railways, although the same as that of Roumania, and there would be no time to make carriages or trucks. Thus country waggons and carts would be the principal means of transport; of such conveyances, from all accounts, there are plenty in Bulgaria and Roumelia, but the difficulty of supplying an army of more than

s

150,000 men in a march of nearly 300 miles by these alone is self-evident.

If, as not impossible, the war were to resolve itself into a series of sieges, knowing as we do the valour of the Turks behind entrenchments, it is scarcely possible that the contest could be brought to a decisive close in one campaign. A prolongation of hostilities would be fatal to Russia, not only in a financial point of view, as hinted by Lord Beaconsfield at the Guildhall, but also because the various Great Powers would have had time to become alarmed, to organise their forces, and to interpose. A lengthened conflict between Russia and Turkey must result in the utter financial ruin of both—certainly of the former power, since the latter may be already termed ruined— and also either in a European war of gigantic proportions, or an armed intervention in favour of the Porte. The only hope which Russia possesses of reaching Constantinople is by a *coup-de-main*; had she the command of the sea there would be but little difficulty in effecting this; under the present circumstances, however, her sole chance is the rapid and unchecked march of a large army, whose supplies would principally be drawn from home, and whose communications would extend over about 400 miles of country. It may here be remarked that some have suggested that an occupation of Bulgaria, opposed by the Porte, would not necessarily imply any attempt to march on the capital. Such an hypothesis is evidently absurd, the present

Russian generals are not likely to fall again into the error of the Emperor Nicholas in 1853, who, when he occupied the Principalities, made a declaration of his peaceful intentions, and imposed on himself the boundary of the Danube, while he in no way bound his adversary to it. Such a strategic error, if repeated, could only result in a repetition of the same disasters to the army that committed it. There is another reason why, in case of war, an attempted march on Constantinople would be inevitable: by this means alone could the war be brought to a conclusion; otherwise, a harassing conflict might go on for years. Muscovite soldiers would die, Muscovite roubles would be squandered, but no result whatever would be gained.

Let us suppose that a Russian army of the required strength, which is not less than 250,000 men, has assembled on the Pruth, that the co-operation or benevolent neutrality of Roumania is assured, and that Austria abstains entirely from all share in the contest, and let us examine the probable lines by which the invaders would advance.

It must be prefaced, before drawing deductions from previous campaigns, that in the present instance the conditions are materially altered from what they were in 1828 and 1829, by the fact that there is now no object in seizing a fortified seaport; hence Varna need no longer be the objective, and the only reason for capturing it would be to make use of the coast road which it commands. Likewise Servia is available as a base, which was not the case formerly, although as there is no railway in that principality south of Belgrade, and as Austrian territory cannot be violated, but little use can be made of this advantage. If, therefore, four corps in the first instance take the field—that is to say about 150,000 men—we may expect to see that, beginning from the Russian left, No. 1 will cross the Danube near Reni, Isakchi, or Brailow into the Dobrudscha and march up the right bank of the river past Matchin and Dovian to Hirsova.

No. 2 will move along the post road from Kischenau to Faltsi or Faltsey, as it is also called, will there cross the Pruth, and march up the right bank of that river and the left bank of the Danube as far as Hirsova, where probably it will cross, and then in conjunction with No. 1 will march onwards towards Schumla, having on its way detached a force to watch Silistria.

Nos. 3 and 4 will probably be conveyed by railway from Kischenau to Jassy, thence by Roumanian railway to Galatz, Bucharest, and Giurgevo, where they will concentrate.

If a fifth corps is available—or the portion of a corps —it may perhaps be despatched to Servia, there to join a contingent of Servians and Montenegrins, to mask Widdin, and march on Nissa or Nisch, which probably is not capable of offering much resistance, and thence *viâ* Sophia and Samakovo on the Philippopolis railway; thus turning the Balkans and the position of any Ottoman army defending those mountains.

It has been calculated that not more than 7,000 men a day could be moved along the Roumanian railway. As will be shown hereafter, it would appear that even this is an over-estimate, considering that the line is single and the curves sharp, which prevent either long trains or a rapid speed. If two corps (in all about 70,000 men), are sent by railway, it would take ten days for them to concentrate at Giurgevo. We must allow at least six to eight days more for artillery and train, so that under the most favourable circumstances about three weeks must elapse after the declaration of war before the passage of the Danube can be effected in any force near the point named. If we turn to corps Nos. 1 and 2, we shall find that the former would have to cross the Danube and march about 80 miles in order to get to Hirscva from the Southern Bessarabian frontier, while No. 2, which is supposed to have been echelloned further north and to have crossed the Pruth at Falsti, would have about 140 miles to march before it reached the same place. At the rate of ten miles a day for five days a week, and allowing four days for crossing the Danube, as probably the passage would be opposed, we find that these two corps would probably arrive at Hirsova about the same time, namely, between the eighteenth and twentieth day after the commencement of their march; perhaps under favourable circumstances a day or two sooner.

It thus appears the passage of the Danube might be

effected almost simultaneously by the three corps on its left bank. Nearly a week would probably be required by the corps Nos. 3 and 4 to cross with their train and artillery, and No. 2 would need about half that time. We have now got to the twenty-seventh day from the commencement of operations. The distance from Hirsova to Schumla is about 150 miles, and from Rustchuk about 75; one column would need about three weeks, and the other a week and three days to perform this distance; therefore, on or about the forty-eighth day from the crossing of the Pruth, if all goes well with the Russian army, we may expect to hear of a concentration and probably of a decisive engagement before Schumla. Of course it is needless to remark that the weather and the condition of the roads will have a very material influence on the pace at which the armies move. The above suggestions are hazarded on the supposition that the campaign begins in May or the end of the April. If it were opened in January with a hard frost and not much snow, the operations would be considerably hastened— the Danube could be crossed on the ice, probably in the space of two days in the place of a week, and the troops might march 60 or even 70 miles a week in the place of 50. If, on the other hand, it were an open winter, it would be almost wholly impossible to move troops at all, and no doubt the Russian Government would continue negotiations, and postpone crossing the Pruth until a time came which suited military expediency. Having thus conducted the invaders so far on their road, let us now turn to the defenders.

As we all know frequently occurs in politics, three distinct courses would be open to the Turks in the event of invasion. The first would be to defend the line of the Danube; the second to concentrate on Schumla and make a stand there; the third and last to leave garrisons only in Rustchuk, Silistria, Schumla, and Varna, to retreat across the Balkans and wait for the enemy at Aidos, Karnabad, and Selimno. The first course would undoubtedly be the one to pursue with an army of anything like the same strength as that opposed to it, provided also that it were movable and fairly provided with a train. Although accounts differ as to the amount of forces which Turkey could put into the field, varying from 300,000 to 120,000, it is probable that the latter is nearer the truth than the former, and that, allowing for garrisons, &c., a field army of 80,000 men is the utmost that could assemble on the Danube. As was shown by Radetzky in 1848 and 1849 in Italy, a small army, if properly handled on a river line, can keep in check one of twice its strength, but then it is necessary that it should possess *têtes-de-pont* on the other side, and should have an efficient train so as to enable it to move quickly. Turkey possesses neither of these advantages. Whereas formerly she had command of the left bank of the Danube, Kalafat, Giurgevo, Oltenitza, Kalarash, &c., are now Roumanian, and will be used against her, also she has absolutely no organised train or transport service. Her fortresses, moreover, on the Danube—Widdin, Nicopolis, Rustchuk, Silistria, and Tulcha—are neither so numerous nor so formidable as in days gone by. Widdin is commanded by Kalafat and practically useless—the two most important ones, Rustchuk and Silistria, are daily being strengthened and, if there is time to make them so, will probably become formidable. An active army pivoting between the two might either check the advance of an invader or cause him to give battle at a disadvantage; it is, however, most improbable that the Turks will thus make use of them.

The second course open to the Ottomans is to retire on Schumla, and this is the one which in all probability they would adopt. The place has so often been spoken of in the preceding pages that it seems now unnecessary to say much of it. The power of modern artillery has much diminished its importance, since the range of hills round it is now its weakness. A large fort, however, has been built lately, capable, it is said, of containing 18,000 men, and various other defensive measures taken to render the place if possible impregnable. As a week's work may entirely alter the whole defensive capabilities of any of these Turkish fortresses, it is impossible to say what resistance, when the time comes, they will or will not offer. From all one hears, however, they have hitherto been much neglected. In its best days Schumla was only a fortified position, requiring a large body of troops to defend it, not a fortress which might be held by a small garrison, and it could always be turned to the west by the route from Eski-Jurna and Osman-Bazar, as well as to the east by the road from Pravadi to Karnabad. At the present time the main line of railway is twelve miles from the town, and is not commanded—a great disadvantage for the defenders, and the opposite for an invading army. If the Turks assembled in force before Schumla it is probable that the Russian army would be forced to give battle; otherwise they would leave a body to mask the place, and march onward over the Balkans. Again, here the question arises as to the strength of the army that could thus move on. We have supposed that 150,000 men actually crossed the Danube about thirty-two days after the declaration of war, about 60,000 being in reserve, and about 35,000 being detached to co-operate in Servia. These numbers are probably much in excess of what in fact would be available. At least 20,000 men would be required to guard each of the fortresses, Silistria and Rustchuk, and 10,000 may be allowed for the casualties and guarding the communications. This leaves 100,000 men to reach Schumla; 30,000 would probably be required for this fortress; hence there only remain 70,000 to cross the Balkans. When the reserves come up, and either Silistria or Rustchuk falls, of course this number would be increased.

The Turks might possibly elect to defend the passes of the Balkans. That such a course would be advisable is undoubted, provided only that the main army were not scattered and rendered liable to be defeated in detail. It is, however, doubtful whether such a defence, in the face of an enterprising and numerous enemy, would be successful. An enemy might be greatly delayed, but from all accounts he could scarcely be repelled in these passes. They have already been named and described. In addition there are numerous sheep-walks along which infantry might be conducted, so as to turn any position that defenders could occupy. The following description given by Lord Albemarle of the Selimno Pass is interesting, and is applicable to the greater proportion of these so-called obstacles to the progress of an invading army. He says:

After a ride of three miles we entered the mountain gorge. The Balkan here runs north-east by south-west. We traversed its side, which is covered with vineyards from the summit to the base. The road, which was paved at the beginning of the ascent, was in good order, and broad enough in the narrowest part to allow two carriages to pass; it is practicable for artillery, and, indeed, for every description of wheeled conveyance. The soil of the country of which the road is made is sandstone, which, containing a portion of common clay, forms quickly, when broken into pieces, a compact substance admirably adapted for the purpose. It is impervious to damp, for it was neither affected by the rain of the four or five preceding days, nor by the fall of snow which was melting at the time. It is easily repairable, the soil itself forming the materials. With so much facility is this road constructed, that any cart actually makes its own road by the track of its wheels. This remark is not only applicable to this part of the Balkan, but is generally to the hilly parts of Roumelia and Bulgaria, which we traversed. Hence it is evident that should an army wish to cross by the Selimno Pass it has nothing to do but cut away the brushwood, draw it out on one side, and the baggage and battering-trains form the road. This, in fact, is what the Russians did in that part of the Balkan by which they advanced. They cut down a few trees and filled up the inequalities of the ground. The number of carriages that accompanied that army is a proof how trifling were the difficulties that had to be encountered. Almost every field-officer had his calèche, and the general officers three or four, and every company a cart for their camp kettles.

It is evident from the above that one pass at least offers no natural obstacles to an invader, and this description is in the main applicable to nearly all the others. It will be remembered that General Diebitsch and his army in 1829 crossed by a route much to the east of the one here named.

As before remarked, the Turks will probably choose the position which they finally select for their principal stand, according as their army is numerous and efficient, or the reverse. If they feel themselves very strong, they will probably defend the line of the Danube; if only moderately strong, they will concentrate round Schumla, and if very weak they will retire behind the Balkans, defending the passes over those mountains as best they can, and finally preparing from some central position such as Aidos, Karnabad, or Selimno, to crush the enemy's columns as they emerge from the defiles of the mountains. The intermediate position is the most likely one, the last would be the most prudent, since it is evident that the further they make the invader fight from his base, the smaller will be the force which they have to encounter. If either of the two retired positions are occupied, the column advancing from Servia by Sophia will have an important influence on the strategic situation. In order that its presence may be felt, it is necessary that its movements should, to a certain extent, coincide with those of the main body. Let us see how this could be arranged.

As there is only one line of railway through Roumania from Galatz to the junction north of Bucharest, in the direction of Servia, and as armed bodies of men could not pass through Austrian territory like the Russian volunteers during the Servian war, much delay must occur before the corps intended to co-operate in the west could arrive at its destination. It might be forwarded by rail, either in advance of the main body destined for Giurgevo, simultaneously with it, or in rear of it. In the two former cases the concentration at Giurgevo would be delayed at least eight days; in the latter case, five corps could scarcely arrive at Verciorova or Orsova, the terminus of the Roumanian railway on the Servian frontier, before the twenty-sixth day after the declaration of war. This would be manifestly too late, so probably a middle course would be pursued: it would be sent on between corps Nos. 3 and 4, and might arrive at the starting-point of its southern march on or about the twenty-first day. It may be remarked that it is a two days' journey by rail from

Bessarabia to the Servian frontier. It might either start from Belgrade, in which case it would have a march of about 300 miles to Philippopolis, or it might cross the Danube at Gladova, and then commence a march of about 270 miles. As probably the Servians do not march better than they fight, forty-two and thirty-seven days would be respectively needed to accomplish these distances. Therefore it may be said that this flanking corps could scarcely exercise an important influence on the main operations before the fifty-eighth day after the declaration of war at earliest. On or about this day it ought to reach Philippopolis—thence to Adrianople by railway is about 120 miles—so on the seventy-fourth day it might be expected to reach the latter place. The main army having arrived opposite Schumla about the forty-eighth day would have had to fight probably once or twice, cross the Balkans, and march 130 miles before it reached Adrianople. If it were fortunately and energetically carried out, from twenty-one to twenty-five days might suffice for this operation, thus the converging columns of the invading army might hope possibly to find themselves united before Adrianople about seventy-four days after the passage of the Pruth. From Adrianople to Constantinople is 150 miles, to the position of Büjuk Chekmedgè 130 miles; therefore supposing the same rate of march were maintained, namely, ten miles a day during five days in the week, more than ninety days must elapse after the declaration of war before the capital of the Turkish empire could be seriously threatened. It may appear to some that the rate of march named is unusually slow: it is certainly less than that accomplished by the Prussian columns either in 1866 or in 1870; but it is probably more than could be actually carried out in Bulgaria; the Prussians, moreover, are notoriously the best marchers in Europe, the Russians by no means the best, and some great authorities, to whom the writer has spoken, agree in considering that this rate is as much as under the most favourable circumstances could be expected.

It may be remarked, why should the main Russian army be weakened by the Servian column being detached, more especially as the latter could only arrive after the decisive actions had probably taken place? To this it may be replied, that such a diversion might be made, first, because it would bring up a not unimportant contingent of Servians and Montenegrins; secondly, because it would neutralise an equal, perhaps even a superior, force of the enemy in its front; thirdly, because in the event of the Turkish army making a successful stand either before or behind the Balkans, it would turn their position and take them in flank and rear of their communications; and lastly, that it would cause the evacuation of Bosnia by any Ottoman force occupying it, or would effectually cut off that force altogether.

There is also another plan of operations, which not impossibly might be adopted by the Russians, more especially were the campaign to be opened in the early spring, when probably the roads through the Dobrudscha and up the left bank of the Danube would be in a soft condition and unfavourable for the passage of troops. If, moreover, as would be the case in the present instance, war had long been threatened, if there had been ample time for preparations, and thus opportunities had been afforded for creating a large amount of rolling stock on the Roumanian railways,[1] the following plan would appear to possess very great advantages.

We will suppose that six corps have been concentrated on the Bessarabian frontier, each corps numbering about 35,000 men, in all about 210,000, and that this force is further supplemented by reserves of regular troops, sufficient to fill up the gaps in the field army, keeping the latter up to its normal strength; while also there are reserves of militia—say about 60,000 strong, and capable of performing valuable service in guarding communications and blockading fortresses, although perhaps unfitted for active operations in the open field. To these forces, possibly the Roumanian army may also be added. From all accounts the troops of this monarchy are not very formidable as regards quality—the probable numbers that would be available have already been estimated in the last chapter. Nevertheless, as a contingent, and employed in the same way as the militia, they would be a most valuable assistance. In any case it is probable that the Moldavian

[1] It is stated that at present there are in Roumania only 1,200 carriages and trucks fit for military transport.

and Wallachian soldiers are fully as efficient as the greater part of the 'men with rifles' now rallied under the flag of the Porte.

Supposing, therefore, that all these forces are available in place of dividing the columns, as previously suggested, it might be decided to concentrate four out of the six corps by rail near Giurgevo, while one corps joined the Servians, and the other protected the left flank of the main army, making diversions on the Lower Danube and threatening the passages of the river below Silistria. Were this plan adopted it would possess the following advantages:—

1st. The main army destined for decisive operations would have a far shorter distance to march than if two columns advanced up the Lower Danube, one on each bank, as has often been done in former wars.

2nd. The unhealthy and barren district of the Dobrudscha would be entirely avoided.

3rd. The line of communications to be defended would be comparatively short and up to within about 90 miles of Schumla would be entirely by rail.

4th. The general advance would be fairly united; and the column on the right flank, advancing from Servia, would be able to co-operate more closely with the movements of the main army than would be the case if the eastern route were adopted.

It may also be added, that with such a splendid screen before them as the Danube, coupled with the notorious inefficiency of the Ottoman cavalry, as it now exists, the movements and intentions of the Russian army might be entirely concealed from their enemies, and were the corps on the left flank skilfully handled, the Turks might be kept in entire ignorance as to whence they would have to expect the principal attack. Hence a large portion of their forces might be neutralized about Tulscha, Silistria, and in the Dobrudscha, leaving but a small body to oppose the main body of the invaders.

Let us now consider the time that would be required to concentrate the four corps about Giurgevo as suggested. Bucharest by rail is 42 miles from the Danube; it is also about 290 miles distant from Roman, on the Jassy railway, according to the railway guide-books, and from Roman to Kischenau, according to the map, is 140 miles. Thus, supposing that these four, or rather five, corps were shipped on the railway at Kischenau, they would have a railway journey of 330 miles before they reached Bucharest, which probably would be the main point of concentration. It is certainly more than doubtful if this distance could be performed in one day with a single line, as ordinary trains in peace time require twelve hours to go from Roman to Bucharest. Under any circumstances, 7,000 men per day may safely be regarded as the very highest number that could be transported between the two points, and this without including either artillery or trains.

It is probable that an effort would be made as soon as possible after the declaration of war to seize and hold the two places Giurgevo and Oltenitza, which, in every war that has taken place on the Danube for the last century and a half, have always been important points for the passage of the river. The amount of force required for this operation would entirely depend on whether the Turks had previously taken any measures for the defence of these passages, and whether they occupied Rustchuk and Turtukai on the opposite bank in force or not. In all probability the Russians would have obtained complete and detailed information as to the movements and position of the Turkish army by means of spies and from other sources, and would regulate their plans accordingly. If the Ottomans had taken no special precautions to prevent a passage of the river at the points named, then probably as soon as one corps with its artillery, or even a smaller force, could be collected near Bucharest—that is, in little more than a week—a forward movement would be made; otherwise, at least two corps would be required for the proposed operation. Allowing, therefore, 7,000 men per day, three days for the artillery and indispensable train of each corps, and four days for the march from Bucharest to the Danube, nothing could be well attempted within a period of twenty days after the declaration of war.

We will therefore suppose that two corps have been safely deposited at Bucharest, and that they have successfully occupied Giurgevo and Oltenitza, and are busy making preparations for effecting the passage of the Danube, and thus preparing for the advance of the main army.

No time probably would now be lost in forwarding on to Servia the corps or the portion of a corps destined for that flank. As before mentioned, this force would have to pass along the same line of railway as the main army, so far as the junction a little to the north of Bucharest; this would delay the arrival of the two remaining corps of the central force for at least eight days, even supposing that the great proportion of the train and reserve ammunition were not forwarded on until later. Thus, at the rate of 7,000 men per day, and allowing three days per corps for the transit of artillery and necessary train, which is a most moderate allowance, it would require sixteen and eight, in all twenty-four more days before the main body would be concentrated on the left bank of the Danube.

It may be presumed that while the rear of the army are thus being forwarded to the front, the advance guard and main body have already effected the passage of the river, have established bridges across it, and have themselves crossed. In this manner each body of troops, as it disembarked from the railway at Bucharest, at Komana, or elsewhere, might at once march on, and there would be but little delay in crossing the Danube. We will allow four days after the concentration of the entire army for this operation, and it will be seen, according to this calculation, that 20 added to 24 and 4, in all about 48 days must elapse after the declaration of war before four corps could assemble on the right bank of the Danube for a combined advance on the Balkans.

The difficulties and delays of a purely railway method of transport are thus self-evident; let us see how long it would require for these same corps to reach the same places on the Danube by march route. According to the map, the distance from Kischenau to Rustchuk by road is about 300 miles. Allowing that they march ten miles a day for five days in the week, and as before require four days to cross the Danube, on or about the forty-sixth day the four corps would be united on the right bank. Under these circumstances it is probable that a medium course would be adopted, that the advance guard, heavy artillery, and supplies would be forwarded by train to Galatz and Rustchuk, while the main body of the infantry, of course the cavalry, and the greater portion of the artillery would follow by road,—in any case much the same time would be needed, namely, about seven weeks and a half from the first crossing of the Pruth before the final advance on the Balkans could be commenced. It may be remarked that, according to recent calculations, about 800 railway trains would be required to concentrate the Russian army on the Danube, and that twenty trains per day is the very maximum that could be despatched.

At present it is by no means improbable that the advance of a corps from Servia would be entirely dispensed with. The great distance that it would have to march—about 470 miles; the long railway journey that it would in the first instance have to perform, namely, 566 miles—330 from Kischenau to Bucharest, and 236 from Bucharest to the Servian frontier—before it could even commence the invasion, would equally tend to make such a detachment from the main army undesirable. When, moreover, we consider the character of the contingent with which such a detached corps would have to co-operate, the small influence it would exercise on the most decisive portion of the operations, and the large force that would be needed with the main body to mask the various Ottoman fortresses, we may safely express our conviction that such a diversion through Servia will not, under existing circumstances, be attempted by the commander-in-chief of the Russian army.

Under all circumstances whatsoever it seems inevitable that the main advance must be based on the Giurgevo and Bucharest railway, and that the main army will find itself, about seven weeks after the commencement of the campaign, somewhere between Rustchuk and Silistria. The subsequent movements will then depend on the attitude of the Turks, of which probably the Russian staff will have ample information. If the Ottomans intend to make a stand near Schumla, the Russian army will have to turn aside and fight them; if, on the other hand, the Turkish generalissimo has concentrated south of the Balkans— about Burghas, Aidos, Praoadi, and Selimno, as before suggested—then the Muscovites will probably detach a force to defend their left flank, and will make a dash for the western passes of the Balkans, entirely ignoring those on the east. From Rustchuk direct there are three good roads leading to the Balkans; the first, beginning from the west, is somewhat circuitous, leading by Tirnova either to Selimno or to Kasanlik; the second, not marked in accompanying map, goes nearly due south to Osman-bazar, where it unites with No. 3, which proceeds *viâ* Rasgrad and Eski-Djuma either to Kasan or to Selimno. The distances to these Balkan passes from Rustchuk are as follows:—

By western road about 100 miles to Selimno pass, and 90 *viâ* Tirnova to Kasanlik pass.

By centre road about 80 miles to Kasan pass, and the same distance to the Selimno defile.

By eastern road (Rasgrad, &c.) 90 miles to Kasan pass.

It is probable that forced marches would be made to seize these important defiles, and therefore about six or seven days would suffice for the Russian army to reach them. The Kasan and Selimno passes are those where in all likelihood fighting would take place, and therefore the description of the latter by Lord Albemarle, as already given, is all the more interesting.

It is impossible to foretell the action of the Turks if they were deceived by a demonstration towards Schumla; it is not impossible that they would form a position at Aidos, direct their principal attention to the passes on the east, neglecting those on the west. In any case their task of defending the Balkans would be a most difficult one, if only from the great range of country which they would have to watch. Doubtless the railway from Adrianople to Zamboli and Philippopolis would much aid them, but still, as in the case of Benedek and the Austrian army in 1866, they would always be liable to have fractions of their army engaged by superior numbers and defeated in detail. Even supposing that, favoured by the advantages of ground, they were temporarily successful in checking an advance guard, they would be liable at any moment to find themselves face to face with the entire Russian army, and probably might share the fate which befell Vandamme at Chulm in 1813.

As before remarked, if the Ottoman army concentrated near Schumla, they would have to be defeated before any advance could be made on the Balkans; if, on the other hand, they assembled round Aidos or anywhere south of the mountains, a general action must take place before Adrianople could be captured. The scene of this action and the date on which it takes place will depend on the dispositions of the Turkish generals, and cannot be predicted any more than its result. If this action is in any way unfavourable to the Turks, it will probably make the Russians masters of the entire country up to the position of Büjuk Chekmedgè, and will decide the campaign, but not the fate of Constantinople, which can scarcely fall before an enemy that has not the command of the sea. In every previous war a great defeat has almost completely prostrated the energies and the defensive powers of the Ottoman Government. Turkish armies never rally after a serious disaster, whereas the soldiers of the Czars have always been celebrated for their steadiness in adversity.

It may be remarked that, whatever plan of operations be adopted, much the same time, namely, about forty-eight days, would be needed after the declaration of war before Schumla could be reached, and if all went well, and the Russian army were sufficiently large to mask and disregard the fortresses, the invaders could scarcely threaten Stamboul within a period of ninety days after they crossed the Pruth.

With respect to the actual force that, after so long a march might arrive at the last position before Constantinople—this could only be a matter of the wildest conjecture; as before mentioned, General Fadéeff considers that if 250,000 men arrived on the Danube, 150,000 ought to reach the capital. Even, however, supposing that this number of men got so far—an improbable contingency under the present circumstances—it by no means follows that Constantinople is lost; there still is the celebrated position of the Chekmedgès to be carried. Although still unfortified, it is so favoured by nature for defence, that but a few weeks' work would suffice to render it impregnable. This position has been often described, but the following account of it, given in General Mackintosh's 'Strategic Tour in Bulgaria,' appears to be the most detailed and graphic that has yet been published. It was written in the year 1854, but of course the physical characteristics are now the same as they were twenty-three years ago.

On the Adrianople side the country resembles the rest of the immediate neighbourhood of Constantinople, but at the distance of two hours it ascends considerably; and beneath the last height in that direction lies the lake of Chekmagee.

This lake is separated from the sea by a marshy tongue or isthmus, narrow, and divided by outlets from the lake, which is brackish. The breadth of the lake is here about three-quarters of a mile, but it increases higher up, and at the distance of three or four miles divides into a fork, that nearest Constantinople receiving the river which anciently bore the name of the Bathynias.

At the Great Lake, about two hours further on, beyond a country of heights and valleys, is also a position which looks down upon the lake and isthmus of Buguk Chekmagee, the latter of which is reached by a zigzag road, descending from the crest above into the town of that name.

The spot is very strong, but nothing has been done by art to render it stronger. A few works on the height above, and to the left of the town near a burying-ground, would command the isthmus and close the road from Adrianople, or even a couple of martello towers in advance of the bridge, not immediately commanded from the heights, in that direction, might possibly lead to the last-mentioned result. As it is, there is not a gun near the spot, and the country is generally smooth and open.

Nothing seems done with judgment, on any side to cover the capital so strongly situated by nature.

The lakes in question form the left of a strong defensible line which has its right on the fort of Kara Bornoo on the Black Sea, which is again strengthened by the proximity to its front of another large salt lake. Between this fort and Domusdereh, near the entry of the Bosphorus, there is no practicable landing-place for a hostile force. The town of Chatsalda is about ten miles from the passage over the marshy ledge which separates the greater lake (Buguk Chekmagee) from the sea. That lake is gradually lost in marsh near Chatsalda, and the advance of troops might be rendered very difficult by taking advantage of the country immediately east of that place, and strengthening it artificially. The distance from Chatsalda to the Black Sea is about thirteen miles, and a little to the north-east the range of little Balkan begins, which runs pretty steeply down to the shore of the Bosphorus, but slopes more gradually towards the Black Sea.

The routes through it are difficult and unmade, and there can be little doubt that this line, if properly strengthened and defended, would put Constantinople beyond the risk of capture. It would cover effectually the great bends or reservoirs on which the city depends for water, and the country which would be inclosed by it might be rendered prosperous and fruitful, so as to yield supplies to the capital.

It may be mentioned that this position was surveyed by Sir John Burgoyne in 1853, that recently also it has been examined, and forts have been projected on it, which now only have to be constructed. A line of railway in rear of the forts by Adhemköi has been marked out.

In another part of his work the same writer gives the following information regarding the position on the Dardanelles:—

Even though the Russians were to be the conquerors in case of hostilities with the Turks, and even though they were to effect the occupation of Constantinople, the Dardanelles might still be held by a power having the command of a fleet, even though that fleet might not be on the very spot at the moment; but this could only be done if that position were to be augmented in strength on the land side. On the Asiatic side of these straits, forts were erected about the time of Mehemet Ali's defection, from a fear of his advancing and seizing on that important channel; but when I last passed through it, no new work had been even commenced on the European side, which is a peninsula connected by a narrow neck with the mainland. In case of a land attack, it could not be defended by the old Turkish castles or batteries, chiefly on the water's edge; and if the peninsula were once occupied they must themselves very soon fall into the hands of the assailants.

To prevent such an occupation by a force passing over the neck or isthmus, I would propose that a strong line of defensive works should be erected across its narrowest part, which is only a few miles broad, and at which point the slope of the land is favourable for the purpose. It lies some miles above, that is, north-east of Gallipoli.

If the Russians were enabled to advance on Constantinople, there is no doubt they would make a simultaneous movement on the Dardanelles, and would easily carry the batteries on the European side by the gorge. I say the gorge, as the works have only thin walls on the land side.

Constantinople itself is so extensive, that an army might occupy its inland portions without fear of being dislodged by a fleet, though it might bombard and batter the districts near the water. A struggle of this kind would cause the entire destruction of the city, but mere operations from the sea would have little other result.

After thus describing the means of defence possessed by Constantinople on the European side, General Mackintosh refers as follows to the manner in which it may be protected in Asia Minor:—

In case of the immediate vicinity of Constantinople being threatened on the Asiatic side, either by the advance of an enemy from the direction of Erzeroom, or in consequence of such a landing having been effected as I have supposed, the country presents an interior line of defence, commencing at the Bay of Chalcedon, without the suburbs of Scutari, and extending to Anatoli-Hissar, the first Asiatic castle above the capital.

The suburb of Scutari is enveloped by a chain of heights descending from Mount Bourgarloo, and connected in an oblique line with an eminence near the castle, but beyond the valley in which it stands. Although, however, this elevated spot commands one of the narrowest parts of the strait, it ought not to be occupied, as it is itself commanded by a higher ridge; but about four hundred yards further on is a plateau embracing a view as far as Therapia, which would cross its fire with the batteries on the European side; and here a fort, aided by another on Mount Bourgarloo, would enable the defenders to hold the enemy at bay, in a line extending from Chalcedon to the Giant's Mountain.

All the positions, in fact, are very strong, being supported on both flanks by precipitous ravines, so that they might be held by a corps very inferior in number to that of the enemy, who would be obliged to occupy a very extensive line, while the defending force could confine itself to one comparatively very limited.

The advance of an enemy, even to the water's edge, would not, on this side, be at once so decisive as on the other, from the obstacle presented by the Bosphorus.

Still the loss of the Asiatic forts, and the destruction of the villages and dwellings, extending nearly ten miles up the strait, which must be the consequence of such an advance, would be a very heavy calamity, tending much to the ultimate success of an enemy.

Even should nothing more effective be done, works on the heights behind are imperatively required for the defence of both shores, for which the only provision yet made is some small wooden blockhouses, erected in 1853, behind the fort of Youska, with six or seven similar constructions at other points, of which one was in the rear of Roomeli-Kavac, on the European side. That at Youska appeared to me to be commanded behind by the Giant's Mountain, and all these blockhouses seemed mean and combustible defences.

They are, however, provided with a small ditch and glacis, and their roofs are covered with earth to deaden the effect of shells and other projectiles.

Such are the natural facilities possessed by Constantinople for defence. A reference to the map will suffice to show her extraordinary commercial advantages, situated as she is between the continents of Europe and Asia, and at the junction of two great inland seas. Hence it can scarcely be wondered that for sixteen centuries she has been coveted by all neighbouring nations; that she enables the Government by which she is held preternaturally to survive the ordinary causes of decay, and that, now as formerly, she is regarded as the chief seat of the empire of the world.

In conclusion, therefore, we may consider that, great as would be the obstacles to a Russian army advancing on Constantinople, these obstacles are by no means insurmountable; although about three-and-half months would be required to reach the Bosphorus, nevertheless the feat might be accomplished, even without the command of the sea. If Russia were mistress of the Euxine, the operation would be enormously facilitated, and most of the real difficulties that now exist, namely those connected with supply and transport, would in a great measure be removed. This being the case, as, by the amendment of the treaty of Paris in 1870, there is nothing to prevent the creation of a formidable Russian fleet in the Black Sea, it seems more than probable that the present time would not voluntarily have been selected for an attack on the Turkish empire. Force of circumstances, not choice, has forced Russia to assume her present attitude. If deep and ulterior designs are nourished against the independence of the Porte, the contest will possibly be postponed at least half a dozen years, until the deficiencies of the Russian railways are supplied; until a Russian fleet has been constructed; until the Slavonian agitation has reached a climax; and until the continued insolvency of the Ottoman Government has permitted her land and sea forces alike to relapse into a condition of inefficiency and decay. It must, however, be added that, from information which the author has received on undoubted authority of the condition of the Turkish armaments at the outbreak of the Servian war, he has no doubt whatever that had the Russian Government been able in May 1876 to mobilise and concentrate 200,000 men in Bessarabia, within a month they might have marched to Constantinople almost without hindrance, and might have encamped on the Bosphorus within nine weeks of the day on which their rear-guard crossed the Danube.

It need scarcely be added that the suggestions made above regarding the probable lines of advance, and the marches of the various columns, are only intended to be conjectural, that the distances given are taken from the map and are only approximate, there being no good itinerary or even guide-book of Turkey-in-Europe; and lastly that, as in the other matters of life, still more in the march of armies, the chapter of accidents has at all times a powerful, and in some cases a decisive influence.

CHAPTER XII.

THE POLITICAL ASPECT OF THE EASTERN QUESTION.

Importance of Austria in a Russo-Turkish War—The Slaves—Policy of Austria—How the action of Austria might be neutralized, externally and internally—Slavonic question—Danger to Austria—Limits of Bulgaria—Interests of England—Traditional policy of Russia—Essentially aggressive in its character—Various lines of policy open to England—Which it is her interest to adopt—Unfortunate natural antagonism between Russia and England—Advantages of the policy suggested.

In the foregoing chapter, and in those that preceded it, no account whatever has been taken of the position of Austria or of the attitude which the Slavonic and Greek population of Turkey might assume in the event of any complication and subsequent war with Russia. A glance at the map will show that in a strategic point of view Austria holds the key of the situation; no Russian army could possibly reach Constantinople from the Danubian frontier, if Austria were to forbid. This fact has been dilated on at considerable length and with great clearness by the Russian General Fadéeff,[1] who thereupon argues that the real enemy of Russia is not Turkey but Austria, since the latter power may prevent any designs of aggression being carried out on the former.

[1] *Vide* Appendix.

This author, however, apparently overshoots the mark: while taking it for granted that Turkey, if unassisted, would prove an easy prey to a Muscovite attack, and that an invading army would only require six weeks to march from the Danube to Constantinople, he considers that not more than 60,000 men could be sent by the maritime powers to assist the Porte. This evidently is an underestimate. France, perhaps, need not be taken into account, as since the '70 campaign her great object has been to establish a Russian alliance; but were either Italy or England to enter into the contest both powers could alone place in the field a far larger force. Considering the enormous amount of shipping at the disposal of England, two corps could be despatched from their shores at a week's notice, and an equal number from India in scarcely a longer time, and could certainly arrive at the Bosphorus before the Russians could get there from the Danube. It is, however, extremely improbable, having in view the present temper of the English people, and the present financial difficulties of the Italian Government, that either one power or the other would, at all events in the first instance, take any part in the quarrel. Hence Turkey would stand alone, having in her favour the possible intervention of Austria, and having against her the probability of an extensive rising on the part of the Slave population.

Let us first turn to Austria. The past political history of this country exhibits a strange mixture of weakness, indecision, temporary boldness, and chronic fear. No

U

country has less reason to desire a Russian occupation of Constantinople, or has greater cause to wish the Danube to remain free and neutralised; nevertheless of all the interested powers, there is not one that has lent herself with greater readiness to Russian designs. We have seen that twice in the last century she allied herself against Turkey, and in only one of the eight wars in which during the last 170 years Russia and Turkey have been engaged has Austria assumed in any way a hostile attitude to the Muscovite armies. That once—in the Crimean War—she took no active part in the contest, although, as clearly shown by Kinglake, she led the Western Powers on the ice, distinctly assuring them that she would support their ultimatum to the Emperor Nicholas, and drawing back at the last moment. In 1829, according to Von Moltke, she encouraged the Turks to continue the contest, hoping from the apparent exhaustion of the combatants that she might eventually step in as an umpire and dictate terms to both. In 1870, when Russia issued her celebrated note, announcing that she could no longer be bound by the treaty of Paris as to the Black Sea, Austria pursued her accustomed and traditional policy of masterly inactivity. It is true at the time she was not supported. The English ministry of the day failed to appreciate the importance of the clauses involved; the Sultan Abdul Aziz was too busy with his palaces and his harems to take much account of the doings of infidels. France and Germany were engaged in mortal strife; Italy had only just got to Rome and hoped to stay there; Austria alone could have said 'No,' and this 'No' would probably have been decisive, but she failed to say it. Thus one of the great safeguards against Russian aggression was swept away by the stroke of a pen; what had cost thousands of lives and millions of pounds to effect was abandoned without a blow or a struggle.

At the present juncture, who can doubt that a simple concentration of Austrian troops on the Transylvanian frontier would make war an impossibility? There would be no more panics on all the bourses in Europe; no more failures from the prostration of trade; but faithful to her ancient policy Austria remains still. War rumours continue, and if peace intervenes we shall owe but few thanks to the Cabinet of Vienna. It cannot be said that Austria is to blame for the policy which she thus consistently pursues; she is perfectly right to allow others to pull the chestnuts out of the fire for her; but it must always be remembered by those who look to Austria to check Russian aggression that, if they trust to her, they trust to a broken reed; not only from habitual policy, but also from external circumstances, she cannot be regarded in any way as a dependable element connected with the Eastern question.

For let us consider how her action might be neutralised, however willing she might be to act. Of course first comes Germany. An understanding between Prince Gortchakoff and Prince Bismarck, and a simple warning issued by the latter, would prevent a single

Austrian soldier moving a foot forwards towards the Principalities; and the bribe that could be offered for this passive assistance might be a tempting one, say Holland, the German-speaking Baltic provinces, or Bohemia, with Austrian Germany. Then, again, there is Italy; lately there were rumours of a Russo-Italian alliance : it is said that wherever there is smoke there is also fire. The action of Italy would much paralyse Austria, and would neutralise a large portion of her troops—the bribe there would not be so tempting, and it could not so certainly be administered ; it would be the Trentino, or perhaps the eastern shores of the Adriatic. It thus may be seen that complications may easily occur, which would render Austria by no means a free agent. It is fortunate for Europe that the statesmen both of Germany and Italy of the present day are notoriously honest and high-minded, otherwise the possibilities here suggested might become realities.

Then again, there is the Slavonic question—so much talked of now, but which has only recently come into prominence. It is somewhat difficult to disentangle the actual truth from the web of falsehood and random assertion with which it is involved. It would appear, however, from the writings of those who are both friendly and hostile to Russia, that for years past a most complicated and deep-seated intrigue has been proceeding—instituted and carried out by secret societies [1]—according to some fostered, and certainly regarded by no means with

---

[1] *Vide* Appendix, Lord Palmerston's opinions.

disfavour, by the Russian Government. The object of this intrigue or conspiracy is nominally the freedom of the Slavonic races from the dominion of Turkey, and the creation of either a number of independent or, as it is termed, ' autonomous ' states, or else of a single Slavonic kingdom under the protection of Russia. What this would ultimately result in, it is unnecessary to point out. The protection of small independent states on the frontier of a great and aggressive empire must result, as in the case of the Crimea, in the word protection being replaced by incorporation.

This scheme, if carried out, would be a double-edged weapon in the hands of Russia—it would tend towards the dismemberment not only of the Ottoman but also of the Austrian empire. The Slave states, that owe allegiance to the Court of Vienna, would inevitably be attracted to a Slave kingdom, just as the minor states of Italy were attracted round Piedmont, and those of Germany round Prussia. Unfortunately the Austrian rule can scarcely be called assimilating, like that of her neighbours; the various races that own allegiance to the yellow and black flag still retain their individuality, and in a great degree their mutual hostilities. It is different in Germany; one of the great triumphs of comparatively free and constitutional governments may be witnessed in the success achieved by the new German empire in reconciling the different and previously hostile Germanic kingdoms to her rule, and in imbuing them with a mutual regard and united patriotism. Undoubtedly the war of 1870 was in a great degree instrumental in bringing this about, nevertheless the complete success is not the less commendable.

The secession of her Slave provinces from Austria would inevitably be followed by an entire disruption of the empire. Hungary would probably become an independent kingdom, the German provinces would go to Prussia, the Italian Tyrol and some other pickings to Italy. That this is an end which would be of enormous benefit to Russia is unquestionable, the road to Constantinople would at once be open, and any danger of a reconstitution of the Polish kingdom would be removed for ever. It has been remarked by many Russian writers that Austria could use Polish disaffection as a most valuable weapon against Russia. An offer to restore Galicia and erect a free Poland at Warsaw would probably neutralise the action of 150,000 Russian troops, and cause disaffection among many thousands more. As directed against Turkey the value of the Slavonic agitation is self-evident, it means insurrection and utter paralysis of resources in case of war—be it remarked, moreover, that this would not be confined to Christians alone, since the Slave Mahomedans are by no means an unimportant body, and might be supposed to side with their brethren of similar race and language. Were this agitation ripe for action, were the Christian population armed, a single great defeat of the Turkish army would result not only in an utter collapse of that army itself, as has always been the case in former wars, but in an utter prostration of all further means of defence; the defenders would be taken in flank and rear, faithful Mussulmans would lose heart—would mutter 'Kismet,' and the Sultan with his advisers would decamp 'bag and baggage' from Constantinople. Even if at the last moment the Western Powers were to take fright and save the capital, a Muscovite army encamped almost within sight of St. Sophia—a Muscovite army in occupation of all the Turkish provinces, and an uprising of all the subject populations, would place the St. Petersburg Cabinet in a very different position from that which it now occupies, with a half-mobilised army encamped in the steppes of Bessarabia, dying of cold and privation on the banks of the Pruth.

Were all that has been written and said regarding Russian designs to be believed, the credulity or, to use a most expressive French word, the *gobemoucherie* of us all would be strained to the utmost. A recent publication [1] has given an elaborate account of all the various intrigues and machinations by which Russia has endeavoured to cause the term 'Bulgaria' to extend south of the Balkans, and thus to give her army after the proposed occupation the advantage of starting from a base which has already surmounted the great strategic obstacle of those mountains. The writer of this pamphlet even goes so far as to say that the 'whole attention of diplomacy

[1] 'Attention aux Balkans,' translated by Edgar Whitaker.

ought to be directed to the Balkans.' Apparently the military value of this defensive line has been enormously over-estimated; as previously shown, the only time that an army has ever got so far, it had no difficulty in marching on. History, moreover, contains but few examples of the successful defence of a mountain range which contains as many as thirteen practicable passes, and which might also be turned, as is the case in the present instance. Nevertheless, both in the interest of the Greeks and in that also of military expediency, the limitation of Bulgaria to the country north of the Balkans is most desirable.

We have hitherto endeavoured to discuss the political elements which might influence the military situation in a Russo-Turkish war; it now only remains for us to consider how far the interests of England may be concerned in the settlement of the 'Eastern,' or, as it has now begun to be termed, the 'Slavonic Question.'

We have all received the assurances of the present Emperor of Russia that he has no designs whatever on Constantinople, and that the only explanation of the recent attitude which the Government of St. Petersburg has been forced to assume is their earnest desire to improve the condition of the Christian subjects of the Porte. The character of the Czar stands so high, his honesty is so undoubted, his regard for England so universally known, and his liberality so great, that the assurance thus gratuitously given has, notwithstanding the unfortunate Khivan affair, carried with it universal confidence; it has done much to calm public feeling in this country, and hence to direct and influence the general policy of the English nation. Possibly, were the present Emperor to live for ever, we might afford to view with indifference all that takes place in the East. Unfortunately, as with all of us, the Czar and his policy are but tenants for life; and in the interests of ourselves, our children, and our grandchildren, we must look farther than the actual present.

The fact remains that for the last two centuries the capture of Constantinople has been the great object to which the efforts and aims of Russian policy have been consistently directed. We put aside the apocryphal will of Peter the Great as probably a fable; we will suppose that some of the eight wars in which since his death Russia has been engaged with Turkey as an antagonist, were undertaken for philanthropic motives like those now professed; but on referring to history we find the Empress Anne in the year 1736 concluded an alliance with Austria for the partition of Turkey; in 1786 a similar convention was made between Catherine II. and Joseph II.; Alexander I. at the peace of Tilsit in 1807 made the same arrangement with Napoleon; and in 1853, as is well known, the Emperor Nicholas made distinct proposals in the same sense to Sir Hamilton Seymour. To say, therefore, that Russia as a nation has no designs on Constantinople is to do the patriotism of her statesmen great injustice. It is, moreover, an historical absurdity, just as much as to say

that 'the possession of Constantinople would be a misfortune for Russia' is a geographical absurdity. The following passage, extracted from General Fadéeff's book, shows the opinion of a patriotic Russian on this point. He says:—
'There is yet another place on the earth immeasurably important to Russia, having no material character, but from its exceptional position too important to belong to any small people—Constantinople, with the surrounding suburbs, country, and straits. The most positive interests of Russia render it desirable that that city—far more eternal than Rome—should become the free city of a tribal union.'

The term ' free city of a tribal union' is indeed a mockery. Can there be anything connected with Russia that is free? Russian writers talk of making the Slaves free! Until the institutions, laws, and entire system of government in the Muscovite empire are changed from the foundation, a transfer from the rule of Turkey to that of Russia would—to use a common expression—be a transfer from the frying-pan to the fire.

In addition to the influence of her traditional policy for centuries, there are other causes which tend to make Russia an aggressive and conquering power. In the first place she possesses but few safety-valves for the energy of her youth, such as are offered in a commercial or colonising country under a constitutional government. There is but one profession—the army—and the entire system of government is a military despotism. Hence a war would, as a rule, be viewed in Russia by all the governing class except the Minister of Finance, as a pleasing variety, more especially as those in whom chief power is vested do not bear the burden of the taxation. There are likewise social dangers of a most serious character, which effect pressure from within that tends to cause expansion outwards. The taxation is levied on principles that are opposed alike to all rules of justice and of political economy. The peasant pays heavily, while the noble and the member of the Imperial family go almost free. The burden of universal military service—a legacy from the year 1870—presses heavily on the population, and, more even than in Germany, tends to arrest all progress and to paralyse all industry. M. Leroy-Beaulieu, in the *Revue des Deux Mondes*, has brought out most vividly the present internal condition of the Muscovite empire, and other recent works on the same subject are equally explicit, so much so that when we see the solicitude exhibited by Russia for the sufferings of Turkish subjects, the saying arises to our lips, 'Physician, heal thyself.'[1]

It seems, therefore, incontestable that whatever may be the disinterested and philanthropic motives that have prompted the action of Russia as regards the Eastern Question during the last year, the natural action of her

[1] It has been remarked by a recent writer on this subject, Mr. Alfred Austin, that the solicitude of Russia for the welfare of Turkish subjects is of recent date, whereas the interest of Russia in Turkish territories is as old as Turkish decline in defensive capacity and Russia's consciousness of offensive strength.

Government is essentially ambitious and aggressive. When opportunity offers that action will be carried out. It only remains for England to decide on a definite policy to be pursued—a policy which will be maintained whatever Government may be in office, whatever events may occur, and which will not be influenced either by Polish or by Bulgarian atrocities.

It may be said that, as frequently happens, three distinct lines of policy are open to us.

The first is that which was pursued at the time of the Crimean War, to support Turkey to the last, to guarantee her integrity and independence, and be prepared to maintain both by force of arms.

The second is to conclude an alliance with Russia, the ultimate object of which, whatever might be its immediate pretext, would be the dismemberment of the Ottoman empire, and a share in the spoils when the day of dismemberment came.

The third and last course is to await the course of events, to lavish on the Porte plenty of excellent advice and as many diplomatic notes as circumstances may render desirable; but beyond this on no account to move, still less to fight, for a continuance of Turkish rule in Europe.

The first line of policy is not one which it is probable will ever again commend itself to the English nation. Were it to be pursued consistently, notwithstanding the great military difficulties of conducting a war thousands of miles from a base, there is no doubt that it could be successfully carried out. The wealth and resources of England are so enormous that certainly for many years to come, with no allies but the Turks, she could effectually arrest the progress of Russia towards the south, even supposing that her resolute attitude did not infuse fresh life and determination into the councils of Austria. It may, however, be well questioned whether the enormous expenditure of money and lives which such a course of policy must entail, would be worth the ends at which it is aimed. If the Turkish rule in Europe were a beneficent, enlightened rule, if it tended to improve the condition of its subjects and to develop the resources of the country which it governs, the case would be different; but as notoriously Turkish pachas are corrupt and oppressive, as the whole system on which the Ottoman government is carried out is essentially rotten, carrying with it the causes of its own decay, any attempt of England to perpetuate it would be equally wrong and in the end unavailing. If the constitution, recently announced, effects such a radical change as is anticipated, then possibly the system of government in the Ottoman states may become of so enlightened a character that it may be deserving of all support from England; and that support we may rest assured, when the day comes, Englishmen will most freely accord.

The second course of policy, namely, a close alliance with Russia, is almost an impossibility. There is no reason why a free country, possessed of a constitutional government, should not ally itself with an enlightened despotism, such as the government of Russia may become, if the wishes and reforms of the present Emperor are carried out. Unfortunately, at present, this enlightened despotism seems just as far distant as beneficent government on the part of Turkey.

There are also other reasons why such an alliance could not be honestly maintained. It would be utterly repugnant to the feelings and traditions of the English nation to assist, even in prospective, in the possible dismemberment of a former ally. Statesmen out of office may talk of the expulsion of the Turk, 'bag and baggage,' out of Europe, but were they in office probably their language and certainly their action would be very differently modelled. Lastly, it is true, however much to be regretted, that the interests of Russia and England are, like their respective politics, in many ways, distinctly antagonistic. Not only in Europe, but still more in the East, this unfortunate antagonism becomes every day more and more apparent. While England is unaggressive, peaceful, and commercial, Russia is aggressive, warlike, and military. While England practises free trade in the purest sense, and grants liberty of the press with absolute freedom as regards the movements and expressed opinions of her subjects, Russia indulges in a protective system of trade suited almost to the dark ages, the press is gagged, and Russian subjects can scarcely venture either to move or to speak without being prepared to face consequences of the most serious description. Doubtless, much has been done by the present Emperor to remedy these matters, but still there is yet much to be desired, and, until this improvement takes place, an Anglo-Russian alliance can only exist in the dim prospect of the future.

We now come to the third and last line of policy— that of awaiting the course of events—of affording our best offices in aid of peace and order, but steering, if possible, clear of any warlike complications. It does not follow that we are at once to give up all that we should not be prepared to maintain by force of arms. Lord Palmerston's opinion on this point is worth remarking.[1] Or that we should proclaim to the world our fixed peaceful determinations. Such a proclamation would materially weaken our influence for good, and would be calculated entirely to mislead the rest of Europe, thereby not impossibly tending to cause the very war which it was specially intended to avert. Moreover such an announcement could not be based on sufficient grounds to justify its being made. The feelings of the English people are most changeable, and their temper on occasions most warlike; at any moment, as before the Crimean war, the Government of the day might find itself carried away by popular enthusiasm and forced to enter on a war the possibility of which it had previously scouted. The prospect of the immediate capture of Constantinople might at any moment evoke an outburst of feeling and excitement

[1] *Vide* Appendix.

in this country of a most violent and unexpected nature. Bulgarian atrocities would at once be forgotten, and probably the old policy of former days would be hurriedly embraced. As regards the presence of Russia at Constantinople, one word must be said.

Until recently it has always been regarded in England as an axiom that the seizure by Russia of the seat of the empire of the world would be a 'pistol levelled at the head of India,' just as the possible occupation of Antwerp by the French in former days could have been regarded as a 'pistol levelled at the head of England.' Since the opening of the Suez Canal this axiom would appear to be even still more self-evident. It has, however, recently been questioned, and hence is no longer an axiom. It is related that recently a large bet was made that the sun went round the earth and not the earth round the sun. A treatise also not long since was written to prove that the surface of the globe was flat and not round. It seems as unnecessary here to discuss the value of Constantinople, as to demonstrate the truth of the facts in physical science which these two statements have called in question. Let it be granted, however, that a Russian occupation of the Bosphorus would be a danger to our communications with our Indian empire, and that we should feel disquieted were such an event to occur, just as a farmer possessed of a field full of valuable stock, and distant from his own house, would feel uneasy if he heard that an ill-conditioned neighbour had suddenly acquired the power to stop up the road to that field, and to cut off the water with which it is supplied. This must be conceded. It now remains for us to consider what material guarantees should we take for our safety.

The abandonment of Corfu, one of our great bases in the Mediterranean, appears now, more than ever, peculiarly unfortunate. It has been termed 'an unaccountable access of sentimental insanity.' The remarks attributed to Prince Bismarck regarding this voluntary surrender are especially appropriate—'When a nation begins to give up, she begins to decline,' or words to that effect. However, the deed is done; being many thousand miles from our natural base it behoves us to establish in the Mediterranean as many artificial bases as we require. The geographical position of Candia, with its admirable harbour of Suda, at once suggests itself, and as a strategic point for land defence the importance of Acre has already been shown in a previous chapter. The occupation of Constantinople presents many difficulties—the principal one being the large number of troops required to carry out such an occupation effectually. Then again, the wishes of the Turks are not an unimportant element in such a proposal. If we have an alliance with Turkey at all it must be an active not a passive alliance. It would be alike detrimental to the interests of England, and incompatible with the honour and feelings of the English army, that British troops should occupy the position of Büjuk-Checkmedgè, while the Turks are doing all the fighting on the Balkans

x

or on the Danube. Such a proposal is not to be for a moment entertained. Lastly there is the position on the Daradnelles; the advantage of occupying this is self-evident, thereby we should possess a guarantee valuable alike in a commercial and in a naval point of view. As long as we hold the Dardanelles, no Russian fleet could suddenly emerge from the Euxine and cut us off from our Indian Empire at a moment when our countrymen there may most urgently need our assistance. It also should not be forgotten that eventually Constantinople must be on the main channel of communication between Europe and Asia. The day must come when a railway will unite London with Calcutta, and the line of this railway will pause at the Bosphorus.

Hitherto, in discussing the political aspect of the Eastern Question, but little mention has been made of Germany, although, as the greatest military power of the West, she must of necessity exercise an all-important influence in the councils of Europe, even if her own immediate interests are only indirectly affected by the progress of Russia in the East. No one who has ever mingled much with the Germans of the present day can be ignorant of their universal and deep-rooted conviction that in order to consolidate and finally to secure the German Empire a war with Russia is an inevitable necessity. Situated between three great military nations, and having vanquished two, it now remains to vanquish the third. The one danger that Germany has to fear is a French and

Russian alliance. Were the Muscovites finally weakened and humbled, the danger would be past; then armaments might be reduced, taxes might be lightened, and the fearful burden under which German industry groans might in a great measure be removed.

The relations now existing between the courts of St. Petersburg and Berlin forbid anything approaching to open hostility, and the Emperor William is far too loyal and true ever to cherish a feeling or to favour an intrigue which could in any way prejudice the cordiality and friendship between himself and his nephew. Nevertheless, when national interests are at stake, family and personal feelings only too often are forgotten; in future years the cordiality which now exists between the Czar and the German Emperor may have passed away. Even at the present time no patriotic German statesman can forget that a war which would weaken Russia would strengthen Germany, and that for the interests of the Fatherland it is far better that this war should be fought on the slopes of the Balkans than on the banks of the Vistula.

In conclusion, it need only be remarked that whatever be the immediate result of the Conference, its ultimate effect must be politically to strengthen the position of Russia. In place of being isolated and 'acting independently,' she has been associated with the other Great Powers; she has induced their representatives to attempt to impose on the Porte conditions such as were utterly incompatible with the integrity and independence of the Ottoman Empire; she has given evidence of her own moderation, whether sincere or feigned it is unnecessary to inquire; and last, but not least, she has succeeded in isolating her traditional antagonist from exterior alliance and support.

APPENDIX.

Extract from 'Opinion on the Eastern Question,' by General Rotislar Fadéeff, of the Russian Army. Translated by T. Mitchell, C.B., late Secretary to Her Majesty's Embassy, and Consul at St. Petersburg.

It is generally considered in Russia that France and England are the principal obstacles to an armed intervention in Turkish affairs; but, in reality, however much they might desire it, France and England are not in a position to defend European Turkey against Russia, provided the hands of Russia are untied on the western frontier. It is a matter of impossibility to struggle, by landing forces, against a power of equal strength which has open access overland into the disputed country Such a struggle is impossible, both in respect to time and to numbers. Of what avail would be the means of maritime transport against an army of 200,000 men acting continuously? In 1854 the allies employed a part of the winter and the whole of the spring in transporting 60,000 soldiers to Turkey; they then required a considerable time for the organisation of their waggon-train; until June they were chained to the sea-coast, and they had not acquired mobility even by the end of that month. Their forces in the Crimea grew to the dimensions of a numerous army only by the gradual transport of fresh troops during the course of a whole year. Meanwhile the Russian army requires only six weeks, and even less, to march from the Danube to Constantinople, provided, of course, it be sufficiently numerous for the blockade of fortresses in the rear, during a forward movement, that shall also be as far as possible uninterrupted. In dealing with the Turks, a war may be pushed on as rapidly as the transport train can be made to advance. It is to be presumed that the war will support itself on the Balkan peninsula, provided the rapidity of the campaign does not permit the enemy to devastate methodically the country which, under such circumstances, would of course not submit to him without opposition. Hitherto, following old traditions, Russia has fought in European Turkey step by step, besieging fortresses to the astonishment of Europe, and without the justification of an unavoidable military necessity. In 1829, however, there was a political reason for such a plan of campaign; it was necessary to secure, as far as possible, the rear of the Russian army against any sudden hostile attack on the part of Austria.

In order to settle the fate of European Turkey, in spite of the maritime powers, it will be sufficient for 150,000 troops to reach the Bosphorus, *i.e.*, that 250,000 men, on the broadest calculation, should reach the Danube. There can be no difficulty in supplying these numbers, even with our present military organisation, allowing also for a sufficient and satisfactory occupation of the shores of the Baltic and Black Seas, and for the employment of 50,000 active troops on the side of the Caucasus. Russia can always forestal the land forces of her Western opponents, not only in the Balkans, but even at Constantinople. Even if they should succeed, after considerable difficulty, in meeting the Russian army in front of that capital with a force like that which, after the lapse of many months, they got together in 1854 at Varna, 60,000 Europeans, supported by any number of Turks, would not be able to defeat a Russian army of 150,000 men. Moreover, there would be no regular Turkish troops in existence at such a time: they would have been dispersed earlier in Europe and in Asia. The Straits would fall into the hands of the captors of Constantinople; their fortifications could not hold out against a land force; and the entrances into the Sea of Marmora, once occupied and properly defended, any serious attempt from seaward to dispute the possession of Turkey would become almost impossible. The largest force that has ever yet been landed was the army of the Crimea, which consisted of 60,000 troops, without cavalry or waggon-train, and with but a small proportion of artillery. The landing was crowned with success in consequence of two special reasons, namely, the shortness of the voyage (only thirty-six hours), and the numerical inferiority—to the extent of one-half—of our troops on shore. But a landing in the face of superior numbers, or of an enemy of equal strength abundantly supplied with warlike resources, would lead to destruction. The army of Wellington, transported in ships supplied from sea, and having a strong place of refuge at the mouth of the Tagus, maintained its footing in Spain against the superior, although divided, forces of the French, only because the country was for that army; but imagine the opposite position. Could a French army, between 1807 and 1812, surrounded by a national insurrection, have held its ground in Spain against superior English forces? And such would be exactly the position of the European allies in Turkey if Russia acted with decision. Indeed, were Russia to act with promptitude and decision, those allies would not, in all probability, be found in Turkey at all. Were the maritime powers to resolve on defending Turkey without having the co-operation of Austria, they would defend it only with their naval forces, and only with such a number of land troops as they could carry on board their fleet without inconvenience; but they would never risk their army. Many are led into error by the fact that the allies of 1854 were able to carry the war into Russia and to maintain themselves there. But how were they able to effect this? Simply by taking up a strong position on the coast, which they succeeded in fortifying before a sufficient force could be collected against them. There are many similar positions on the Turkish coast, but it would be impossible to save the Turkish dominions by encamping a small force on a sea-shore. In reality France and England can as little protect European Turkey against Russia with their land forces as they can protect Canada or Mexico against the Americans.

The difficulty is this, that it is impossible for Russia to carry on a war on the Balkan peninsula without the permission of Austria, and that permission she can under no circumstances obtain. Look at the map. Russia can reach European Turkey only by one road through the gate formed by the south-east angle of the Carpathians and the mouth of the Danube: the key of that gate is in the hands of Austria. By crossing the Danube or even the Pruth, a Russian army would expose her rear to Austria. In this awkward position the first threatening demonstration on the part of Russia's good neighbour would compel the army to beat a hasty retreat as in 1854. The Lower Danube is accessible only with an Austrian passport. In relation to Russia, the geographical position of European Turkey may be compared to a strong chest, of which Austria forms the lid; without lifting that lid, it is impossible to get anything out of the chest. Russia has had sufficient experience of that.

It was rumoured in 1854 that Prince Paskewitch strongly represented to the late Emperor that, once resolved on a war with Turkey, it was necessary, above all, to prepare for a war with Austria. He affirmed that the Eastern question could be solved only at Vienna, not in Turkey. Events have proved the correctness of the views of that celebrated warrior.

While Russia held possession of the Black Sea, an attempt might have been made to break open the chest from the other side, *i.e.*, to knock out the bottom of it by a landing in the Bosphorus. The result would have been a rising of the entire Christian population, the paralysing of Turkey during the following months, and probably her final dissolution; but in whose favour? The siege of Constantinople and the straits would not settle that question. It would have to be settled by a war on land against a coalition of which Austria would be the soul. During the continuance of such a war the Christian population of the Balkan peninsula would be in a chaotic condition. It would fight the Mussulman inhabitants of the towns, but it would not be able to give Russia any assistance beyond its own territory. In order to occupy the straits and the entire peninsula, it would be necessary to detach forces greater than those which would be required in case of a war in the West to defend the shores and land frontier of Russia against a live Turkey; so that, in reality, the seizure of Constantinople from seaward, while such a seizure was yet possible, would have increased but very little the material probabilities of the final success of Russia. In questions of the character of the last Greek question a fleet in the Black Sea might have exercised a weighty influence: it might have been used as a strong diplomatic expedient, but it would have been no very important military weapon in view of the objects that appertain to Russia. It is naturally impossible to estimate speculatively the moral effect of such a stupendous event as the entry of the Russian troops into Constantinople, even if it were unexpected, but such an event would in any case be a double-edged weapon.

OPINION OF LORD PALMERSTON.

The following extracts from Lord Palmerston's letters and opinions on the Eastern Question appeared in the 'Morning Post' of December 30, 1876. As they appear peculiarly appropriate at the present time, they are here reproduced.

It is nearly forty years since Lord Palmerston wrote to the Secretary of the Embassy at Constantinople in these words:—

'People go on talking of the inevitable and progressive decay of the Turkish empire, which they say is crumbling to pieces. In the first place, no empire is likely to fall to pieces if left to itself, and if no kind neighbours tear it to pieces. In the next place, I much question that there is any process of decay going on in the Turkish empire; and I am inclined to suspect that those who say that the Turkish empire is rapidly going from bad to worse, ought rather to say that the other countries of Europe are year by year becoming better acquainted with the manifest and manifold defects of the organisation of Turkey. . . . Half the conclusions at which mankind arrive are reached by the abuse of metaphors, and by mistaking general resemblance or imaginary similarity for real identity. Thus people compare an ancient monarchy with an old building, an old tree, or an old man, and because the building, tree, or man must, from the nature of things, crumble, or decay, or die, they imagine that the same thing holds good with a community, and that the same laws which govern inanimate matter, or vegetable and animal life, govern also nations and states; than which there cannot be a greater or more utterly unphilosophical mistake. For, besides all other points of difference, it is to be remembered that the component parts of the building, tree, or man remain the same, or are either decomposed by external causes or are altered in their internal structure by the process of life, so as ultimately to be unfit for their original functions; while, on the contrary, the component parts of a community are undergoing daily the process of physical renovation and of moral improvement. Therefore all that we hear every day of the week about the decay of the Turkish empire, and its being a dead body or a sapless trunk, and so forth, is pure and unadulterated nonsense.' Still, as he says elsewhere, ' you can't expect much energy of a people with no heels to their shoes.'

In a letter to Lord Clarendon of May 22, 1853, Lord Palmerston writes as follows :—

' The policy and practice of the Russian Government have always been to push forward its encroachments as fast and as far as the apathy or want of firmness of other Governments would allow it to go, but always to stop and retire when it was met with decided resistance, and then to wait for the next favourable opportunity to make another spring on its intended victim. In furtherance of this policy, the Russian Government has always had two strings to its bow—moderate language and disinterested professions at Petersburg and at London; active aggression by its agents on the scene of operations. If the aggression succeed locally, the Petersburg Government adopts them as *a fait accompli* which it did not intend, but cannot, in honour, recede from. If the local agents fail, they are disavowed and recalled, and the language previously held is appealed to as a proof that the agents have overstepped their instructions. This was exemplified in the treaty of Unkiar Skelessi and in the exploits of Simonivitch and Vikovitch in Persia. Orloff succeeded in extorting the treaty of Unkiar Skelessi from the Turks, and it was represented as a sudden thought, suggested by the circumstances of the time and place, and not the result of any previous instructions; but having been done it could not be undone. On the other hand, Simonivitch and Vikovitch failed in getting possession of Herat in consequence of our vigorous measures of resistance; and as they failed, and when they failed, they were disavowed and recalled, and the language previously held at St. Petersburg was appealed to as a proof of the sincerity of the disavowal, although no human being with two ideas in his head could for a moment doubt that they had acted under specific instructions.'

Again, on September 21, 1853, he says in a letter to Mr. Sidney Herbert:—

'I am coming reluctantly to the conclusion that war between the Emperor of Russia and Turkey is becoming inevitable. If such war should happen, upon his head be the responsibility of the consequences. I by no means think with you that he will have an easy victory over the Turks. On the contrary, if the betting is not even, I would lay odds on the Turks. All that the Turkish army wants is directing officers, and it would be strange indeed if England, France, Poland and Hungary could not amply supply that deficiency. I do not believe in the disaffection of the Turkish provinces—this is an oft-repeated tale got up by the Russians. The best refutation is that for many months past the Russian agents have been trying *per fas et nefas* to provoke insurrection in Turkey, and have failed. The fact is that the Christian subjects in Turkey know too well what Russian *régime* is not to be aware that it is of all things the most to be dreaded.'

Here is a striking passage on the 'bag-and-baggage' policy:

'I have no partiality for the Turks as Mohammedans, and should be very glad if they could be turned into Christians; but as to the character of the Turkish Government in regard to its treatment of Christians, I am well convinced that there are a vast number of Christians under the Governments of Russia, Austria, Rome, and Naples, who would be rejoiced to be as well treated and to enjoy as much security for person and property as the Christian subjects of the Sultan. To expel from Europe the Sultan and his two million of Mussulman subjects, including the army and the bulk of the landowners, might not be an easy task; still the five Powers might effect it, and play the Polish drama over again. But they would find the building up still more difficult than the pulling down. There are no sufficient Christian elements as yet for a Christian State in European Turkey capable of performing its functions as a component part of the European system. The Greeks are a small minority, and could not be the governing race. The Sclavonians, who are the majority, do not possess the conditions necessary for becoming the bones and sinews of a new State. A reconstruction of Turkey means neither more nor less than its subjection to Russia, direct or indirect, immediate or for a time delayed.'

In the following letter to Lord Clarendon, which is dated May 14, 1855, he summarises the most necessary reforms for Turkey, and anticipates part of the Constitution just promulgated:—

'What remains to be done for the nonconformists in Turkey would be, I apprehend, speaking generally:—(*a*.) Capacity for military service by voluntary enlistment, and eligibility to rise to any rank in the army. (*b*.) Admission of non-Mussulman evidence in civil as well as criminal cases. (*c*.) Establishment of mixed courts of justice (with an equal number of Christian and Mussulman judges) for all cases in which Mohammedans and non-Mohammedans are parties. (*d*.) Appointment of a Christian officer as assessor to every governor of a province, when that governor is a Mussulman; such assessor to be of suitable rank, and to have full liberty to appeal to Constantinople against any act of the governor unjust, oppressive, or corrupt. (*e*.) Eligibility of Christians to all places in the Administration, whether at Constantinople or in the Provinces, and a practical application of this rule by the appointment of Christians at once to some places of trust, civil and military. (*f.*) The total abolition of the present system, by which offices at Constantinople and in the province are bought and sold, and given to unfit and unworthy men for money paid or promised. Such men become tyrants in their offices, either from incapacity or bad passions, or from a desire to repay themselves the money paid for their appointments. There ought not only to be complete toleration of non-Mussulman religions, but all punishment on converts from Islam, whether natives or foreigners, ought to be abolished.'

The following forms part of a letter to Baron Brunnow, the Russian Ambassador, on the occasion of the Polish insurrection in 1863:—

'Je regrette beaucoup les insurrections qui ont éclaté en Pologne et en plusieurs des provinces de la Russie. . . . Mais, quant au Gouvernement Russe, je considère ces insurrections, comme une juste punition du Ciel pour les menées dont ce Gouvernement a été coupable, pour préparer pour le printemps des révoltes et des insurrections dans la Moldo-Wallachie, en Servie et en Bosnie, contre le Sultan.

Non lex est justior ulla
Quam necis artifices arte perire sua.

'Il est vrai que ces insurrections, ou éclatées ou préparées, ne menacent de mort ni l'Empire Russe ni l'Empire Ottoman; la Russie saura mettre ordre dans les provinces, et la Porte saura apprendre à Couza, au Prince de Servie, et aux Bosniacs, qu'il est mieux de rester fidèle à son Souverain que d'écouter les conseils subversifs d'un voisin ambitieux. Mais, pour le moment, la Russie souffre dans son intérieur le mal qu'elle a l'intention d'infliger à un voisin inoffensif. Vous concevez bien que je parle maintenant des cent mille et plus de fusils que la Gouvernement Russe a envoyés en Servie et en Bosnie par des chemins détournés et avec toutes les précautions pour cacher, autant que possible, ce que l'on faisait ; et je fais allusion aussi à cette nuée d'agents provocateurs qui, venant de la Russie, abondent et travaillent dans les provinces Européennes de la Turquie.'

The letter just quoted was written, it must be remembered, seven years after the close of the Crimean war ; and it shows how systematic and how sustained has been the agitation carried on by Russian agents in Servia. We may conclude this series of extracts with one from Lord Dalling's 'Biography of Lord Palmerston,' which we specially commend to those agitators who recommended that, before entering into negotiations at Constantinople, we should take care to announce, beyond the possibility of misconstruction, that no possible action on the part of Russia would induce England to take up arms.

'Lord Palmerston maintained, indeed, as may have been learnt from his correspondence relative to Belgium, that the true policy of England was never to put forward any pretension that was unjust, but to give up none which justice supported so long as there was a possibility of defending it by arms, if its value justified our having recourse to arms ; by negotiating if we carried our defence no farther than argument ; leaving our adversary in doubt, however, till the last as to whether we should finally protest or fight. He laughed to scorn the theory that you should yield immediately everything for which you are not prepared to go to war. "Why," he used to say, "every State would be disposed to give up three out of every four questions sooner than go to war to maintain them. If you choose to give way hastily on these because you are not prepared to go to war for them, you will most frequently anticipate your antagonist. Nor is this all. It is not concession on this matter or that which is of national importance; it is the habit of making concessions, and creating a belief that you will make them, which is fatal to a nation's interest, tranquillity, and honour. To create such a belief in a Democratic Government, especially a Government which is prone to seek at all times to please the multitude, is a sure way to have constant troubles with that Government; from every difficulty you avoid to-day will arise twenty difficulties round you to-morrow; for every man who seeks popularity will attempt to gain it at your expense."'

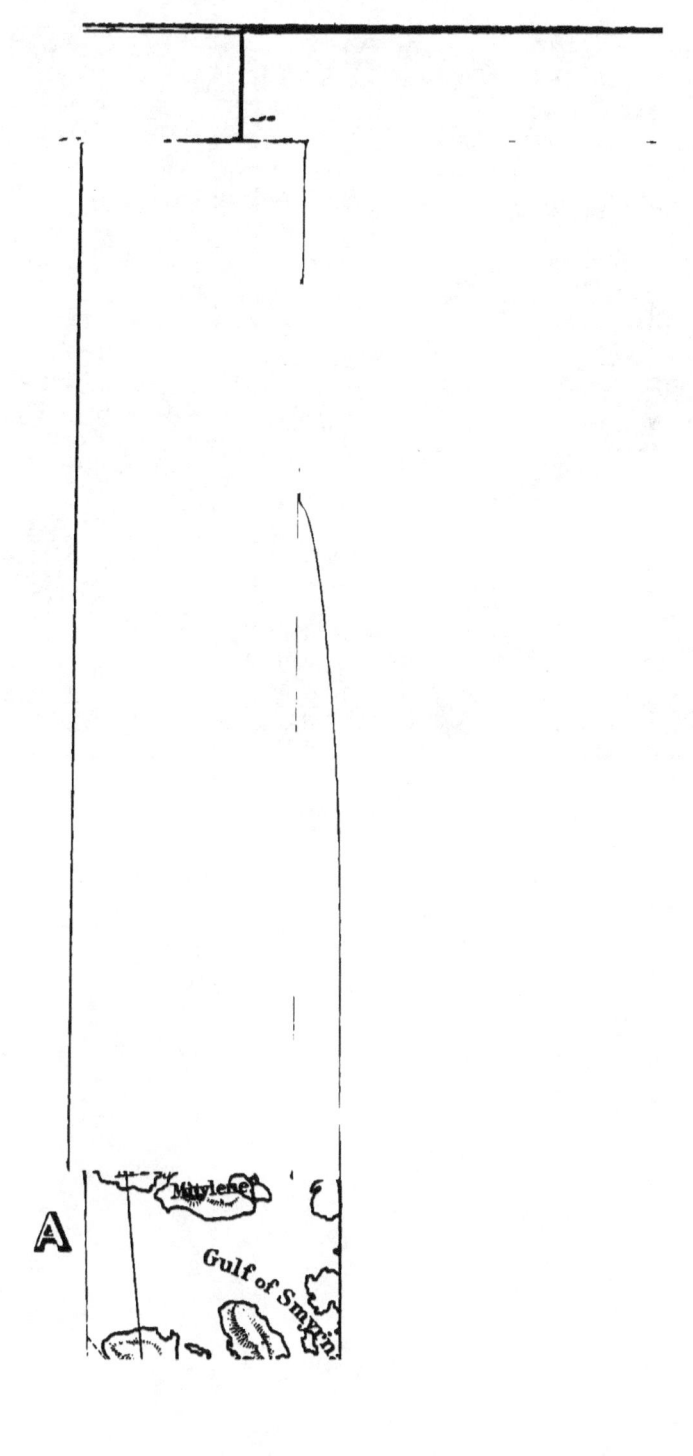

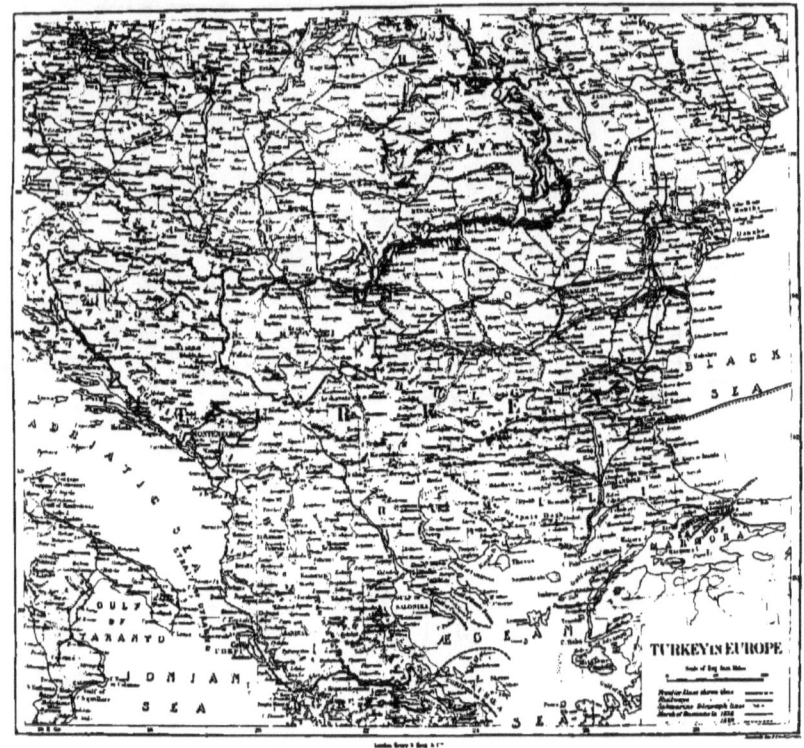

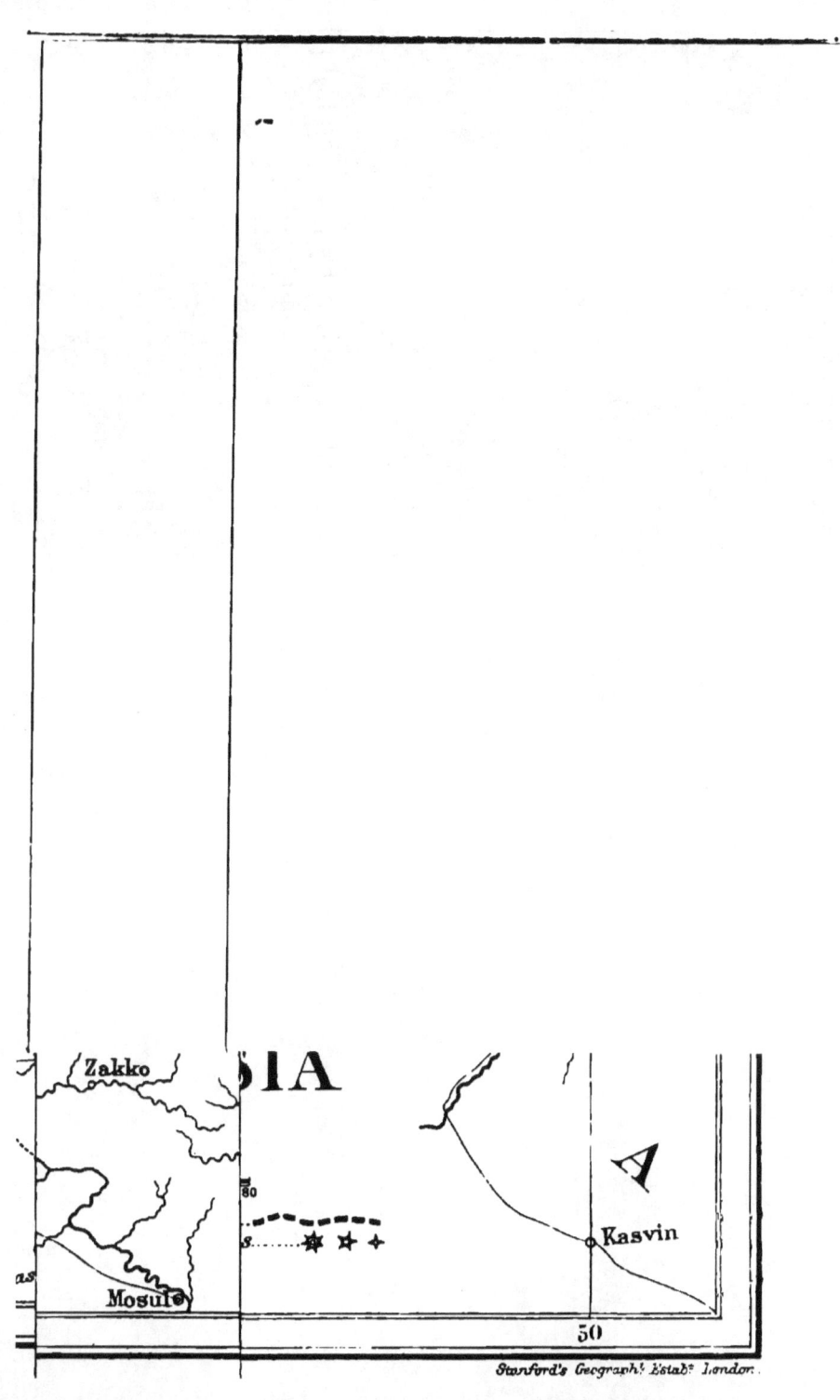

The Russians in Central Asia.

A Critical Examination, down to the Present Time, of the Geography and History of Central Asia.

By Baron F. Von Hellwald.

Translated by Lieut.-Col. Theodore Wirgman, LL.B.

With Map. Large post 8vo. cloth, price 12s.

Explorations in Central Asia are being simultaneously carried on by the Russians and the English, the two great rivals in the Asiatic world. Scientific research follows in the footsteps of military operations. Russia gives to Asia culture and civilisation. Every disinterested man must admit that this opening of new spheres to the development of civilisation is the greatest gain which mankind derives from warlike expeditions.

'A learned account of the geography of this still ill-known land, of the characteristics of its main divisions, of the nature and habits of its numerous races, and of the progress through it of Russian influence......It contains a large amount of valuable information.'—TIMES.

'A lucidly written and apparently accurate account of Turkestan, its geographical features and its history. Its worth to the reader is further enhanced by a well-executed map, based on the most recent Russian surveys.'—GLASGOW NEWS.

'We think that the book is important; the author has done us signal service in bringing the facts so forcibly before us that they must arrest attention. Nor is our debt a slight one to Lieutenant Wirgman, who has accomplished his task of translation thoroughly well.'
WESTMINSTER REVIEW.

'We have reason to thank Herr Von Hellwald for his highly interesting and right-minded work, which is by far the best on this subject which has been produced in England........ Colorel Wirgman has done a good service to his mother country in publishing his translation, and has accomplished his task well.'—PALL MALL GAZETTE.

HENRY S. KING & CO., London.

EASTERN EXPERIENCES.

By L. BOWRING, C.S.I., Lord Canning's Private Secretary, and for many years Chief Commissioner of Mysore and Coorg.

Illustrated with Maps and Diagrams.

Demy 8vo. cloth, price 16s.

The sketches contained in this volume are based upon notes made during the course of several tours through the provinces of Mysore and Coorg. Information has been added from published official reports and such other sources as could be comprised within moderate limits.

'An admirable and exhaustive geographical, political, and industrial survey.'—ATHENÆUM.

'Interesting even to the general reader, but especially so those who may have a special concern in that portion of our Indian Empire.'—MORNING POST.

'This compact and methodical summary of the most authentic information relating to countries whose welfare is intimately connected with our own.'—DAILY NEWS.

THE ASHANTEE WAR.

A Popular Narrative.

By the Special Correspondent of the *Daily News*.

Crown 8vo. cloth, price 6s.

This account of the Ashantee War does not pretend to the dignity of a HISTORY, but attempts to provide a connected narrative of what took place, with descriptions of the country and scenes passed through.

'Trustworthy and readable, and well fitted to serve its purpose as a popular narrative. ......The *Daily News* correspondent secures interest chiefly by bringing together suggestive incidents, and by clearing up points that his readers would naturally be desirous of knowing.'—EXAMINER.

'What this writer has to tell us is well told, and it forms a valuable and welcome addition to the literature of the Ashantee War.'—NAVAL AND MILITARY GAZETTE.

HENRY S. KING & CO., London.

The History of Japan

FROM THE EARLIEST PERIOD TO THE PRESENT TIME.

By F. O. ADAMS, H.B.M.'s Secretary of Embassy at Paris, formerly H.B.M.'s Chargé d'Affaires, and Secretary of Legation at Yedo.

New Edition, revised. In 2 vols. with Maps and Plans, demy 8vo. cloth, price 21s. each.

This is the only History of Japan accessible to English readers. It is compiled from official sources, and the high diplomatic position long held by the Author gave him an insight into Japanese politics possessed by few Europeans.

'He marshals his facts with skill and judgment; and he writes with an elegance worthy of a very skilled craftsman in literary work......We hope Mr. Adams will not keep the public long without the second volume, for the appearance of which all who read the first will anxiously look.'—STANDARD.

'As a diplomatic study, and as referring to a deeply interesting episode in contemporary history, it is well worth reading. The information it contains is trustworthy, and is carefully compiled, and the style is all that can be desired.'—SATURDAY REVIEW.

'A most valuable contribution to our knowledge of an interesting people.'—EXAMINER.

'It will form a valuable record of the stirring events which have marked the annals of this strange country during the last twenty years, long after the immediate interest now attaching to its transformation has ceased.'—ACADEMY.

The Inner Life of Syria, Palestine, and the Holy Land.

By Mrs. RICHARD BURTON.

With Photographic Portraits, Coloured Illustrations, and Map.

Second Edition, revised, 2 vols. demy 8vo. cloth, price 24s.

This volume is intended to present a sketch of the *vie intime* of the Holy Land in general and of Damascus in particular, and to convey an idea of the life which an Englishwoman may make for herself in the East.

'We must commend heartily to our readers Mrs. Burton's account of "The Inner Life of Syria."'—EXAMINER.

'Mrs. Burton presents us with vivid pictures of the outer as well as the inner life of the Syrians. We welcome her book the more warmly because it may be long before any one with equal powers of observation enjoys equal opportunities of instructing us.'—PALL MALL GAZETTE.

'A more delightful and instructive book on "The Inner Life of Syria, Palestine, and the Holy Land" we have never read. We heartily recommend a perusal thereof to every one interested in this most attractive subject.'—JEWISH CHRONICLE.

HENRY S. KING & CO., London.

WESTERN INDIA
BEFORE AND DURING THE MUTINIES.

Pictures Drawn from Life.

By Major-General G. LE GRAND JACOB, K.C.S.I., C.B.

Second Edition.   Crown 8vo. cloth, price 7s. 6d.

'The most important contribution to the history of Western India during the Mutinies which has yet, in a popular form, been made public.'—ATHENÆUM.

'Few men are more competent than himself to speak authoritatively concerning Indian affairs.'—STANDARD.

'This volume is interesting, and contains many valuable remarks on the policy of the Government of India, the result of a large experience in a department which is the best school for Indian statesmen.'—ENGLISHMAN OF INDIA.

'We cannot leave this book without a word of commendation for the fresh and pleasant style in which it is written.'—WESTMINSTER REVIEW.

PERSIA—ANCIENT AND MODERN.

By JOHN PIGGOTT, F.S.A., F.R.G.S.

Post 8vo. cloth, price 10s. 6d.

A general view of Ancient and Modern Persia is here presented to the reader. It is supplemented by chapters on the religion, literature, commerce, arts, sciences, army education, language, sport, &c., of the country. In the chapter on travelling, the routes to the country, its climate, roads, modes of conveyance, and all other necessary details are described.

'That Mr. Piggott has spared no pains or research in the execution of his work is apparent in the list of authorities, classic and modern, which he continually quotes; his style, also, when not recounting history, is lively and pleasant, and the anecdotes which he culls from the writings of travellers are frequently amusing.'—HOUR.

'Mr. Piggott has made good use of the materials collected by others, and the result is a clear, readable, and truthful account of the political history of modern Persia.'—ATHENÆUM.

'He has read up to the level of his subject; old and new authorities have been explored and digested; the style is clear and unambitious; and his compilation is well planned and is not too long.'—SATURDAY REVIEW.

HENRY S. KING & CO., London.

65, Cornhill, and 1, Paternoster Square,
London, December, 1876.

A LIST OF
HENRY S. KING AND CO.'S PUBLICATIONS.

ABBEY (Henry).
Ballads of Good Deeds, and Other Verses. Fcap. 8vo. Cloth gilt, price 5s.

ABDULLA (Hakayit).
Autobiography of a Malay Munshi. Translated by J. T. Thomson, F.R.G.S. With Photolithograph Page of Abdulla's MS. Post 8vo. Cloth, price 12s.

ADAMS (A. L.), M.A., M.B, F.R.S., F.G.S.
Field and Forest Rambles of a Naturalist in New Brunswick. With Notes and Observations on the Natural History of Eastern Canada. Illustrated. 8vo. Cloth, price 14s.

ADAMS (F. O.), F.R.G.S.
The History of Japan. From the Earliest Period to the Present Time. New Edition, revised. 2 volumes. With Maps and Plans. Demy 8vo. Cloth, price 21s. each.

ADAMS (W. D., Jun.).
Lyrics of Love, from Shakespeare to Tennyson. Selected and arranged by. Fcap. 8vo. Cloth extra, gilt edges, price 3s. 6d.

ADAMS (John), M.A.
St. Malo's Quest, and other Poems. Fcap. 8vo. Cloth, 5s.

ADON.
Through Storm & Sunshine. Illustrated by M. E. Edwards, A. T. H. Paterson, and the Author. Crown 8vo Cloth, price 7s. 6d.

A. K. H. B.
A Scotch Communion Sunday, to which are added Certain Discourses from a University City. By the Author of "The Recreations of a Country Parson." Second Edition. Crown 8vo. Cloth, price 5s.

ALLEN (Rev. R.), M.A.
Abraham; his Life, Times, and Travels, as told by a Contemporary 3,800 years ago. With Map. Post 8vo. Cloth, price 10s. 6d.

AMOS (Prof. Sheldon).
Science of Law. Second Edition. Crown 8vo. Cloth, price 5s.
Volume X. of The International Scientific Series.

ANDERSON (Rev. C.), M.A.
New Readings of Old Parables. Demy 8vo. Cloth, price 4s. 6d.

Church Thought and Church Work. Edited by. Second Edition. Demy 8vo. Cloth, price 7s. 6d.

Words and Works in a London Parish. Edited by. Second Edition. Demy 8vo. Cloth, price 6s.

The Curate of Shyre. Second Edition. 8vo. Cloth, price 7s. 6d.

ANDERSON (Col. R. P.).
Victories and Defeats. An Attempt to explain the Causes which have led to them. An Officer's Manual. Demy 8vo. Cloth, price 14s.

ANDERSON (R. C.), C.E.
Tables for Facilitating the Calculation of every Detail in connection with Earthen and Masonry Dams. Royal 8vo. Cloth, price £2 2s.

A

ANSON (Lieut.-Col. The Hon. A.), V.C., M.P.
The Abolition of Purchase and the Army Regulation Bill of 1871. Crown 8vo. Sewed, price 1s.
Army Reserves and Militia Reforms. Crown 8vo. Sewed, price 1s.
Story of the Supersessions. Crown 8vo. Sewed, price 6d.

ARCHER (Thomas).
About my Father's Business. Work amidst the Sick, the Sad, and the Sorrowing. Crown 8vo. Cloth, price 5s.

ARGYLE (Duke of).
Speeches on the Second Reading of the Church Patronage (Scotland) Bill in the House of Lords, June 2, 1874; and Earl of Camperdown's Amendment, June 9, 1874, placing the Election of Ministers in the hands of Ratepayers. Crown 8vo. Sewed, price 1s.

Army of the North German Confederation.
A Brief Description of its Organization, of the Different Branches of the Service and their *rôle* in War, of its Mode of Fighting, &c., &c. Translated from the Corrected Edition, by permission of the Author, by Colonel Edward Newdigate. Demy 8vo. Cloth, price 5s.

Ashantee War (The).
A Popular Narrative. By the Special Correspondent of the "Daily News." Crown 8vo. Cloth, price 6s.

ASHTON (J.).
Rough Notes of a Visit to Belgium, Sedan, and Paris, in September, 1870-71. Crown 8vo. Cloth, price 3s. 6d.

Aunt Mary's Bran Pie.
By the author of "St. Olave's." Illustrated. Cloth, price 3s. 6d.

Aurora.
A Volume of Verse. Fcap. 8vo. Cloth, price 5s.

AYRTON (J. C.).
A Scotch Wooing. 2 vols. Crown 8vo. Cloth.

BAGEHOT (Walter).
Physics and Politics; or, Thoughts on the Application of the Principles of "Natural Selection" and "Inheritance" to Political Society. Third Edition. Crown 8vo. Cloth, price 4s.
Volume II. of The International Scientific Series.
The English Constitution. A New Edition, Revised and Corrected, with an Introductory Dissertation on Recent Changes and Events. Crown 8vo. Cloth, price 7s. 6d.
Lombard Street. A Description of the Money Market. Sixth Edition. Crown 8vo. Cloth, price 7s. 6d.

BAIN (Alexander), LL.D.
Mind and Body: the Theories of their relation. Fifth Edition. Crown 8vo. Cloth, price 4s.
Volume IV. of The International Scientific Series.

BALDWIN (Capt. J. H.), F.Z.S., Bengal Staff Corps.
The Large and Small Game of Bengal and the North-Western Provinces of India. 4to. With numerous Illustrations. Cloth, price 21s.

BANKS (Mrs. G. L.).
God's Providence House. New Edition. Crown 8vo. Cloth, price 3s. 6d.

BARING (T. C.), M.A., M.P.
Pindar in English Rhyme. Being an Attempt to render the Epinikian Odes with the principal remaining Fragments of Pindar into English Rhymed Verse. Small Quarto. Cloth, price 7s.

BARLEE (Ellen).
Locked Out: a Tale of the Strike. With a Frontispiece. Royal 16mo. Cloth, price 1s. 6d.

BAUR (Ferdinand), Dr. Ph., Professor in Maulbronn.
A Philological Introduction to Greek and Latin for Students. Translated and adapted from the German of. By C. KEGAN PAUL, M.A. Oxon., and the Rev. E. D. STONE, M.A., late Fellow of King's College, Cambridge, and Assistant Master at Eton. Crown 8vo. Cloth, price 6s.

BAYNES (Rev. Canon R. H.), M.A.

Home Songs for Quiet Hours. Third Edition. Fcap. 8vo. Cloth extra, price 3s. 6d.
This may also be had handsomely bound in Morocco with gilt edges.

BECKER (Bernard H.).

The Scientific Societies of London. Crown 8vo. Cloth, price 5s.

BENNETT (Dr. W. C.).

Baby May. Home Poems and Ballads. With Frontispiece. Crown 8vo. Cloth elegant, price 6s.

Baby May and Home Poems. Fcap. 8vo. Sewed in Coloured Wrapper, price 1s.

Narrative Poems & Ballads. Fcap. 8vo. Sewed in Coloured Wrapper, price 1s.

Songs for Sailors. Dedicated by Special Request to H. R. H. the Duke of Edinburgh. With Steel Portrait and Illustrations. Crown 8vo. Cloth, price 3s. 6d.
An Edition in Illustrated Paper Covers, price 1s.

Songs of a Song Writer. Crown 8vo. Cloth, price 6s.

BENNIE (Rev. J. N.), M.A.

The Eternal Life. Sermons preached during the last twelve years. Crown 8vo. Cloth, price 6s.

BERNARD (Bayle).

Samuel Lover, the Life and Unpublished Works of. In 2 vols. With a Steel Portrait. Post 8vo. Cloth, price 21s.

BERNSTEIN (Prof.).

The Five Senses of Man. With 91 Illustrations. Second Edition. Crown 8vo. Cloth, price 5s.
Volume XXI. of The International Scientific Series.

BETHAM - EDWARDS (Miss M.).

Kitty. With a Frontispiece. Crown 8vo. Cloth, price 3s. 6d.

Mademoiselle Josephine's Fridays, and Other Stories. Crown 8vo. Cloth, price 7s. 6d.

BISCOE (A. C.).

The Earls of Middleton, Lords of Clermont and of Fettercairn, and the Middleton Family. Crown 8vo. Cloth, price 10s. 6d.

BISSET (A.)

History of the Struggle for Parliamentary Government in England. 2 vols. Demy 8vo. Cloth, price 24s.

BLANC (H.), M.D.

Cholera: How to Avoid and Treat it. Popular and Practical Notes. Crown 8vo. Cloth, price 4s. 6d.

BLASERNA (Prof. Pietro).

The Theory of Sound in its Relation to Music. With numerous Illustrations. Crown 8vo. Cloth, price 5s.
Volume XXII. of The International Scientific Series.

BLUME (Major W.).

The Operations of the German Armies in France, from Sedan to the end of the war of 1870-71. With Map. From the Journals of the Head-quarters Staff. Translated by the late E. M. Jones, Maj. 20th Foot, Prof. of Mil. Hist., Sandhurst. Demy 8vo. Cloth, price 9s.

BOGUSLAWSKI (Capt. A. von).

Tactical Deductions from the War of 1870-71. Translated by Colonel Sir Lumley Graham, Bart., late 18th (Royal Irish) Regiment. Third Edition, Revised and Corrected. Demy 8vo. Cloth, price 7s.

BONWICK (J.), F.R.G.S.

The Tasmanian Lily. With Frontispiece. Crown 8vo. Cloth, price 5s.

Mike Howe, the Bushranger of Van Diemen's Land. With Frontispiece. Crown 8vo. Cloth, price 5s.

BOSWELL (R. B.), M.A., Oxon.

Metrical Translations from the Greek and Latin Poets, and other Poems. Crown 8vo. Cloth, price 5s.

BOTHMER (Countess von).

Cruel as the Grave. A Novel. 3 vols. Crown 8vo. Cloth.

BOWEN (H. C.), M.A., Head Master of the Grocers' Company's Middle Class School at Hackney.

Studies in English, for the use of Modern Schools. Small Crown 8vo. Cloth, price 1s. 6d.

BOWRING (L.), C.S.I.

Eastern Experiences. Illustrated with Maps and Diagrams. Demy 8vo. Cloth, price 16s.

BRADLEY (F. H.).

Ethical Studies. Critical Essays in Moral Philosophy. Large post 8vo. Cloth, price 9s.

Brave Men's Footsteps. By the Editor of "Men who have Risen." A Book of Example and Anecdote for Young People. With Four Illustrations by C. Doyle. Third Edition. Crown 8vo. Cloth, price 3s. 6d.

BRIALMONT (Col. A.).

Hasty Intrenchments. Translated by Lieut. Charles A. Empson, R.A. With Nine Plates. Demy 8vo. Cloth, price 6s.

Briefs and Papers. Being Sketches of the Bar and the Press. By Two Idle Apprentices. Second Edition. Crown 8vo. Cloth, price 7s. 6d.

BROOKE (Rev. J. M. S.), M.A.

Heart, be Still. A Sermon preached in Holy Trinity Church, Southall. Imperial 32mo. Sewed, price 6d.

BROOKE (Rev. S. A.), M.A., Chaplain in Ordinary to Her Majesty the Queen, and Minister of Bedford Chapel, Bloomsbury.

The Late Rev. F. W. Robertson, M.A., Life and Letters of. Edited by.

I. Uniform with the Sermons. 2 vols. With Steel Portrait. Price 7s. 6d.

II. Library Edition. 8vo. With Two Steel Portraits. Price 12s.

III. A Popular Edition, in 1 vol. 8vo. Price 6s.

Theology in the English Poets. — COWPER, COLERIDGE, WORDSWORTH, and BURNS. Third Edition. Post 8vo. Cloth, price 9s.

Christ in Modern Life. Ninth Edition. Crown 8vo. Cloth, price 7s. 6d.

Sermons. First Series. Ninth Edition. Crown 8vo. Cloth, price 6s.

Sermons. Second Series. Third Edition. Crown 8vo. Cloth, price 7s.

Frederick Denison Maurice: The Life and Work of. A Memorial Sermon. Crown 8vo. Sewed, price 1s.

BROOKE (W. G.), M.A.

The Public Worship Regulation Act. With a Classified Statement of its Provisions, Notes, and Index. Third Edition, revised and corrected. Crown 8vo. Cloth, price 3s. 6d.

Six Privy Council Judgments—1850-1872. Annotated by. Third Edition. Crown 8vo. Cloth, price 9s.

BROUN (J. A.).

Magnetic Observations at Trevandrum and Augustia Malley. Vol. I. 4to. Cloth, price 63s.

The Report from above, separately sewed, price 21s.

BROWN (Rev. J. Baldwin), B.A.

The Higher Life. Its Reality, Experience, and Destiny. Fourth Edition. Crown 8vo. Cloth, price 7s. 6d.

Doctrine of Annihilation in the Light of the Gospel of Love. Five Discourses. Second Edition. Crown 8vo. Cloth, price 2s. 6d.

BROWN (J. Croumbie), LL.D.

Reboisement in France; or, Records of the Replanting of the Alps, the Cevennes, and the Pyrenees with Trees, Herbage, and Bush. Demy 8vo. Cloth, price 12s. 6d.

The Hydrology of Southern Africa. Demy 8vo. Cloth, price 10s. 6d.

BROWNE (Rev. M. E.)

Until the Day Dawn. Four Advent Lectures. Crown 8vo. Cloth, price 2s. 6d.

BRYANT (W. C.)

Poems. Red-line Edition. With 24 Illustrations and Portrait of the Author. Crown 8vo. Cloth extra, price 7s. 6d.

A Cheaper Edition, with Frontispiece. Small crown 8vo. Cloth, price 3s. 6d.

BUCHANAN (Robert).

Poetical Works. Collected Edition, in 3 vols., with Portrait. Crown 8vo. Cloth, price 6s. each.

Master-Spirits. Post 8vo. Cloth, price 10s. 6d.

BULKELEY (Rev. H. J.).

Walled in, and other Poems. Crown 8vo. Cloth, price 5s.

BUNNETT (F. E.).

Linked at Last. Crown 8vo. Cloth.

BURTON (Mrs. Richard).

The Inner Life of Syria, Palestine, and the Holy Land. With Maps, Photographs, and Coloured Plates. 2 vols. Second Edition. Demy 8vo. Cloth, price 24s.

CADELL (Mrs. H. M.).

Ida Craven: A Novel. 2 vols. Crown 8vo. Cloth.

CALDERON.

Calderon's Dramas: The Wonder-Working Magician,—Life is a Dream—The Purgatory of St. Patrick. Translated by Denis Florence MacCarthy. Post 8vo. Cloth, price 10s.

CARLISLE (A. D.), B. A.

Round the World in 1870. A Volume of Travels, with Maps. New and Cheaper Edition. Demy 8vo. Cloth, price 6s.

CARNE (Miss E. T.).

The Realm of Truth. Crown 8vo. Cloth, price 5s. 6d.

CARPENTER (E.).

Narcissus and other Poems. Fcap. 8vo. Cloth, price 5s.

CARPENTER (W. B.), LL.D., M.D., F.R.S., &c.

The Principles of Mental Physiology. With their Applications to the Training and Discipline of the Mind, and the Study of its Morbid Conditions. Illustrated. Fourth Edition. 8vo. Cloth, price 12s.

CARR (Lisle).

Judith Gwynne. 3 vols. Second Edition. Crown 8vo. Cloth.

CHRISTOPHERSON (The late Rev. Henry), M.A.

Sermons. With an Introduction by John Rae, LL.D., F.S.A. First Series. Crown 8vo. Cloth, price 7s. 6d.

Sermons. With an Introduction by John Rae, LL.D., F.S.A. Second Series. Crown 8vo. Cloth price 6s.

CLAYTON (Cecil).

Effie's Game; How She Lost and How She Won. A Novel. 2 vols. Cloth.

CLERK (Mrs. Godfrey).

'Ilâm en Nâs. Historical Tales and Anecdotes of the Times of the Early Khalifahs. Translated from the Arabic Originals. Illustrated with Historical and Explanatory Notes. Crown 8vo. Cloth, price 7s.

CLERY (C.), Capt.

Minor Tactics. With 26 Maps and Plans. Third and revised Edition. Demy 8vo. Cloth, price 16s.

CLODD (Edward), F.R.A.S.

The Childhood of the World: a Simple Account of Man in Early Times. Third Edition. Crown 8vo. Cloth, price 3s.
 A Special Edition for Schools. Price 1s.

The Childhood of Religions. Including a Simple Account of the Birth and Growth of Myths and Legends. Crown 8vo. Cloth, price 5s.

COLERIDGE (Sara).

Pretty Lessons in Verse for Good Children, with some Lessons in Latin, in Easy Rhyme. A New Edition. Illustrated. Fcap. 8vo. Cloth, price 3s. 6d.

Phantasmion. A Fairy Tale. With an Introductory Preface by the Right Hon. Lord Coleridge, of Ottery St. Mary. A New Edition. Illustrated. Crown 8vo. Cloth, price 7s. 6d.

Memoir and Letters of Sara Coleridge. Edited by her Daughter. With Index. 2 vols. With Two Portraits. Third Edition, Revised and Corrected. Crown 8vo. Cloth, price 24s.
 Cheap Edition. With one Portrait. Cloth, price 7s. 6d.

COLLINS (Mortimer).

The Princess Clarice. A Story of 1871. 2 vols. Cloth.

Squire Silchester's Whim. 3 vols. Cloth.

Miranda. A Midsummer Madness. 3 vols. Cloth.

Inn of Strange Meetings, and other Poems. Crown 8vo. Cloth, price 5s.

The Secret of Long Life. Dedicated by special permission to Lord St. Leonards. Fourth Edition. Large crown 8vo. Cloth, price 5s.

COLLINS (Rev. R.), M.A.

Missionary Enterprise in the East. With special reference to the Syrian Christians of Malabar, and the results of modern Missions. With Four Illustrations. Crown 8vo. Cloth, price 6s.

CONGREVE (Richard), M.A., M.R.C.P.L.

Human Catholicism. Two Sermons delivered at the Positivist School on the Festival of Humanity, 87 and 88, January 1, 1875 and 1876. Demy 8vo. Sewed, price 1s.

CONWAY (Moncure D.).

Republican Superstitions. Illustrated by the Political History of the United States. Including a Correspondence with M. Louis Blanc. Crown 8vo. Cloth, price 5s.

CONYERS (Ansley).

Chesterleigh. 3 vols. Crown 8vo. Cloth.

COOKE (M. C.), M.A., LL.D.

Fungi; their Nature, Influences, Uses, &c. Edited by the Rev. M. J. Berkeley, M.A., F.L.S. With Illustrations. Second Edition. Crown 8vo. Cloth, price 5s.
 Volume XIV. of The International Scientific Series.

COOKE (Prof. J. P.), of the Harvard University.

The New Chemistry. With 31 Illustrations. Third Edition. Crown 8vo. Cloth, price 5s.
 Volume IX. of The International Scientific Series.

Scientific Culture. Crown 8vo. Cloth, price 1s.

COOPER (T. T.), F.R.G.S.

The Mishmee Hills: an Account of a Journey made in an Attempt to Penetrate Thibet from Assam, to open New Routes for Commerce. Second Edition. With Four Illustrations and Map. Post 8vo. Cloth, price 10s. 6d.

Cornhill Library of Fiction (The). Crown 8vo. Cloth, price 3s. 6d. per volume.
 Half-a-Dozen Daughters. By J. Masterman.
 The House of Raby. By Mrs. G. Hooper.
 A Fight for Life. By Moy Thomas.
 Robin Gray. By Charles Gibbon.
 Kitty. By Miss M. Betham-Edwards.
 One of Two; or, The Left-Handed Bride. By J. Hain Friswell.
 Ready-Money Mortiboy. A Matter-of-Fact Story.
 God's Providence House. By Mrs. G. L. Banks.
 For Lack of Gold. By Charles Gibbon.
 Abel Drake's Wife. By John Saunders.
 Hirell. By John Saunders.

CORY (Lieut. Col. Arthur).

The Eastern Menace; or, Shadows of Coming Events. Crown 8vo. Cloth, price 5s.

Cosmos.

A Poem. Fcap. 8vo. Cloth, price 3s. 6d.

COTTON (R. T.).

Mr. Carington. A Tale of Love and Conspiracy. 3 vols. Crown 8vo. Cloth.

CRESSWELL (Mrs. G.).

The King's Banner. Drama in Four Acts. Five Illustrations. 4to. Cloth, price 10s. 6d.

CROMPTON (Henry).

Industrial Conciliation. Fcap. 8vo. Cloth, price 2s. 6d.

CUMMINS (H. I.), M. A.

Parochial Charities of the City of London. Sewed, price 1s.

CURWEN (Henry).

Sorrow and Song: Studies of Literary Struggle. Henry Mürger—Novalis—Alexander Petöfi—Honoré de Balzac—Edgar Allan Poe—André Chénier. 2 vols. Crown 8vo. Cloth, price 15s.

DANCE (Rev. C. D.).

Recollections of Four Years in Venezuela. With Three Illustrations and a Map. Crown 8vo. Cloth, price 7s. 6d.

D'ANVERS (N. R.).

The Suez Canal: Letters and Documents descriptive of its Rise and Progress in 1854-56. By Ferdinand de Lesseps. Translated by. Demy 8vo. Cloth, price 10s. 6d.

Little Minnie's Troubles. An Every-day Chronicle. With Four Illustrations by W. H. Hughes. Fcap. Cloth, price 3s. 6d.

DAVIDSON (Rev. Samuel), D.D., LL.D.

The New Testament, translated from the Latest Greek Text of Tischendorf. A new and thoroughly revised Edition. Post 8vo. Cloth, price 10s. 6d.

Canon of the Bible: Its Formation, History, and Fluctuations. Small crown 8vo. Cloth, price 5s.

DAVIES (G. Christopher).

Mountain, Meadow, and Mere: a Series of Outdoor Sketches of Sport, Scenery, Adventures, and Natural History. With Sixteen Illustrations by Bosworth W. Harcourt. Crown 8vo. Cloth, price 6s.

Rambles and Adventures of Our School Field Club. With Four Illustrations. Crown 8vo. Cloth, price 5s.

DAVIES (Rev. J. L.), M.A.

Theology and Morality. Essays on Questions of Belief and Practice. Crown 8vo. Cloth, price 7s. 6d.

DE KERKADEC (Vicomtesse Solange).

A Chequered Life, being Memoirs of the Vicomtesse de Leoville Meilhan. Edited by. Crown 8vo. Cloth, price 7s. 6d.

DE L'HOSTE (Col. E. P.).

The Desert Pastor, Jean Jarousseau. Translated from the French of Eugène Pelletan. With a Frontispiece. New Edition. Fcap. 8vo. Cloth, price 3s. 6d.

DE REDCLIFFE (Viscount Stratford), P.C., K.G., G.C.B.

Why am I a Christian? Fifth Edition. Crown 8vo. Cloth, price 3s.

DE TOCQUEVILLE (A.).

Correspondence and Conversations of, with Nassau William Senior, from 1834 to 1859. Edited by M. C. M. Simpson. 2 vols. Post 8vo. Cloth, price 21s.

DE VERE (Aubrey).

Alexander the Great. A Dramatic Poem. Small crown 8vo. Cloth, price 5s.

The Infant Bridal, and Other Poems. A New and Enlarged Edition. Fcap. 8vo. Cloth, price 7s. 6d.

DE VERE (Aubrey)—*continued:*

The Legends of St. Patrick, and Other Poems. Small crown 8vo. Cloth, price 5s.

St. Thomas of Canterbury. A Dramatic Poem. Large fcap. 8vo. Cloth, price 5s.

DE WILLE (E.).

Under a Cloud; or, Johannes Olaf. A Novel. Translated by F. E. Bunnètt. 3 vols. Crown 8vo. Cloth.

DENNIS (J.).

English Sonnets. Collected and Arranged. Elegantly bound. Fcap. 8vo. Cloth, price 3s. 6d.

DOBSON (Austin).

Vignettes in Rhyme and Vers de Société. Third Edition. Fcap. 8vo. Cloth, price 5s.

DONNÉ (A.), M.D.

Change of Air and Scene. A Physician's Hints about Doctors, Patients, Hygiene, and Society; with Notes of Excursions for Health. Second Edition. Large post 8vo. Cloth, price 9s.

DOWDEN (Edward), LL.D.

Shakspere: a Critical Study of his Mind and Art. Second Edition. Post 8vo. Cloth, price 12s.

Poems. Fcap. 8vo. Cloth, price 5s.

DOWNTON (Rev. H.), M.A.

Hymns and Verses. Original and Translated. Small crown 8vo. Cloth, price 3s. 6d.

DRAPER (J. W.), M.D., LL.D., Professor in the University of New York.

History of the Conflict between Religion and Science. Seventh Edition. Crown 8vo. Cloth, price 5s.
  Volume XIII. of The International Scientific Series.

DREW (Rev. G. S.), M.A.
Scripture Lands in connection with their History. Second Edition. 8vo. Cloth, price 10s. 6d.

Nazareth: Its Life and Lessons. Third Edition. Crown 8vo. Cloth, price 5s.

The Divine Kingdom on Earth as it is in Heaven. 8vo. Cloth, price 10s. 6d.

The Son of Man: His Life and Ministry. Crown 8vo. Cloth, price 7s. 6d.

DREWRY (G. O.), M.D.
The Common-Sense Management of the Stomach. Third Edition. Fcap. 8vo. Cloth, price 2s. 6d.

DREWRY (G. O.), M.D., and BARTLETT (H. C.), Ph.D., F.C.S.
Cup and Platter: or, Notes on Food and its Effects. Small 8vo. Cloth, price 2s. 6d.

DRUMMOND (Miss).
Tripps Buildings. A Study from Life, with Frontispiece. Small crown 8vo. Cloth, price 3s. 6d.

DURAND (Lady).
Imitations from the German of Spitta and Terstegen. Fcap. 8vo. Cloth, price 4s.

DU VERNOIS (Col. von Verdy).
Studies in leading Troops. An authorized and accurate Translation by Lieutenant H. J. T. Hildyard, 71st Foot. Parts I. and II. Demy 8vo. Cloth, price 7s.

EDEN (Frederick).
The Nile without a Dragoman. Second Edition. Crown 8vo. Cloth, price 7s. 6d.

EDWARDS (Rev. Basil).
Minor Chords; Or, Songs for the Suffering: a Volume of Verse. Fcap. 8vo. Cloth, price 3s. 6d.; paper, price 2s. 6d.

EILOART (Mrs.).
Lady Moretoun's Daughter. 3 vols. Crown 8vo. Cloth.

ELLIOTT (Ebenezer), The Corn Law Rhymer.
Poems. Edited by his son, the Rev. Edwin Elliott, of St. John's, Antigua. 2 vols. Crown 8vo. Cloth, price 18s.

ENGLISH CLERGYMAN.
An Essay on the Rule of Faith and Creed of Athanasius. Shall the Rubric preceding the Creed be removed from the Prayer-book? Sewed. 8vo. Price 1s.

Epic of Hades (The).
By a New Writer. Author of "Songs of Two Worlds." Fcap. 8vo. Cloth, price 5s.

Eros Agonistes.
Poems. By E. B. D. Fcap. 8vo. Cloth, price 3s. 6d.

Essays on the Endowment of Research.
By Various Writers.

LIST OF CONTRIBUTORS.
Mark Pattison, B. D.
James S. Cotton, B. A.
Charles E. Appleton, D. C. L.
Archibald H. Sayce, M. A.
Henry Clifton Sorby, F. R. S.
Thomas K. Cheyne, M. A.
W. T. Thiselton Dyer, M. A.
Henry Nettleship, M. A.

Square crown octavo. Cloth, price 10s. 6d.

EVANS (Mark).
The Story of our Father's Love, told to Children; being a New and Enlarged Edition of Theology for Children. With Four Illustrations. Fcap. 8vo. Cloth, price 3s. 6d.

A Book of Common Prayer and Worship for Household Use, compiled exclusively from the Holy Scriptures. Fcap. 8vo. Cloth, price 2s. 6d.

EYRE (Maj.-Gen. Sir V.), C.B., K.C.S.I., &c.
Lays of a Knight-Errant in many Lands. Square crown 8vo. With Six Illustrations. Cloth, price 7s. 6d.

FAITHFULL (Mrs. Francis G.).
  Love Me, or Love Me Not.
  3 vols. Crown 8vo. Cloth.

FARQUHARSON (M.).
  I. Elsie Dinsmore. Crown 8vo. Cloth, price 3s. 6d.
  II. Elsie's Girlhood. Crown 8vo. Cloth, price 3s. 6d.
  III. Elsie's Holidays at Roselands. Crown 8vo. Cloth, price 3s. 6d.

FAVRE (Mons. J.).
  The Government of the National Defence. From the 30th June to the 31st October, 1870. Translated by H. Clark. Demy 8vo. Cloth, price 10s. 6d.

FERRIS (Henry Weybridge).
  Poems. Fcap. 8vo. Cloth, price 5s.

FISHER (Alice).
  His Queen. 3 vols. Crown 8vo. Cloth.

FOOTMAN (Rev. H.), M.A.
  From Home and Back; or, Some Aspects of Sin as seen in the Light of the Parable of the Prodigal. Crown 8vo. Cloth, price 5s.

FORBES (A.).
  Soldiering and Scribbling. A Series of Sketches. Crown 8vo. Cloth, price 7s. 6d.

FOTHERGILL (Jessie).
  Aldyth: A Novel. 2 vols. Crown 8vo. Cloth.
  Healey. A Romance. 3 vols. Crown 8vo. Cloth.

FOWLE (Rev. T. W.), M.A.
  The Reconciliation of Religion and Science. Being Essays on Immortality, Inspiration, Miracles, and the Being of Christ. Demy 8vo. Cloth, price 10s. 6d.

FOX-BOURNE (H. R.).
  The Life of John Locke, 1632—1704. 2 vols. Demy 8vo. Cloth, price 28s.

FRASER (Donald).
  Exchange Tables of Sterling and Indian Rupee Currency, upon a new and extended system, embracing Values from One Farthing to One Hundred Thousand Pounds, and at Rates progressing, in Sixteenths of a Penny, from 1s. 9d. to 2s. 3d. per Rupee. Royal 8vo. Cloth, price 10s. 6d.

FRERE (Sir H. Bartle E.), G.C.B., G.C.S.I.
  The Threatened Famine in Bengal: How it may be Met, and the Recurrence of Famines in India Prevented. Being No. 1 of "Occasional Notes on Indian Affairs." With 3 Maps. Crown 8vo. Cloth, price 5s.

FRISWELL (J. Hain).
  The Better Self. Essays for Home Life. Crown 8vo. Cloth, price 6s.
  One of Two; or, The Left-Handed Bride. With a Frontispiece. Crown 8vo. Cloth, price 3s. 6d.

GARDNER (H.).
  Sunflowers. A Book of Verses. Fcap. 8vo. Cloth, price 5s.

GARDNER (J.), M.D.
  Longevity: The Means of Prolonging Life after Middle Age. Third Edition, revised and enlarged. Small crown 8vo. Cloth, price 4s.

GARRETT (E.).
  By Still Waters. A Story for Quiet Hours. With Seven Illustrations. Crown 8vo. Cloth, price 6s.

GIBBON (Charles).
  For Lack of Gold. With a Frontispiece. Crown 8vo. Cloth, price 3s. 6d.
  Robin Gray. With a Frontispiece. Crown 8vo. Cloth, price 3s. 6d.

GILBERT (Mrs.).

Autobiography and other Memorials. Edited by Josiah Gilbert. Second Edition. In 2 vols. With 2 Steel Portraits and several Wood Engravings. Post 8vo. Cloth, price 24s.

GILL (Rev. W. W.), B.A.

Myths and Songs from the South Pacific. With a Preface by F. Max Müller, M.A., Professor of Comparative Philology at Oxford. Post 8vo. Cloth, price 9s.

GODKIN (James).

The Religious History of Ireland: Primitive, Papal, and Protestant. Including the Evangelical Missions, Catholic Agitations, and Church Progress of the last half Century. 8vo. Cloth, price 12s.

GODWIN (William).

William Godwin: His Friends and Contemporaries. With Portraits and Facsimiles of the handwriting of Godwin and his Wife. By C. Kegan Paul. 2 vols. Demy 8vo. Cloth, price 28s.

The Genius of Christianity Unveiled. Being Essays never before published. Edited, with a Preface, by C. Kegan Paul. Crown 8vo. Cloth, price 7s. 6d.

GOETZE (Capt. A. von).

Operations of the German Engineers during the War of 1870-1871. Published by Authority, and in accordance with Official Documents. Translated from the German by Colonel G. Graham, V.C., C.B., R.E. With 6 large Maps. Demy 8vo. Cloth, price 21s.

GOODENOUGH (Commodore J. G.), R.N., C.B., C.M.G.

Journals of, during his Last Command as Senior Officer on the Australian Station, 1873-1875. Edited, with a Memoir, by his Widow. With Maps, Woodcuts, and Steel Engraved Portrait. Square post 8vo. Cloth, price 14s.

GOODMAN (W.).

Cuba, the Pearl of the Antilles. Crown 8vo. Cloth, price 7s. 6d.

GOULD (Rev. S. Baring), M.A.

The Vicar of Morwenstow: a Memoir of the Rev. R. S. Hawker. With Portrait. Third Edition, revised. Square post 8vo. Cloth, 10s. 6d.

GRANVILLE (A. B.), M.D., F.R.S., &c.

Autobiography of A. B. Granville, F.R.S., etc. Edited, with a brief account of the concluding years of his life, by his youngest Daughter, Paulina B. Granville. 2 vols. With a Portrait. Second Edition. Demy 8vo. Cloth, price 32s.

GRAY (Mrs. Russell).

Lisette's Venture. A Novel. 2 vols. Crown 8vo. Cloth.

GREEN (T. Bowden).

Fragments of Thought. Dedicated by permission to the Poet Laureate. Crown 8vo. Cloth, price 7s. 6d.

GREENWOOD (J.), "The Amateur Casual."

In Strange Company; or, The Note Book of a Roving Correspondent. Second Edition. Crown 8vo. Cloth, price 6s.

GREY (John), of Dilston.

John Grey (of Dilston): Memoirs. By Josephine E. Butler. New and Revised Edition. Crown 8vo. Cloth, price 3s. 6d.

GRIFFITH (Rev. T.), A.M.

Studies of the Divine Master. Demy 8vo. Cloth, price 12s.

GRIFFITHS (Capt. Arthur).

Memorials of Millbank, and Chapters in Prison History. With Illustrations by R. Goff and the Author. 2 vols. Post 8vo. Cloth, price 21s.

The Queen's Shilling. A Novel. 2 vols. Cloth.

GRIMLEY (Rev. H. N.), M.A., Professor of Mathematics in the University College of Wales, and Chaplain of Tremadoc Church.

Tremadoc Sermons, chiefly on the SPIRITUAL BODY, the UNSEEN WORLD, and the DIVINE HUMANITY. Crown 8vo. Cloth, price 7s. 6d.

GRÜNER (M. L.).

Studies of Blast Furnace Phenomena. Translated by L. D. B. Gordon, F.R.S.E., F.G.S. Demy 8vo. Cloth, price 7s. 6d.

GURNEY (Rev. A. T.).

Words of Faith and Cheer. A Mission of Instruction and Suggestion. Crown 8vo. Cloth, price 6s.

First Principles in Church and State. Demy 8vo. Sewed, price 1s. 6d.

HAECKEL (Prof. Ernst).

The History of Creation. Translation revised by Professor E. Ray Lankester, M.A., F.R.S. With Coloured Plates and Genealogical Trees of the various groups of both plants and animals. 2 vols. Second Edition. Post 8vo. Cloth, price 32s.

HARCOURT (Capt. A. F. P.).

The Shakespeare Argosy. Containing much of the wealth of Shakespeare's Wisdom and Wit, alphabetically arranged and classified. Crown 8vo. Cloth, price 6s.

HAWEIS (Rev. H. R.), M.A.

Current Coin. Materialism—The Devil—Crime—Drunkenness—Pauperism—Emotion—Recreation—The Sabbath. Crown 8vo. Cloth, price 6s.

Speech in Season. Third Edition. Crown 8vo. Cloth, price 9s.

Thoughts for the Times. Ninth Edition. Crown 8vo. Cloth, price 7s. 6d.

Unsectarian Family Prayers, for Morning and Evening for a Week, with short selected passages from the Bible. Square crown 8vo. Cloth, price 3s. 6d.

HAWTHORNE (Julian).

Bressant. A Romance. 2 vols. Crown 8vo. Cloth.

Idolatry. A Romance. 2 vols. Crown 8vo. Cloth.

HAWTHORNE (Nathaniel).

Nathaniel Hawthorne. A Memoir with Stories, now first published in this country. By H. A. Page. Post 8vo. Cloth, price 7s. 6d.

Septimius. A Romance. Second Edition. Crown 8vo. Cloth, price 9s.

HAYMAN (H.), D.D., late Head Master of Rugby School.

Rugby School Sermons. With an Introductory Essay on the Indwelling of the Holy Spirit. Crown 8vo. Cloth, price 7s. 6d.

Heathergate. A Story of Scottish Life and Character. By a New Author. 2 vols. Crown 8vo. Cloth.

HELLWALD (Baron F. von).

The Russians in Central Asia. A Critical Examination, down to the present time, of the Geography and History of Central Asia. Translated by Lieut.-Col. Theodore Wirgman, LL.B. Large post 8vo. With Map. Cloth, price 12s.

HELVIG (Capt. H.).

The Operations of the Bavarian Army Corps. Translated by Captain G. S. Schwabe. With Five large Maps. In 2 vols. Demy 8vo. Cloth, price 24s.

HINTON (James).

The Place of the Physician. To which is added ESSAYS ON THE LAW OF HUMAN LIFE, AND ON THE RELATION BETWEEN ORGANIC AND INORGANIC WORLDS. Second Edition. Crown 8vo. Cloth, price 3s. 6d.

Physiology for Practical Use. By various Writers. With 50 Illustrations. 2 vols. Second Edition. Crown 8vo. Cloth, price 12s. 6d.

HINTON (James)—*continued*:

An Atlas of Diseases of the Membrana Tympani. With Descriptive Text. Post 8vo. Price £6 6s.

The Questions of Aural Surgery. With Illustrations. 2 vols. Post 8vo. Cloth, price 12s. 6d.

H. J. C.

The Art of Furnishing. A Popular Treatise on the Principles of Furnishing, based on the Laws of Common Sense, Requirement, and Picturesque Effect. Small crown 8vo. Cloth, price 3s. 6d.

HOCKLEY (W. B.).

Tales of the Zenana; or, A Nuwab's Leisure Hours. By the Author of "Pandurang Hari." With a Preface by Lord Stanley of Alderley. 2 vols. Crown 8vo. Cloth, price 21s.

Pandurang Hari; or, Memoirs of a Hindoo. A Tale of Mahratta Life sixty years ago. With a Preface by Sir H. Bartle E. Frere, G.C.S.I., &c. 2 vols. Crown 8vo. Cloth, price 21s.

HOFFBAUER (Capt.).

The German Artillery in the Battles near Metz. Based on the official reports of the German Artillery. Translated by Capt. E. O. Hollist. With Map and Plans. Demy 8vo. Cloth, price 21s.

Hogan, M.P.

A Novel. 3 vols. Crown 8vo. Cloth.

HOLMES (E. G. A.).

Poems. Fcap. 8vo. Cloth, price 5s.

HOLROYD (Major W. R. M.)

Tas-hil ul Kālām; or, Hindustani made Easy. Crown 8vo. Cloth, price 5s.

HOPE (James L. A.).

In Quest of Coolies. With Illustrations. Second Edition. Crown 8vo. Cloth, price 6s.

HOOPER (Mary).

Little Dinners: How to Serve them with Elegance and Economy. Eleventh Edition. Crown 8vo. Cloth, price 5s.

Cookery for Invalids, Persons of Delicate Digestion, and Children. Crown 8vo. Cloth, price 3s. 6d.

HOOPER (Mrs. G.).

The House of Raby. With a Frontispiece. Crown 8vo. Cloth, price 3s. 6d.

HOPKINS (M.).

The Port of Refuge; or, Counsel and Aid to Shipmasters in Difficulty, Doubt, or Distress. Second Edition. Crown 8vo. Cloth, price 6s.

HORNE (William), M.A.

Reason and Revelation: an Examination into the Nature and Contents of Scripture Revelation, as compared with other Forms of Truth. Demy 8vo. Cloth, price 12s.

HOWARD (Mary M.).

Beatrice Aylmer, and other Tales. Crown 8vo. Cloth, price 6s.

HOWARD (Rev. G. B.).

An Old Legend of St. Paul's. Fcap. 8vo. Cloth, price 4s. 6d.

HOWELL (James).

A Tale of the Sea, Sonnets, and other Poems. Fcap. 8vo. Cloth, price 5s.

HUGHES (Allison).

Penelope and other Poems. Fcap. 8vo. Cloth, price 4s. 6d.

HULL (Edmund C. P.).

The European in India. With a MEDICAL GUIDE FOR ANGLO-INDIANS. By R. R. S. Mair, M.D., F.R.C.S.E. Second Edition, Revised and Corrected. Post 8vo. Cloth, price 6s.

HUMPHREY (Rev. W.).
Mr. Fitzjames Stephen and Cardinal Bellarmine. Demy 8vo. Sewed, price 1s.

HUTTON (James).
Missionary Life in the Southern Seas. With Illustrations. Crown 8vo. Cloth, price 7s. 6d.

IGNOTUS.
Culmshire Folk. A Novel. New and Cheaper Edition. Crown 8vo. Cloth, price 6s.

INCHBOLD (J. W.).
Annus Amoris. Sonnets. Foolscap 8vo. Cloth, price 4s. 6d.

INGELOW (Jean).
The Little Wonder-horn. A Second Series of "Stories Told to a Child." With Fifteen Illustrations. Square 24mo. Cloth, price 3s. 6d.

Off the Skelligs. (Her First Romance.) 4 vols. Crown 8vo. Cloth.

International Scientific Series (The).
I. **The Forms of Water in Clouds and Rivers, Ice and Glaciers.** By J. Tyndall, LL.D., F.R.S. With 25 Illustrations. Sixth Edition. Crown 8vo. Cloth, price 5s.
II. **Physics and Politics;** or, Thoughts on the Application of the Principles of "Natural Selection" and "Inheritance" to Political Society. By Walter Bagehot. Third Edition. Crown 8vo. Cloth, price 4s.
III. **Foods.** By Edward Smith, M.D., LL.B., F.R.S. With numerous Illustrations. Fourth Edition. Crown 8vo. Cloth, price 5s.
IV. **Mind and Body:** The Theories of their Relation. By Alexander Bain, LL.D. With Four Illustrations. Fifth Edition. Crown 8vo. Cloth, price 4s.
V. **The Study of Sociology.** By Herbert Spencer. Sixth Edition. Crown 8vo. Cloth, price 5s.
VI. **On the Conservation of Energy.** By Balfour Stewart, M.A., LL.D., F.R.S. With 14 Illustrations. Third Edition. Crown 8vo. Cloth, price 5s.

International Scientific Series (The)—*continued.*
VII. **Animal Locomotion;** or, Walking, Swimming, and Flying. By J. B. Pettigrew, M.D., F.R.S., etc. With 130 Illustrations. Second Edition. Crown 8vo. Cloth, price 5s.
VIII. **Responsibility in Mental Disease.** By Henry Maudsley, M.D. Second Edition. Crown 8vo. Cloth, price 5s.
IX. **The New Chemistry.** By Professor J. P. Cooke, of the Harvard University. With 31 Illustrations. Third Edition. Crown 8vo. Cloth, price 5s.
X. **The Science of Law.** By Professor Sheldon Amos. Second Edition. Crown 8vo. Cloth, price 5s.
XI. **Animal Mechanism.** A Treatise on Terrestrial and Aerial Locomotion. By Professor E. J. Marey. With 117 Illustrations. Second Edition. Crown 8vo. Cloth, price 5s.
XII. **The Doctrine of Descent and Darwinism.** By Professor Oscar Schmidt (Strasburg University). With 26 Illustrations. Third Edition. Crown 8vo. Cloth, price 5s.
XIII. **The History of the Conflict between Religion and Science.** By J. W. Draper, M.D., LL.D. Eighth Edition. Crown 8vo. Cloth, price 5s.
XIV. **Fungi;** their Nature, Influences, Uses, &c. By M. C. Cooke, M.A., LL.D. Edited by the Rev. M. J. Berkeley, M.A., F.L.S. With numerous Illustrations. Second Edition. Crown 8vo. Cloth, price 5s.
XV. **The Chemical Effects of Light and Photography.** By Dr. Hermann Vogel (Polytechnic Academy of Berlin). Translation thoroughly revised. With 100 Illustrations. Third Edition. Crown 8vo. Cloth, price 5s.
XVI. **The Life and Growth of Language.** By William Dwight Whitney, Professor of Sanskrit and Comparative Philology in Yale College, New Haven. Second Edition. Crown 8vo. Cloth, price 5s.

International Scientific Series (The)—*continued.*

XVII. **Money and the Mechanism of Exchange.** By W. Stanley Jevons, M.A., F.R.S. Third Edition. Crown 8vo. Cloth, price 5s.

XVIII. **The Nature of Light:** With a General Account of Physical Optics. By Dr. Eugene Lommel, Professor of Physics in the University of Erlangen. With 188 Illustrations and a table of Spectra in Chromo-lithography. Second Edition. Crown 8vo. Cloth, price 5s.

XIX. **Animal Parasites and Messmates.** By Monsieur Van Beneden, Professor of the University of Louvain, Correspondent of the Institute of France. With 83 Illustrations. Second Edition. Crown 8vo. Cloth, price 5s.

XX. **Fermentation.** By Professor Schützenberger, Director of the Chemical Laboratory at the Sorbonne. With 28 Illustrations. Second Edition. Crown 8vo. Cloth, price 5s.

XXI. **The Five Senses of Man.** By Professor Bernstein, of the University of Halle. With 91 Illustrations. Second Edition. Crown 8vo. Cloth, price 5s.

XXII. **The Theory of Sound in its Relation to Music.** By Professor Pietro Blaserna, of the Royal University of Rome. With numerous Illustrations. Second Edition. Crown 8vo. Cloth, price 5s.

Forthcoming Volumes.

Prof. W. KINGDON CLIFFORD, M.A. The First Principles of the Exact Sciences explained to the Non-mathematical.

Prof. T. H. HUXLEY, LL.D., F.R.S. Bodily Motion and Consciousness.

Dr. W. B. CARPENTER, LL.D., F.R.S. The Physical Geography of the Sea.

W. LAUDER LINDSAY, M.D., F.R.S.E. Mind in the Lower Animals.

Sir JOHN LUBBOCK, Bart., F.R.S. On Ants and Bees.

Prof. W. T. THISELTON DYER, B.A., B.Sc. Form and Habit in Flowering Plants.

International Scientific Series (The)—*continued.*

Mr. J. N. LOCKYER, F.R.S. Spectrum Analysis.

Prof. MICHAEL FOSTER, M.D. Protoplasm and the Cell Theory.

H. CHARLTON BASTIAN, M.D., F.R.S. The Brain as an Organ of Mind.

Prof. A. C. RAMSAY, LL.D., F.R.S. Earth Sculpture: Hills, Valleys, Mountains, Plains, Rivers, Lakes; how they were Produced, and how they have been Destroyed.

Prof. J. ROSENTHAL. General Physiology of Muscles and Nerves.

P. BERT (Professor of Physiology, Paris). Forms of Life and other Cosmical Conditions.

Prof. CORFIELD, M.A., M.D. (Oxon.) Air in its relation to Health.

JACKSON (T. G.).

Modern Gothic Architecture. Crown 8vo. Cloth, price 5s.

JACOB (Maj.-Gen. Sir G. Le Grand), K.C.S.I., C.B.

Western India Before and during the Mutinies. Pictures drawn from life. Second Edition. Crown 8vo. Cloth, price 7s. 6d.

JENKINS (E.) and RAYMOND (J.), Esqs.

A Legal Handbook for Architects, Builders, and Building Owners. Second Edition Revised. Crown 8vo. Cloth, price 6s.

JENKINS (Rev. R. C.), M.A.

The Privilege of Peter and the Claims of the Roman Church confronted with the Scriptures, the Councils, and the Testimony of the Popes themselves. Fcap. 8vo. Cloth, price 3s. 6d.

JENNINGS (Mrs. Vaughan).

Rahel: Her Life and Letters. With a Portrait from the Painting by Daffinger. Square post 8vo. Cloth, price 7s. 6d.

JEVONS (W. Stanley), M.A., F.R.S.
  Money and the Mechanism of Exchange. Second Edition. Crown 8vo. Cloth, price 5s.
    Volume XVII. of The International Scientific Series.

KAUFMANN (Rev. M.), B.A.
  Socialism: Its Nature, its Dangers, and its Remedies considered. Crown 8vo. Cloth, price 7s. 6d.

KEATINGE (Mrs.).
  Honor Blake: The Story of a Plain Woman. 2 vols. Crown 8vo. Cloth.

KER (David).
  On the Road to Khiva. Illustrated with Photographs of the Country and its Inhabitants, and a copy of the Official Map in use during the Campaign, from the Survey of Captain Leusilin. Post 8vo. Cloth, price 12s.

  The Boy Slave in Bokhara. A Tale of Central Asia. With Illustrations. Crown 8vo. Cloth, price 5s.

  The Wild Horseman of the Pampas. Illustrated. Crown 8vo. Cloth, price 5s.

KING (Alice).
  A Cluster of Lives. Crown 8vo. Cloth, price 7s. 6d.

KING (Mrs. Hamilton).
  The Disciples. A New Poem. Second Edition, with some Notes. Crown 8vo. Cloth, price 7s. 6d.

  Aspromonte, and other Poems. Second Edition. Fcap. 8vo. Cloth, price 4s. 6d.

KINGSFORD (Rev. F.W.), M.A., Vicar of St. Thomas's, Stamford Hill; late Chaplain H. E. I. C. (Bengal Presidency).
  Hartham Conferences; or, Discussions upon some of the Religious Topics of the Day. "Audi alteram partem." Crown 8vo. Cloth, price 3s. 6d.

KNIGHT (A. F. C.).
  Poems. Fcap 8vo. Cloth, price 5s.

KINGSLEY (Charles).
  Letters and Memories of his Life. Edited by his WIFE. 2 vols. Demy 8vo. With 2 Steel engraved Portraits and numerous Illustrations on Wood, and a Facsimile of his Handwriting. Cloth, price 36s.

LACORDAIRE (Rev. Père).
  Life: Conferences delivered at Toulouse. A New and Cheaper Edition. Crown 8vo. Cloth, price 3s. 6d.

Lady of Lipari (The).
  A Poem in Three Cantos. Fcap. 8vo. Cloth, price 5s.

LAURIE (J. S.).
  Educational Course of Secular School Books for India:
  The First Hindustani Reader. Stiff linen wrapper, price 6d.
  The Second Hindustani Reader. Stiff linen wrapper, price 6d.
  The Oriental (English) Reader. Book I., price 6d.; II., price $7\frac{1}{2}d$.; III., price 9d.; IV., price 1s.
  Geography of India; with Maps and Historical Appendix, tracing the Growth of the British Empire in Hindustan. Fcap. 8vo. Cloth, price 1s. 6d.

LAYMANN (Capt.).
  The Frontal Attack of Infantry. Translated by Colonel Edward Newdigate. Crown 8vo. Cloth, price 2s. 6d.

L. D. S.
  Letters from China and Japan. With Illustrated Title-page. Crown 8vo. Cloth, price 7s. 6d.

LEANDER (Richard).
  Fantastic Stories. Translated from the German by Paulina B. Granville. With Eight full-page Illustrations by M. E. Fraser-Tytler. Crown 8vo. Cloth, price 5s.

LEATHES (Rev. S.), M.A.
  The Gospel Its Own Witness. Crown 8vo. Cloth, price 5s.

LEE (Rev. F. G.), D.C.L.
The Other World; or, Glimpses of the Supernatural. 2 vols. A New Edition. Crown 8vo. Cloth, price 15s.

LEE (Holme).
Her Title of Honour. A Book for Girls. New Edition. With a Frontispiece. Crown 8vo. Cloth, price 5s.

LENOIR (J.).
Fayoum; or, Artists in Egypt. A Tour with M. Gérome and others. With 13 Illustrations. A New and Cheaper Edition. Crown 8vo. Cloth, price 3s. 6d.

Leonora Christina, Memoirs of, Daughter of Christian IV. of Denmark. Written during her Imprisonment in the Blue Tower of the Royal Palace at Copenhagen, 1663-1685. Translated by F. E. BUNNETT. With an Autotype Portrait of the Princess. A New and Cheaper Edition. Medium 8vo. Cloth, price 5s.

LEWIS (Mary A.).
A Rat with Three Tales. With Four Illustrations by Catherine F. Frere. Cloth, price 5s.

LISTADO (J. T.).
Civil Service. A Novel. 2 vols. Crown 8vo. Cloth.

LOCKER (F.).
London Lyrics. A New and Revised Edition, with Additions and a Portrait of the Author. Crown 8vo. Cloth, elegant, price 7s. 6d.

LOMMEL (Dr. E.).
The Nature of Light: With a General Account of Physical Optics. Second Edition. With 188 Illustrations and a Table of Spectra in Chromo-lithography. Crown 8vo. Cloth, price 5s.
Volume XVIII. of The International Scientific Series.

LORIMER (Peter), D.D.
John Knox and the Church of England: His Work in her Pulpit, and his Influence upon her Liturgy, Articles, and Parties. Demy 8vo. Cloth, price 12s.

LOTHIAN (Roxburghe).
Dante and Beatrice from 1282 to 1290. A Romance. 2 vols. Post 8vo. Cloth, price 24s.

LOVEL (Edward).
The Owl's Nest in the City: A Story. Crown 8vo. Cloth.

LOVER (Samuel), R.H.A.
The Life of Samuel Lover, R.H.A.; Artistic, Literary, and Musical. With Selections from his Unpublished Papers and Correspondence. By Bayle Bernard. 2 vols. With a Portrait. Post 8vo. Cloth, price 21s.

LOWER (M. A.), M.A., F.S.A.
Wayside Notes in Scandinavia. Being Notes of Travel in the North of Europe. Crown 8vo. Cloth, price 9s.

LUCAS (Alice).
Translations from the Works of German Poets of the 18th and 19th Centuries. Fcap. 8vo. Cloth, price 5s.

LYONS (R. T.), Surg.-Maj. Bengal Army.
A Treatise on Relapsing Fever. Post 8vo. Cloth, price 7s. 6d.

MACAULAY (J.), M.A., M.D., Edin.
The Truth about Ireland: Tours of Observation in 1872 and 1875. With Remarks on Irish Public Questions. Being a Second Edition of "Ireland in 1872," with a New and Supplementary Preface. Crown 8vo. Cloth, price 3s. 6d.

MAC DONALD (G.).
Malcolm. A Novel. 3 vols. Second Edition. Crown 8vo. Cloth.
St. George and St. Michael. 3 vols. Crown 8vo. Cloth.

MACLACHLAN (A. N. C.), M.A.
William Augustus, Duke of Cumberland: being a Sketch of his Military Life and Character, chiefly as exhibited in the General Orders of His Royal Highness, 1745—1747. With Illustrations. Post 8vo. Cloth, price 15s.

MAC KENNA (S. J.).
   Plucky Fellows. A Book for Boys. With Six Illustrations. Second Edition. Crown 8vo. Cloth, price 3s. 6d.
   At School with an Old Dragoon. With Six Illustrations. Second Edition. Crown 8vo. Cloth, price 5s.

McCLINTOCK.
   Sir Spangle and the Dingy Hen. Illustrated. Imperial 16mo. Cloth, price 2s. 6d.

MAIR (R. S.), M.D., F.R.C.S.E.
   The Medical Guide for Anglo-Indians. Being a Compendium of Advice to Europeans in India, relating to the Preservation and Regulation of Health. With a Supplement on the Management of Children in India. Crown 8vo. Limp cloth, price 3s. 6d.

MANNING (His Eminence Cardinal).
   Essays on Religion and Literature. By various Writers. Third Series. Demy 8vo. Cloth, price 10s. 6d.

MAREY (E. J.).
   Animal Mechanics. A Treatise on Terrestrial and Aerial Locomotion. With 117 Illustrations. Second Edition. Crown 8vo. Cloth, price 5s.
   Volume XI. of The International Scientific Series.

MARKEWITCH (B.).
   The Neglected Question. Translated from the Russian, by the Princess Ourousoff, and dedicated by Express Permission to Her Imperial and Royal Highness Marie Alexandrovna, the Duchess of Edinburgh. 2 vols. Crown 8vo. Cloth, price 14s.

MARRIOTT (Maj.-Gen. W. F.), C.S.I.
   A Grammar of Political Economy. Crown 8vo. Cloth, price 6s.

MARSHALL (H.).
   The Story of Sir Edward's Wife. A Novel. Crown 8vo. Cloth, price 10s. 6d.

MASTERMAN (J.).
   Half-a-dozen Daughters. With a Frontispiece. Crown 8vo. Cloth, price 3s. 6d.

MAUDSLEY (Dr. H.).
   Responsibility in Mental Disease. Second Edition. Crown 8vo. Cloth, price 5s.
   Volume VIII. of The International Scientific Series.

MAUGHAN (W. C.).
   The Alps of Arabia; or, Travels through Egypt, Sinai, Arabia, and the Holy Land. With Map. Second Edition. Demy 8vo. Cloth, price 5s.

MAURICE (C. E.).
   Lives of English Popular Leaders. No. 1.—STEPHEN LANGTON. Crown 8vo. Cloth, price 7s. 6d. No. 2.—TYLER, BALL, and OLDCASTLE. Crown 8vo. Cloth, price 7s. 6d.

Mazzini (Joseph).
   A Memoir. By E. A. V. Two Photographic Portraits. Crown 8vo. Cloth, price 3s. 6d.

MEDLEY (Lieut.-Col. J. G.), R.E.
   An Autumn Tour in the United States and Canada. Crown 8vo. Cloth, price 5s.

MENZIES (Sutherland).
   Memoirs of Distinguished Women. 2 vols. Post 8vo. Cloth, price 10s. 6d.

MICKLETHWAITE (J. T.), F.S.A.
   Modern Parish Churches: Their Plan, Design, and Furniture. Crown 8vo. Cloth, price 7s. 6d.

MILNE (James).
   Tables of Exchange for the Conversion of Sterling Money into Indian and Ceylon Currency, at Rates from 1s. 8d. to 2s. 3d. per Rupee. Second Edition. Demy 8vo. Cloth, price £2 2s.

MIRUS (Maj.-Gen. von).

Cavalry Field Duty. Translated by Major Frank S. Russell, 14th (King's) Hussars. Crown 8vo. Cloth limp, price 7s. 6d.

MIVART (St. George), F.R.S.

Contemporary Evolution: An Essay on some recent Social Changes. Post 8vo. Cloth, price 7s. 6d.

MOORE (Rev. D.), M.A.

Christ and His Church. By the Author of "The Age and the Gospel," &c. Crown 8vo. Cloth, price 3s. 6d.

MOORE (Rev. T.).

Sermonettes: on Synonymous Texts, taken from the Bible and Book of Common Prayer, for the Study, Family Reading, and Private Devotion. Small crown 8vo. Cloth, price 4s. 6d.

MORELL (J. R.).

Euclid Simplified in Method and Language. Being a Manual of Geometry. Compiled from the most important French Works, approved by the University of Paris and the Minister of Public Instruction. Fcap. 8vo. Cloth, price 2s. 6d.

MORICE (Rev. F. D.), M.A.

The Olympian and Pythian Odes of Pindar. A New Translation in English Verse. Crown 8vo. Cloth, price 7s. 6d.

MORLEY (Susan).

Aileen Ferrers. A Novel. 2 vols. Crown 8vo. Cloth.

Throstlethwaite. A Novel. 3 vols. Crown 8vo. Cloth.

MORSE (E. S.), Ph.D.

First Book of Zoology. With numerous Illustrations. Crown 8vo. Cloth, price 5s.

MOSTYN (Sydney).

Perplexity. A Novel. 3 vols. Crown 8vo. Cloth.

MUSGRAVE (Anthony).

Studies in Political Economy. Crown 8vo. Cloth, price 6s.

My Sister Rosalind.

A Novel. By the Author of "Christiana North," and "Under the Limes." 2 vols. Cloth.

NAAKÉ (J. T.).

Slavonic Fairy Tales. From Russian, Servian, Polish, and Bohemian Sources. With Four Illustrations. Crown 8vo. Cloth, price 5s.

NEWMAN (J. H.), D.D.

Characteristics from the Writings of. Being Selections from his various Works. Arranged with the Author's personal approval. Second Edition. With Portrait. Crown 8vo. Cloth, price 6s.

*** A Portrait of the late Rev. Dr. J. H. Newman, mounted for framing, can be had, price 2s. 6d.

NEWMAN (Mrs.).

Too Late. A Novel. 2 vols. Crown 8vo. Cloth.

NEW WRITER (A).

Songs of Two Worlds. By a New Writer. Third Series. Second Edition. Fcap. 8vo. Cloth, price 5s.

The Epic of Hades. Fcap. 8vo. Cloth, price 5s.

NOBLE (J. A.).

The Pelican Papers. Reminiscences and Remains of a Dweller in the Wilderness. Crown 8vo. Cloth, price 6s.

NORMAN PEOPLE (The).

The Norman People, and their Existing Descendants in the British Dominions and the United States of America. Demy 8vo. Cloth, price 21s.

NORRIS (Rev. Alfred).

The Inner and Outer Life Poems. Fcap. 8vo. Cloth, price 6s.

Northern Question (The); Or, Russia's Policy in Turkey unmasked. Demy 8vo. Sewed, price 1s.

NOTREGE (John), A.M.
The Spiritual Function of a Presbyter in the Church of England. Crown 8vo. Cloth, red edges, price 3s. 6d.

Oriental Sporting Magazine (The).
A Reprint of the first 5 Volumes, in 2 Volumes. Demy 8vo. Cloth, price 28s.

Our Increasing Military Difficulty, and one Way of Meeting it. Demy 8vo. Stitched, price 1s.

PAGE (Capt. S. F.).
Discipline and Drill. Cheaper Edition. Crown 8vo. Price 1s.

PALGRAVE (W. Gifford).
Hermann Agha. An Eastern Narrative. 2 vols. Crown 8vo. Cloth, extra gilt, price 18s.

**PANDURANG HARI;
Or Memoirs of a Hindoo.** With an Introductory Preface by Sir H. Bartle E. Frere, G.C.S.I., C.B. 2 vols. Crown 8vo. Cloth, price 21s.

PARKER Joseph), D.D.
The Paraclete: An Essay on the Personality and Ministry of the Holy Ghost, with some reference to current discussions. Second Edition. Demy 8vo. Cloth, price 12s.

PARR (Harriet).
Echoes of a Famous Year. Crown 8vo. Cloth, price 8s. 6d.

PAUL (C. Kegan).
Goethe's Faust. A New Translation in Rime. Crown 8vo. Cloth, price 6s.

William Godwin: His Friends and Contemporaries. With Portraits and Facsimiles of the Handwriting of Godwin and his Wife. 2 vols. Square post 8vo. Cloth, price 28s.

The Genius of Christianity Unveiled. Being Essays never before published. By William Godwin. Edited, with a Preface, by C. Kegan Paul. Crown 8vo. Cloth, price 7s. 6d.

PAYNE (John).
Songs of Life and Death. Crown 8vo. Cloth, price 5s.

PAYNE (Prof.).
Lectures on Education. Price 6d. each.
I. Pestalozzi: the Influence of His Principles and Practice.
II. Fröbel and the Kindergarten System. Second Edition.
III. The Science and Art of Education.
IV. The True Foundation of Science Teaching.

A Visit to German Schools: Elementary Schools in Germany. Notes of a Professional Tour to inspect some of the Kindergartens, Primary Schools, Public Girls' Schools, and Schools for Technical Instruction in Hamburgh, Berlin, Dresden, Weimar, Gotha, Eisenach, in the autumn of 1874. With Critical Discussions of the General Principles and Practice of Kindergartens and other Schemes of Elementary Education. Crown 8vo. Cloth, price 4s. 6d.

PEACOCKE (Georgiana).
Rays from the Southern Cross: Poems. Crown 8vo. With Sixteen Full-page Illustrations by the Rev. P. Walsh. Cloth elegant, price 10s. 6d.

PELLETAN (E.).
The Desert Pastor, Jean Jarousseau. Translated from the French. By Colonel E. P. De L'Hoste. With a Frontispiece. New Edition. Fcap. 8vo. Cloth, price 3s. 6d.

PENRICE (Maj. J.), B.A.
A Dictionary and Glossary of the Ko-ran. With copious Grammatical References and Explanations of the Text. 4to. Cloth, price 21s.

PERCEVAL (Rev. P.).
Tamil Proverbs, with their English Translation. Containing upwards of Six Thousand Proverbs. Third Edition. Demy 8vo. Sewed, price 9s.

PERRIER (A.).
A Winter in Morocco.
With Four Illustrations. A New and Cheaper Edition. Crown 8vo. Cloth, price 3s. 6d.
A Good Match. A Novel. 2 vols. Crown 8vo. Cloth.

PERRY (Rev. S. J.), F.R.S.
Notes of a Voyage to Kerguelen Island, to observe the Transit of Venus. Demy 8vo. Sewed, price 2s.

PESCHEL (Dr. Oscar).
The Races of Man and their Geographical Distribution. Large crown 8vo. Cloth, price 9s.

PETTIGREW (J. Bell), M.D., F.R.S.
Animal Locomotion; or, Walking, Swimming, and Flying. With 130 Illustrations. Second Edition. Crown 8vo. Cloth, price 5s. Volume VII. of The International Scientific Series.

PIGGOT (J.), F.S.A., F.R.G.S.
Persia—Ancient and Modern. Post 8vo. Cloth, price 10s. 6d.

POUSHKIN (A. S.).
Russian Romance. Translated from the Tales of Belkin, etc. By Mrs. J. Buchan Telfer (née Mouravieff). Crown 8vo. Cloth, price 7s. 6d.

POWER (H.).
Our Invalids: How shall we Employ and Amuse Them? Fcap. 8vo. Cloth, price 2s. 6d.

POWLETT (Lieut. N.), R.A.
Eastern Legends and Stories in English Verse. Crown 8vo. Cloth, price 5s.

PRESBYTER.
Unfoldings of Christian Hope. An Essay showing that the Doctrine contained in the Damnatory Clauses of the Creed commonly called Athanasian is unscriptural. Small crown 8vo. Cloth, price 4s. 6d.

PRICE (Prof. Bonamy).
Currency and Banking. Crown 8vo. Cloth, price 6s.

PROCTOR (Richard A.), B.A.
Our Place among Infinities. A Series of Essays contrasting our little abode in space and time with the Infinities around us. To which are added Essays on "Astrology," and "The Jewish Sabbath." Second Edition. Crown 8vo. Cloth, price 6s.

The Expanse of Heaven. A Series of Essays on the Wonders of the Firmament. With a Frontispiece. Second Edition. Crown 8vo. Cloth, price 6s.

PUBLIC SCHOOLBOY.
The Volunteer, the Militiaman, and the Regular Soldier. Crown 8vo. Cloth, price 5s.

RANKING (B. M.).
Streams from Hidden Sources. Crown 8vo. Cloth, price 6s.

Ready-Money Mortiboy. A Matter-of-Fact Story. With Frontispiece. Crown 8vo. Cloth, price 3s. 6d.

REANEY (Mrs. G. S.).
Waking and Working; or, from Girlhood to Womanhood. With a Frontispiece. Crown 8vo. Cloth, price 5s.

Sunbeam Willie, and other Stories. Three Illustrations. Royal 16mo. Cloth, price 1s. 6d.

Reginald Bramble.
A Cynic of the Nineteenth Century. An Autobiography. Crown 8vo. Cloth, price 10s. 6d.

REID (T. Wemyss).
Cabinet Portraits. Biographical Sketches of Statesmen of the Day. Crown 8vo. Cloth, price 7s. 6d.

RHOADES (James).
Timoleon. A Dramatic Poem. Fcap. 8vo. Cloth, price 5s.

RIBOT (Prof. Th.).

Contemporary English Psychology. Second Edition. A Revised and Corrected Translation from the latest French Edition. Large post 8vo. Cloth, price 9s.

Heredity : A Psychological Study on its Phenomena, its Laws, its Causes, and its Consequences. Large crown 8vo. Cloth, price 9s.

ROBERTSON (The Late Rev. F. W.), M.A., of Brighton.

The Late Rev. F. W. Robertson, M.A., Life and Letters of. Edited by the Rev. Stopford Brooke, M.A., Chaplain in Ordinary to the Queen.
I. 2 vols., uniform with the Sermons. With Steel Portrait. Crown 8vo. Cloth, price 7s. 6d.
II. Library Edition, in Demy 8vo., with Two Steel Portraits. Cloth, price 12s.
III. A Popular Edition, in 1 vol. Crown 8vo. Cloth, price 6s.

New and Cheaper Editions:—
Sermons. Four Series. Small crown 8vo. Cloth, price 3s. 6d. each.

Notes on Genesis. Crown 8vo. Cloth, price 5s.

Expository Lectures on St. Paul's Epistles to the Corinthians. A New Edition. Small crown 8vo. Cloth, price 5s.

Lectures and Addresses, with other literary remains. A New Edition. Crown 8vo. Cloth, price 5s.

An Analysis of Mr. Tennyson's "In Memoriam." (Dedicated by Permission to the Poet-Laureate.) Fcap. 8vo. Cloth, price 2s.

The Education of the Human Race. Translated from the German of Gotthold Ephraim Lessing. Fcap. 8vo. Cloth, price 2s. 6d.
The above Works can also be had bound in half-morocco.
*** A Portrait of the late Rev. F. W. Robertson, mounted for framing, can be had, price 2s. 6d.

ROSS (Mrs. E.), ("Nelsie Brook").

Daddy's Pet. A Sketch from Humble Life. With Six Illustrations. Royal 16mo. Cloth, price 1s.

RUSSELL (E. R.).

Irving as Hamlet. Second Edition. Demy 8vo. Sewed, price 1s.

RUSSELL (W. C.).

Memoirs of Mrs. Lætitia Boothby. Crown 8vo. Cloth, price 7s. 6d.

SADLER (S. W.), R.N.

The African Cruiser. A Midshipman's Adventures on the West Coast. With Three Illustrations. Second Edition. Crown 8vo. Cloth, price 3s. 6d.

SAMAROW (G.).

For Sceptre and Crown. A Romance of the Present Time. Translated by Fanny Wormald. 2 vols. Crown 8vo. Cloth, price 15s.

SAUNDERS (Katherine).

The High Mills. A Novel. 3 vols. Crown 8vo. Cloth.

Gideon's Rock, and other Stories. Crown 8vo. Cloth, price 6s.

Joan Merryweather, and other Stories. Crown 8vo. Cloth, price 6s.

Margaret and Elizabeth. A Story of the Sea. Crown 8vo. Cloth, price 6s.

SAUNDERS (John).

Israel Mort, Overman. A Story of the Mine. 3 vols. Crown 8vo.

Hirell. With Frontispiece. Crown 8vo. Cloth, price 3s. 6d.
Cheap Edition. With Frontispiece, price 2s.

Abel Drake's Wife. With Frontispiece. Crown 8vo. Cloth, price 3s. 6d.
Cheap Edition. With Frontispiece, price 2s.

SCHELL (Maj. von).

The Operations of the First Army under Gen. Von Goeben. Translated by Col. C. H. von Wright. Four Maps. Demy 8vo. Cloth, price 9s.

The Operations of the First Army under Gen. Von Steinmetz. Translated by Captain E. O. Hollist. Demy 8vo. Cloth, price 10s. 6d.

SCHERFF (Maj. W. von).

Studies in the New Infantry Tactics. Parts I. and II. Translated from the German by Colonel Lumley Graham. Demy 8vo. Cloth, price 7s. 6d.

SCHMIDT (Prof. Oscar).

The Doctrine of Descent and Darwinism. With 26 Illustrations. Third Edition. Crown 8vo. Cloth, price 5s.
Volume XII. of The International Scientific Series.

SCHÜTZENBERGER (Prof. F.).

Fermentation. With Numerous Illustrations. Crown 8vo. Cloth, price 5s.
Volume XX. of The International Scientific Series.

SCOTT (Patrick).

The Dream and the Deed, and other Poems. Fcap. 8vo. Cloth, price 5s.

SCOTT (W. T.).

Antiquities of an Essex Parish; or, Pages from the History of Great Dunmow. Crown 8vo. Cloth, price 5s. Sewed, 4s.

SCOTT (Robert H.).

Weather Charts and Storm Warnings. Illustrated. Crown 8vo. Cloth, price 3s. 6d.

Seeking his Fortune, and other Stories. With Four Illustrations. Crown 8vo. Cloth, price 3s. 6d.

SENIOR (N. W.).

Alexis De Tocqueville. Correspondence and Conversations with Nassau W. Senior, from 1833 to 1859. Edited by M. C. M. Simpson. 2 vols. Large post 8vo. Cloth, price 21s.

Journals Kept in France and Italy. From 1848 to 1852. With a Sketch of the Revolution of 1848. Edited by his Daughter, M. C. M. Simpson. 2 vols. Post 8vo. Cloth, price 24s.

Seven Autumn Leaves from Fairyland. Illustrated with Nine Etchings. Square crown 8vo. Cloth, price 3s. 6d.

SEYD (Ernest), F.S.S.

The Fall in the Price of Silver. Its Causes, its Consequences, and their Possible Avoidance, with Special Reference to India. Demy 8vo. Sewed, price 2s. 6d.

SHADWELL (Maj.-Gen.), C.B.

Mountain Warfare. Illustrated by the Campaign of 1799 in Switzerland. Being a Translation of the Swiss Narrative compiled from the Works of the Archduke Charles, Jomini, and others. Also of Notes by General H. Dufour on the Campaign of the Valtelline in 1635. With Appendix, Maps, and Introductory Remarks. Demy 8vo. Cloth, price 16s.

SHELDON (Philip).

Woman's a Riddle; or, Baby Warmstrey. A Novel. 3 vols. Crown 8vo. Cloth.

SHELLEY (Lady).

Shelley Memorials from Authentic Sources. With (now first printed) an Essay on Christianity by Percy Bysshe Shelley. With Portrait. Third Edition. Crown 8vo. Cloth, price 5s.

SHERMAN (Gen. W. T.).

Memoirs of General W. T. Sherman, Commander of the Federal Forces in the American Civil War. By Himself. 2 vols. With Map. Demy 8vo. Cloth, price 24s. *Copyright English Edition.*

SHIPLEY (Rev. Orby), M.A.

Church Tracts, or Studies in Modern Problems. By various Writers. 2 vols. Crown 8vo. Cloth, price 5s. each.

SMEDLEY (M. B.).

Boarding-out and Pauper Schools for Girls. Crown 8vo. Cloth, price 3s. 6d.

SMITH (Edward), M.D., LL.B., F.R.S.

Health and Disease, as Influenced by the Daily, Seasonal, and other Cyclical Changes in the Human System. A New Edition. Post 8vo. Cloth, price 7s. 6d.

Foods. Profusely Illustrated. Fourth Edition. Crown 8vo. Cloth, price 5s.
Volume III. of The International Scientific Series.

Practical Dietary for Families, Schools, and the Labouring Classes. A New Edition. Post 8vo. Cloth, price 3s. 6d.

Tubercular Consumption in its Early and Remediable Stages. Second Edition. Crown 8vo. Cloth, price 6s.

SMITH (Hubert).

Tent Life with English Gipsies in Norway. With Five full-page Engravings and Thirty-one smaller Illustrations by Whymper and others, and Map of the Country showing Routes. Third Edition. Revised and Corrected. Post 8vo. Cloth, price 21s.

Some Time in Ireland.

A Recollection. Crown 8vo. Cloth, price 7s. 6d.

Songs for Music.

By Four Friends. Square crown 8vo. Cloth, price 5s.
Containing songs by Reginald A. Gatty, Stephen H. Gatty, Greville J. Chester, and Juliana Ewing.

SPENCER (Herbert).

The Study of Sociology. Fifth Edition. Crown 8vo. Cloth, price 5s.
Volume V. of The International Scientific Series.

SPICER (H.).

Otho's Death Wager. A Dark Page of History Illustrated. In Five Acts. Fcap. 8vo. Cloth, price 5s.

STEVENSON (Rev. W. F.).

Hymns for the Church and Home. Selected and Edited by the Rev. W. Fleming Stevenson.
The most complete Hymn Book published.
The Hymn Book consists of Three Parts:—I. For Public Worship.—II. For Family and Private Worship.—III. For Children.
⁎ *Published in various forms and prices, the latter ranging from 8d. to 6s. Lists and full particulars will be furnished on application to the Publishers.*

STEWART (Prof. Balfour), M.A., LL.D., F.R.S.

On the Conservation of Energy. Third Edition. With Fourteen Engravings. Crown 8vo. Cloth, price 5s.
Volume VI. of The International Scientific Series.

STONEHEWER (Agnes).

Monacella: A Legend of North Wales. A Poem. Fcap. 8vo. Cloth, price 3s. 6d.

STRETTON (Hesba). Author of "Jessica's First Prayer."

The Storm of Life. With Ten Illustrations. Royal 16mo. Cloth, price 1s. 6d.

The Crew of the Dolphin. Illustrated. Eighth Thousand. Royal 16mo. Cloth, price 1s. 6d.

Cassy. Twenty-ninth Thousand. With Six Illustrations. Royal 16mo. Cloth, price 1s. 6d.

STRETTON (Hesba)—*continued:*

The King's Servants. Thirty-fifth Thousand. With Eight Illustrations. Royal 16mo. Cloth, price 1s. 6d.

Lost Gip. Forty-eighth Thousand. With Six Illustrations. Royal 16mo. Cloth, price 1s. 6d.

** Also a handsomely bound Edition, with Twelve Illustrations, price 2s. 6d.

Michel Lorio's Cross. Strongly bound in blue cloth, gilt, price 1s. 6d.

Friends till Death, and other Stories. Strongly bound in blue cloth, gilt, price 1s. 6d.

David Lloyd's Last Will. Illustrated. Fcap. 8vo. Cloth, price 2s. 6d.

The Wonderful Life. Ninth Thousand. Fcap. 8vo. Cloth, price 2s. 6d.

Friends till Death. With Frontispiece. Fourteenth Thousand. Royal 16mo. Limp cloth, price 6d.

Two Christmas Stories. With Frontispiece. Eleventh Thousand. Royal 16mo. Limp cloth, price 6d.

Michel Lorio's Cross, and Left Alone. With Frontispiece. Seventh Thousand. Royal 16mo. Limp cloth, price 6d.

Old Transome. With Frontispiece. Ninth Thousand. Royal 16mo. Limp cloth, price 6d.

** Taken from "The King's Servants."

The Worth of a Baby, and how Apple-Tree Court was won. With Frontispiece. Ninth Thousand. Royal 16mo. Limp cloth, price 6d.

A Night and a Day. With Frontispiece. Sixth Thousand. Royal 16mo. Limp cloth, price 6d.

Hester Morley's Promise. 3 vols. Crown 8vo. Cloth.

The Doctor's Dilemma. vols. Crown 8vo. Cloth.

STUMM (Lieut. Hugo), German Military Attaché to the Khivan Expedition.

Russia's advance Eastward. Based on the Official Reports of. Translated by Capt. C. E. H. VINCENT. With Map. Crown 8vo. Cloth, price 6s.

SULLY (James), M.A.

Sensation and Intuition. Demy 8vo. Cloth, price 10s. 6d.

Sunnyland Stories.
By the Author of "Aunt Mary's Bran Pie." Illustrated. Small 8vo. Cloth, price 3s. 6d.

SYME (David).

Outlines of an Industrial Science. Crown 8vo. Cloth, price 6s.

Tales of the Zenana.
By the Author of "Pandurang Hari." 2 vols. Crown 8vo. Cloth, price 21s.

TAYLOR (Rev. J. W. A.), M.A.

Poems. Fcap. 8vo. Cloth, price 5s.

TAYLOR (Sir H.).

Edwin the Fair and Isaac Comnenus. A New Edition. Fcap. 8vo. Cloth, price 3s. 6d.

A Sicilian Summer and other Poems. A New Edition. Fcap. 8vo. Cloth, price 3s. 6d.

Philip Van Artevelde. A Dramatic Poem. A New Edition. Fcap. 8vo. Cloth, price 5s.

TAYLOR (Col. Meadows), C.S.I., M.R.I.A.

The Confessions of a Thug. Crown 8vo. Cloth, price 6s.

Tara: a Mahratta Tale. Crown 8vo. Cloth, price 6s.

TELFER (J. Buchan), F.R.G.S., Commander R.N.

The Crimea and Trans-Caucasia. With numerous Illustrations and Maps. 2 vols. Medium 8vo. Cloth, price 36s.

TENNYSON (Alfred).

Harold. A Drama. Crown 8vo. Cloth, price 6s.

Queen Mary. A Drama. New Edition. Crown 8vo. Cloth, price 6s.

TENNYSON (Alfred).

Cabinet Edition. Ten Volumes. Each with Frontispiece. Fcap. 8vo. Cloth. price 2s. 6d. each.

CABINET EDITION. 10 vols. Complete in handsome Ornamental Case. Price 28s.

TENNYSON (Alfred).

Author's Edition. Complete in Five Volumes. Post 8vo. Cloth gilt; or half-morocco, Roxburgh style.

VOL. I. Early Poems, and English Idylls. Price 6s.; Roxburgh, 7s. 6d.

VOL. II. Locksley Hall, Lucretius, and other Poems. Price 6s.; Roxburgh, 7s. 6d.

VOL. III. The Idylls of the King (*Complete*). Price 7s. 6d.; Roxburgh, 9s.

VOL. IV. The Princess, and Maud. Price 6s.; Roxburgh, 7s. 6d.

VOL. V. Enoch Arden, and In Memoriam. Price 6s.; Roxburgh, 7s. 6d.

TENNYSON (Alfred).

Original Editions.

Poems. Small 8vo. Cloth, price 6s.

Maud, and other Poems. Small 8vo. Cloth, price 3s. 6d.

The Princess. Small 8vo. Cloth, price 3s. 6d.

TENNYSON (Alfred).

Original Editions.

Idylls of the King. Small 8vo. Cloth, price 5s.

Idylls of the King. Complete. Small 8vo. Cloth, price 6s.

The Holy Grail, and other Poems. Small 8vo. Cloth, price 4s. 6d.

Gareth and Lynette. Small 8vo. Cloth, price 3s.

Enoch Arden, &c. Small 8vo. Cloth, price 3s. 6d.

Selections from the above Works. Super royal 16mo. Cloth. price 3s. 6d. Cloth gilt extra, price 4s

Songs from the above Works. Super royal 16mo. Cloth extra, price 3s. 6d.

In Memoriam. Small 8vo. Cloth, price 4s.

TENNYSON (Alfred).

The Illustrated Edition. 1 vol. Large 8vo. Gilt extra, price 25s.

Library Edition. In 6 vols. Demy 8vo. Cloth, price 10s. 6d. each.

Pocket Volume Edition. 11 vols. In neat case, price 31s. 6d. Ditto, ditto. Extra cloth gilt, in case price 35s.

Tennyson's Idylls of the King, and other Poems. Illustrated by Julia Margaret Cameron. 2 vols. Folio. Half-bound morocco, cloth sides, price £6 6s. each.

THOMAS (Moy).

A Fight for Life. With Frontispiece. Crown 8vo. Cloth, price 3s. 6d.

Thomasina.
A Novel. 2 vols. Crown 8vo. Cloth.

THOMPSON (Alice C.).
Preludes. A Volume of Poems. Illustrated by Elizabeth Thompson (Painter of "The Roll Call"). 8vo. Cloth, price 7s. 6d.

THOMPSON (Rev. A. S.).
Home Words for Wanderers. A Volume of Sermons. Crown 8vo. Cloth, price 6s.

Thoughts in Verse.
Small Crown 8vo. Cloth, price 1s. 6d.

THRING (Rev. Godfrey), B.A.
Hymns and Sacred Lyrics. Fcap. 8vo. Cloth, price 5s.

TODD (Herbert), M.A.
Arvan; or, The Story of the Sword. A Poem. Crown 8vo. Cloth, price 7s. 6d.

TODHUNTER (Dr. J.)
Laurella; and other Poems. Crown 8vo. Cloth, price 6s. 6d.

TRAHERNE (Mrs. A.).
The Romantic Annals of a Naval Family. A New and Cheaper Edition. Crown 8vo. Cloth, price 5s.

TRAVERS (Mar.).
The Spinsters of Blatchington. A Novel. 2 vols. Crown 8vo. Cloth.

TREMENHEERE (Lieut.-Gen. C. W.)
Missions in India: the System of Education in Government and Mission Schools contrasted. Demy 8vo. Sewed, price 2s.

TURNER (Rev. C. Tennyson).
Sonnets, Lyrics, and Translations. Crown 8vo. Cloth, price 4s. 6d.

TYNDALL (John), LL.D., F.R.S.
The Forms of Water in Clouds and Rivers, Ice and and Glaciers. With Twenty-five Illustrations. Sixth Edition. Crown 8vo. Cloth, price 5s.
Volume I. of The International Scientific Series.

UMBRA OXONIENSIS.
Results of the expostulation of the Right Honourable W. E. Gladstone, in their Relation to the Unity of Roman Catholicism. Large fcap. 8vo. Cloth, price 5s.

UPTON (Richard D.), Capt.
Newmarket and Arabia. An Examination of the Descent of Racers and Coursers. With Pedigrees and Frontispiece. Post 8vo. Cloth, price 9s.

VAMBERY (Prof. A.).
Bokhara: Its History and Conquest. Second Edition. Demy 8vo. Cloth, price 18s.

VAN BENEDEN (Mons.).
Animal Parasites and Messmates. With 83 Illustrations. Second Edition. Cloth, price 5s.
Volume XIX. of The International Scientific Series.

VANESSA.
By the Author of "Thomasina" &c. A Novel. 2 vols. Second Edition. Crown 8vo. Cloth.

VAUGHAN (Rev. C. J.), D.D.
Words of Hope from the Pulpit of the Temple Church. Third Edition. Crown 8vo. Cloth, price 5s.

The Solidity of true Religion, and other Sermons. Preached in London during the Election and Mission Week, February, 1874. Crown 8vo. Cloth, price 3s. 6d.

VAUGHAN (Rev. C. J.), D.D.—
continued.

Forget Thine own People.
An Appeal for Missions. Crown 8vo. Cloth, price 3s. 6d.

The Young Life equipping Itself For God's Service. Being Four Sermons Preached before the University of Cambridge, in November, 1872. Fourth Edition. Crown 8vo. Cloth, price 3s. 6d.

VINCENT (Capt. C. E. H.).

Elementary Military Geography, Reconnoitring, and Sketching. Compiled for Non-Commissioned Officers and Soldiers of all Arms. Square crown 8vo. Cloth, price 2s. 6d.

Vizcaya; or, Life in the Land of the Carlists at the Outbreak of the Insurrection, with some Account of the Iron Mines and other Characteristics of the Country. With a Map and Eight Illustrations. Crown 8vo. Cloth, price 9s.

VOGEL (Dr. Hermann).

The Chemical effects of Light and Photography, in their application to Art, Science, and Industry. The translation thoroughly revised. With 100 Illustrations, including some beautiful specimens of Photography. Third Edition. Crown 8vo. Cloth, price 5s.

Volume XV. of The International Scientific Series.

VYNER (Lady Mary).

Every day a Portion.
Adapted from the Bible and 'the Prayer Book, for the Private Devotions of those living in Widowhood. Collected and edited by Lady Mary Vyner. Square crown 8vo. Cloth extra, price 5s.

Waiting for Tidings.
By the Author of "White and Black." 3 vols. Crown 8vo. Cloth.

WARTENSLEBEN (Count H. von).

The Operations of the South Army in January and February, 1871. Compiled from the Official War Documents of the Head-quarters of the Southern Army. Translated by Colonel C. H. von Wright. With Maps. Demy 8vo. Cloth, price 6s.

The Operations of the First Army under Gen. von Manteuffel. Translated by Colonel C. H. von Wright. Uniform with the above. Demy 8vo. Cloth, price 9s.

WAY (A.), M.A.

The Odes of Horace Literally Translated in Metre. Fcap. 8vo. Cloth, price 2s.

WEDMORE (F.).

Two Girls. 2 vols. Crown 8vo. Cloth.

WELLS (Capt. John C.), R.N.

Spitzbergen—The Gateway to the Polynia; or, A Voyage to Spitzbergen. With numerous Illustrations by Whymper and others, and Map. New and Cheaper Edition. Demy 8vo. Cloth, price 6s.

WETMORE (W. S.).

Commercial Telegraphic Code. Second Edition. Post 4to. Boards, price 42s.

What 'tis to Love.
By the Author of "Flora Adair," "The Value of Fosterstown." 3 vols. Crown 8vo. Cloth.

WHITAKER (Florence).

Christy's Inheritance. A London Story. Illustrated. Royal 16mo. Cloth, price 1s. 6d.

WHITE (A. D.), LL.D.

Warfare of Science. With Prefatory Note by Professor Tyndall. Crown 8vo. Cloth, price 3s. 6d.

WHITE (Capt. F. B. P.).

The Substantive Seniority Army List—Majors and Captains. 8vo. Sewed, price 2s. 6d.

WHITNEY (Prof. W. D.), of Yale College, New Haven.

The Life and Growth of Language. Second Edition. Crown 8vo. Cloth, price 5s. *Copyright Edition.*
Volume XVI. of The International Scientific Series.

WHITTLE (J. L.), A.M.

Catholicism and the Vatican. With a Narrative of the Old Catholic Congress at Munich. Second Edition. Crown 8vo. Cloth, price 4s. 6d.

WICKHAM (Capt. E. H., R.A.)

Influence of Firearms upon Tactics: Historical and Critical Investigations. By an OFFICER OF SUPERIOR RANK (in the German Army). Translated by Captain E. H. Wickham, R.A. Demy 8vo. Cloth, price 7s. 6d.

WILBERFORCE (H. W.).

The Church and the Empires. Historical Periods. Preceded by a Memoir of the Author by John Henry Newman, D.D. of the Oratory. With Portrait. Post 8vo. Cloth, price 10s. 6d.

WILKINSON (T. L.).

Short Lectures on the Land Laws. Delivered before the Working Men's College. Crown 8vo. Limp Cloth, price 2s.

WILLIAMS (A. Lukyn).

Famines in India; their Causes and Possible Prevention. The Essay for the Le Bas Prize, 1875. Demy 8vo. Cloth, price 5s.

WILLIAMS (Rowland), D.D.

Life and Letters of, with Extracts from his Note-Books. Edited by Mrs. Rowland Williams. With a Photographic Portrait. 2 vols. Large post 8vo. Cloth, price 24s.

WILLIAMS (Rowland), D.D.— *continued.*

The Psalms, Litanies, Counsels and Collects for Devout Persons. Edited by his Widow. New and Popular Edition. Crown 8vo. Cloth, price 3s. 6d.

WILLOUGHBY (The Hon. Mrs.).

On the North Wind—Thistledown. A Volume of Poems. Elegantly bound. Small crown 8vo. Cloth, price 7s. 6d.

WILSON (H. Schütz).

Studies and Romances. Crown 8vo. Cloth, price 7s. 6d.

WILSON (Lieut.-Col. C. T.).

James the Second and the Duke of Berwick. Demy 8vo. Cloth, price 12s. 6d.

WINTERBOTHAM (Rev. R.), M.A., B.Sc.

Sermons and Expositions. Crown 8vo. Cloth, price 7s. 6d.

WOINOVITS (Capt. I.).

Austrian Cavalry Exercise. Translated by Captain W. S. Cooke. Crown 8vo. Cloth, price 7s.

WOOD (C. F.).

A Yachting Cruise in the South Seas. With Six Photographic Illustrations. Demy 8vo. Cloth, price 7s. 6d.

WRIGHT (Rev. David), M.A.

Man and Animals: A Sermon. Crown 8vo. Stitched in wrapper, price 1s.

WRIGHT (Rev. David), M.A.

Waiting for the Light, and other Sermons. Crown 8vo. Cloth, price 6s.

WYLD (R. S.), F.R.S.E.

The Physics and the Philosophy of the Senses; or, The Mental and the Physical in their Mutual Relation. Illustrated by several Plates. Demy 8vo. Cloth, price 16s.

YONGE (C. D.).
History of the English Revolution of 1688. Crown 8vo. Cloth, price 6s.

YORKE (Stephen).
Cleveden. A Novel. 2 vols. Crown 8vo. Cloth.

YOUMANS (Eliza A.).
An Essay on the Culture of the Observing Powers of Children, especially in connection with the Study of Botany. Edited, with Notes and a Supplement, by Joseph Payne, F.C.P., Author of "Lectures on the Science and Art of Education," &c. Crown 8vo. Cloth, price 2s. 6d.

YOUMANS (Eliza A.)—*continued*.
First Book of Botany. Designed to Cultivate the Observing Powers of Children. With 300 Engravings. New and Enlarged Edition. Crown 8vo. Cloth, price 5s.

YOUMANS (Edward L.), M.D.
A Class Book of Chemistry. on the Basis of the New System. With 200 Illustrations. Crown 8vo. Cloth, price 5s.

ZIMMERN (H.).
Stories in Precious Stones. With Six Illustrations. Third Edition. Crown 8vo. Cloth, price 5s.

December, 1876.

NEW BOOKS NOW IN THE PRESS.

THE HISTORY OF THE EVOLUTION OF MAN. By Professor E. HAECKEL, Author of "The History of Creation." Translated by Professor VAN RHYN. 2 vols., profusely illustrated.

SERMONS. Third Series. By the Rev. STOPFORD A. BROOKE, M.A., Chaplain in Ordinary to Her Majesty the Queen, and Minister at Bedford Chapel, Bloomsbury. Crown 8vo. Cloth.

INTERNATIONAL LAW OR RULES REGULATING THE INTERCOURSE OF STATES IN PEACE AND WAR. By H. W. HALLECK, A.M., Author of "Elements of Military Art and Science," "Mining Laws of Spain and Mexico," &c. Edited, with copious Notes and Additions, by G. SHERSTON BAKER, Barrister-at-Law. 2 vols. Demy 8vo. Cloth, price 38s.

HISTORY OF THE ORGANIZATION, EQUIPMENT, AND WAR SERVICES OF THE REGIMENT OF BENGAL ARTILLERY. Compiled from published Official Records, and various private Sources. By FRANCIS W. STUBBS, Major Royal (late Bengal) Artillery. With numerous Maps and Illustrations. 2 vols. Demy 8vo. Cloth.

GREENLAND AND ITS INHABITANTS. By the Chevalier Dr. HENRY RINK, President of the Greenland Board of Trade. With sixteen Illustrations, drawn by the Eskimo, and a Map. Edited by Dr. ROBERT BROWN.

New Books now in the Press.

TRAVELS IN THE FOOTSTEPS OF BRUCE IN ALGERIA AND TUNIS. Illustrated by Facsimiles of his Original Drawings. By Lieut.-Col. R. L. PLAYFAIR, H. B. M.'s Consul-General in Algeria.

A BALOOCHEE GRAMMAR. By Capt. E. C. MOCKLER, Assistant Political Agent on the Mekran Coast. Fcap. 8vo.

NEW READINGS AND RENDERINGS OF SHAKE-SPEARE'S TRAGEDIES. By H. H. VAUGHAN. Demy 8vo. Cloth.

AUTOBIOGRAPHICAL RECOLLECTIONS OF SIR JOHN BOWRING. Edited by his son, LEWIN B. BOWRING. One Vol. Demy 8vo. With a Steel Engraving after the Medallion by David.

A TRIP TO CASHMERE AND LADAK. By COWLEY LAMBERT, F.R.G.S. One Vol. Crown 8vo. Illustrated.

A DISCOURSE ON TRUTH. By RICHARD SHUTE, M.A., Christ Church, Oxon. One Vol. Large crown 8vo.

POEMS: MEDITATIVE AND LYRICAL. By AUBREY DE VERE. Large fcap. 8vo.

PUDDINGS AND SWEETS, being Three Hundred and Sixty-Five Receipts approved by experience. Crown 8vo. price 2s. 6d.

TENNYSON. EXTRACTS FOR SCHOOLS AND RECITATIONS. In foolscap 8vo.

THE SWEET SILVERY SAYINGS OF SHAKE-SPEARE ON THE SOFTER SEX. Compiled by an Old Soldier. Crown 8vo. Cloth gilt extra.

IONE. A Poem, in four Parts. By the Author of "Shadows of Coming Events." Foolscap 8vo. Cloth, price 5s.

THE EPIC OF HADES. Parts I. and III. Completing the Work. By a New Writer. Foolscap 8vo. Cloth, price 3s. 6d.

HEBE: A Tale. By Lieutenant M. H. G. GOLDIE. Foolscap 8vo. Cloth.

Henry S. King & Co., London.

www.ingramcontent.com/pod-product-compliance
Lightning Source LLC
Chambersburg PA
CBHW032044220426
43664CB00008B/857